C000070816

HIGHER

HISTORY
Specimen Question Paper, 2011 & 2012

BrightRED
PUBLISHING

First exam published in 2011.
Published by Bright Red Publishing Ltd, 6 Stafford Street, Edinburgh EH3 7AU
tel: 0131 220 5804 fax: 0131 220 6710 info@brightredpublishing.co.uk www.brightredpublishing.co.uk

ISBN 978-1-84948-291-2

A CIP Catalogue record for this book is available from the British Library.

Bright Red Publishing is grateful to the copyright holders, as credited on the final page of the book, for permission to use their material. Every effort has been made to trace the copyright holders and to obtain their permission for the use of copyright material. Bright Red Publishing will be happy to receive information allowing us to rectify any error or omission in future editions.

HIGHER | SPECIMEN PAPER

[BLANK PAGE]

[C259/SQP351]

History
Higher
Paper 1
Specimen Question Paper

Time: 1 hour 20 minutes

NATIONAL QUALIFICATIONS

Candidates should answer **two** questions, **one** from Historical Study: British History and **one** from Historical Study: European and World History.

All questions are worth 20 marks.

Historical Study: British History

Answer ONE question. Each question is worth 20 marks.

Church, State and Feudal Society

1. "Poor, brutal and without hope." How accurate is this view of the lives of peasants in the Middle Ages?

2. "The main role of the Church in medieval society was more political than religious." How valid is this statement?

3. To what extent was the desire to develop the economy the main reason why David I and Henry II centralised royal power?

The Century of Revolutions 1603–1702

4. How important was finance as a cause of the challenge to the authority of James I in England?

5. How successfully did Charles I impose his authority in Scotland?

6. To what extent was the failure to find an alternative to monarchy, 1649–1660, a result of Cromwell's dependence on the army?

The Atlantic Slave Trade

7. "The need for labour on West Indian plantations was the sole reason for the development of the Atlantic Slave Trade." How valid is this view?

8. How important was the slave trade in the development of the British economy in the 18th century?

9. Was the impact of the Slave Trade on African societies wholly negative?

Britain 1851–1951

10. To what extent was the growth of democracy in Britain after 1860 due to social and economic change?

11. "By 1928, Britain was a fully democratic country." How accurate is this view?

12. How important were concerns about the extent of poverty in Britain in the Liberal Government's decision to introduce social reforms between 1906 and 1914?

Britain and Ireland 1900–1985

13. How far was the growth of Irish Nationalism the main reason for the increasing tension in Ireland up to 1914?

14. To what extent did the First World War change the political situation in Ireland?

15. To what extent was the Civil War of 1922–1923 due to the differences between De Valera and Collins?

Historical Study: European and World

Answer ONE question. Each question is worth 20 marks.

The Crusades, 1071–1204

1. How important was fear about the expansion of Islam in the calling of the First Crusade?

2. To what extent was the desire to acquire territory in the Holy Land the main motive behind the popularity of the crusading movement?

3. To what extent was the fall of Jerusalem in 1187 due to the defeat of the Christian forces at Hattin?

The American Revolution 1763–1787

4. To what extent did colonial resentment towards the Navigation Acts endanger British control of the American colonies by 1763?

5. How important were disputes over taxation in turning colonists' opinion towards independence between 1763 and 1776?

6. How justified is the view that the American War of Independence was a global conflict?

The French Revolution, to 1799

7. How far were the grievances of the Bourgeoisie the most serious challenge to the Ancien Regime in the years before 1789?

8. "The financial problems of the Ancien Regime ultimately brought about its collapse in 1789." How valid is this view?

9. How far can Robespierre alone be blamed for the Region of Terror in France from 1793 to 1794?

Germany 1815–1939

10. How important were economic factors in the growth of national feeling in Germany during the period 1815 to 1850?

11. To what extent was there a real growth in German nationalism between 1815 and 1850?

12. How important was Bismarck's leadership in the achievement of German unification?

Italy 1815–1939

13. How important were economic factors in the growth of national feeling in Italy during the period 1815 to 1850?

14. To what extent was there a real growth in Italian nationalism between 1815 and 1850?

15. How significant was the military leadership of Garibaldi in the achievement of Italian unification?

Russia from Tsarism to Bolshevism

16. "In the period before 1905, opposition groups had little chance of mounting an effective challenge to the authority of the Tsarist state." How accurate is this statement?

17. How significant was military defeat in causing the revolution of 1905 in Russia?

18. To what extent was Nicholas II himself responsible for the collapse of the Tsarist state in February 1917?

USA 1918–1968

19. "Simply part of the post-war desire to isolate America from the outside world." How far does this explain changing attitudes towards immigration in the USA during the 1920s?

20. To what extent was the "separate but equal" decision of the Supreme Court the main obstacle facing black Americans in achieving civil rights before 1941?

21. How effective were the increased powers of the federal government, as adopted in the New Deal, in solving the social and economic problems of the 1930s?

Appeasement and the Road to War, to 1939

22. To what extent do economic difficulties explain the aggressive nature of fascist foreign policies in the 1930s?

23. "Bullying and bluff." How accurate is this description of the methods used by the fascist powers to pursue their foreign policy aims in the years after 1933?

24. How successfully did British governments achieve their aims in foreign policy before the outbreak of the Czechoslovakian Crisis in 1938?

The Cold War 1945–1989

25. To what extent was the development of the Cold War up to 1955 caused by America's decision to use the atom bomb against Japan in 1945?

26. To what extent was Soviet control of Eastern Europe seriously challenged between 1945 and 1961?

27. "America's withdrawal from Vietnam was mainly due to public protests at home." How far is this an accurate statement?

[END OF SPECIMEN QUESTION PAPER]

[C259/SQP351]

History

Higher
Paper 2
Specimen Question Paper

Time: 1 hour 25 minutes

NATIONAL QUALIFICATIONS

Candidates should answer all the questions on one Special Topic.

The marks total for this paper is 30 marks.

SQA

1: THE WARS OF INDEPENDENCE, 1286–1328

Study the sources below and answer the questions which follow.

Source A: from a speech by Roger Barbazon, given on behalf of Edward I at Norham, May 1291.

Our King [Edward I], sees that the peace of the kingdom of Scotland has been disturbed by the deaths of King Alexander, his children and his grandchildren, who were relatives of Edward and by those deaths he is greatly distressed. He wishes to do justice to all who can lay any claim to the inheritance of the kingdom of Scotland. He wishes to keep the peace among the people; therefore he has asked you, the good people of the realm, to come here because of something he wishes to explain to you. He himself has come here from a distant country so that, by the virtue of the overlordship which he has, he may do justice to the peace of Scotland.

So that this matter may be concluded satisfactorily our lord King asks for your agreement and for recognition of his overlordship and he wishes to act with your advice in doing and effecting justice.

Source B: is an account of the Battle of Dunbar from the Chronicle of Guisborough, 1296.

The Earl of Warenne and barely a fifth of the King Edward's army were preparing to go to bed. The Scots army showed themselves boldly on the brow of a steep hill. Although the Scots columns were in close order and strong in numbers, before it was possible for the English to come close, they broke up and scattered more swiftly than smoke. The fiercest of the Scots were the first to flee. Yet their foot soldiers would have stood firm had not the knights shown their heels and fled so readily.

In this way no fewer than 10,000 rebels were killed and several monks were found amongst the dead. On the English side not one man fell, except a single foolhardy knight.

Source C: from *Robert Bruce, King of Scots* by Ronald McNair Scott (1982).

Edward I, ordered his army to march northwards. The disciplined columns of the English met their opponents on 27th April and began to deploy their troops in the deep valley beneath the slopes of the Lammermuir Hills on which the Scots were massed. Although the Scottish knights had shown themselves to be brave in tournaments, they had no experience of the tactics of serious warfare. As the English began to disappear into the dead ground below the hill, the Scots assumed they were seeking to escape. Breaking their ranks they charged down the hillside in a tumultuous rabble only to meet an ordered English battle line which overwhelmed them at the first onslaught. Thousands of Scottish foot soldiers were slain and the knights surrounded and made prisoner.

Source D: from James Mackay, *William Wallace: Braveheart* (1996).

For all that Falkirk was a major blow to the Scots; it was in no sense a decisive victory for the English. The cavalry, the officer corps, got away unscathed to fight another day, redeem the slur on its character and organise resistance in the remoter districts, especially north of the Tay and in the hills of Galloway. The people who had been cowed into submission after Dunbar were not the people whom Edward defeated at Falkirk. They were tempered by the fire of battle and found a new resilience, making them more determined than ever that they would not be subjugated. But defeat at Falkirk meant the end of Wallace's rule and shortly afterwards he gave up his guardianship; whether voluntarily or not is immaterial.

Source E: is a description of a Scots raid into Northern England in 1322; taken from the Lanercost Chronicle.

Now after 6th January 1322, when the truce between the kingdoms lapsed, the Scottish army invaded England and marched into the bishopric of Durham and the Earl of Moray remained at Darlington. But James Douglas and the Steward of Scotland went forward plundering the country in all directions. One of them raided towards Hartlepool and the district of Cleveland, the other towards Richmond. The people of Richmond County, neither having nor hoping to have any defender, bought off the invaders with a great sum of money.

[END OF SOURCES FOR THE WARS OF INDEPENDENCE, 1286–1328]

1: THE WARS OF INDEPENDENCE, 1286–1328

Marks

Answer all of the following questions.

1. How far does **Source A** illustrate the problems caused by the death of Alexander III?
   Use the source and recalled knowledge.   **10**

2. To what extent do **Sources B** and **C** agree about the Scottish defeat at the Battle of Dunbar?
   Compare the content overall and in detail.   **5**

3. How fully does **Source D** show the Scottish resistance to Edward I, 1296–1305?
   Use the source and recalled knowledge   **10**

4. How useful is **Source E** in showing the tactics used by Robert I to persuade the English to accept him as King of Scots?
   In reaching a conclusion you should refer to:
   * *the origin and possible purpose of the source;*
   * *the content of the source;*
   * *recalled knowledge.*   **5**

    (30)

[END OF QUESTIONS ON THE WARS OF INDEPENDENCE, 1286–1328]

2: THE AGE OF REFORMATION, 1542-1603

Study the sources below then answer the questions which follow.

Source A: from the Statutes of the Reforming Councils of the Roman Catholic Church
in Scotland, 1549 & 1552.

This Church Council strongly advises that neither bishops nor priests keep their children born from their mistresses in their company. They should not allow them to be promoted in their churches nor for any reason, marry their daughters to Barons or make their sons Barons using the income of the Church.

Priests of parish churches – who, in the judgement of the bishop, shall be reckoned capable and suitable for preaching the faith to the parishioners – must preach at least four times in the year.

The clergy of this realm have not sufficient knowledge of the Holy Scriptures to be able to instruct the people in the Catholic faith. This present council decrees that a certain book shall be written in the common Scottish tongue. This shall be put into the hands of the clergy, as much for their own instruction as for the Christian people in their care; which book it orders to be called a catechism, that is to say a plain and easy statement and explanation of the basics of the faith.

Source B: from F. Mignet, *The History of Mary, Queen of Scots* (1851).

Mary's actions before and after the murder are quite sufficient to convince us that she was involved in the murder plot. Her journey to Glasgow took place at a time when she was openly expressing her distrust and hatred of Darnley. She showed tenderness towards him and expressed hopes of being reconciled with him in order to persuade him to come with her to Edinburgh. Kirk o' Field was selected as the most convenient place to commit the crime. Mary consented to reside at this house so that Darnley would not refuse to live there. On the evening before the murder she removed from the house all the furniture of any value that it contained.

Source C: from S. Cowan, *Mary Queen of Scots and Who Wrote the Casket Letters?* (1907).

Mary went to Glasgow with nothing in her heart but the most loving devotion to her husband. From that time, until his death, any other interpretation of her actions would be inconsistent with the best historical narratives of her life. She nursed him day and night during her visit, after which he proposed that she should take him with her to Edinburgh. She suggested Craigmillar as it was situated on higher ground and very healthy. Curiously enough, he refused to go there. Mary wrote to Maitland to provide a house. Maitland recommended Kirk o' Field, allegedly after showing Bothwell the letter. We think this is very unlikely as Bothwell was in Liddesdale, seventy miles away. It is clear that Maitland was a member of the conspiracy who wanted to put Darnley into Kirk o' Field.

Source D: from Caroline Bingham, *James VI of Scotland* (1979).

The serious challenge to the authority of King James VI came not from the nobility but from the Kirk, and principally from the extremist Presbyterian party led by Andrew Melville. It is important to stress that James himself remained a convinced Calvinist. To all except the extreme Presbyterians who wanted a theocracy, he might have appeared to be the ideal ruler. He had been educated within the Kirk; he respected it and accepted its beliefs. It was unfortunate for both the monarchy and the Kirk that Andrew Melville should have opposed the King's reasonable and basically favourable views.

The clash between them is usually and probably correctly summed up by quoting James Melville's report of an interview which took place at Falkland Palace in 1596.

Andrew Melville addressed the King with the following words: 'Sir, I must tell you there are two Kings and two kingdoms in Scotland. There is Christ Jesus the King, and his kingdom the Kirk; whose subject King James the sixth is, and of whose kingdom not a king, nor a lord, nor a head, but a member.'

Source E: from St Andrews Kirk Session Registers, 1570 & 1597.

It is agreed that from this moment onwards that the church officers in their areas make no distribution of alms to the poor, except to those who come to the sermons and public prayers, examination and communion. They must present their children to baptism, and give account of their faith. They must be able to say the Lord's Prayer, the Creed and Commandments of God, or at least shall learn the same within a month.

It is concluded that when any poor person cries for alms in any part of the city, that they be taken and arrested by Thomas Wilson and put in the thieves' prison until judgment be made of their state.

[END OF SOURCES FOR THE AGE OF REFORMATION, 1542–1603]

2: THE AGE OF REFORMATION, 1542-1603

Answer all of the following questions.   *Marks*

1. How far does **Source A** illustrate the weaknesses of the Catholic Church in Scotland in the years before the Reformation of 1560?
    Use the source and recalled knowledge.   **10**

2. To what extent do **Sources B** and **C** agree about the involvement of Mary, Queen of Scots, in the death of Darnley?
    Compare the content overall and in detail.   **5**

3. How fully does **Source D** explain the relationship between Monarch and Kirk that existed in the reign of King James VI, to 1603?
    Use the source and recalled knowledge   **10**

4. How useful is **Source E** as evidence of how the Kirk dealt with social issues in Scotland after the Reformation?
    In reaching a conclusion you should refer to:
    • *the origin and possible purpose of the source;*
    • *the content of the source;*
    • *recalled knowledge.*   **5**

                                                                        (30)

[END OF QUESTIONS ON THE AGE OF REFORMATION, 1542–1603]

3: THE TREATY OF UNION, 1689-1740

Study the sources below and answer the questions which follow.

Source A: from P.H. Scott, *Andrew Fletcher and the Treaty of Union* (1992).

It was the question of the succession to the throne which brought the relationship between the two countries to a critical point which had to be resolved one way or another. On 30 July 1700, William, Duke of Gloucester, the last survivor of Queen Anne's eighteen children, died. There was no longer any obvious and automatic heir to the throne. The legitimate line of descent from James VII and II, the Jacobite Pretender, could not be re-established without overthrowing the Protestant settlement of the "Glorious Revolution". The English Parliament, again with no consultation with Scotland, in the Act of Succession of 1701, offered the throne to the Protestant Sophia, Electress of Hanover, and her descendants. The English Parliament seems to have assumed that Scotland would meekly accept their decision.

Source B: from a pamphlet by Seton of Pitmedden, *Scotland's Great Advantages by a Union in England*, (1706).

England secures an old and dangerous enemy to be their friend, and thereby ensures peace at home, and in more safety can carry on designs abroad. Scotland will not be alarmed by the threatenings of a powerful and rich neighbour, nor so easily put under the yoke of a foreign enemy. England gains a considerable addition of brave and courageous men to their fleet, armies and plantations, and we are secured by their protection, and enriched by their labours. We send our commodities and useful manufactures to them and have money and other necessaries remitted to us. They have free access to all our seas and ports and are capable of all privileges of citizens. We are the same among them, can plant colonies at a cheaper rate and, with more assurance than formerly, will see our craftsmen improve and our land better cultivated and manured.

Source C: from a speech by Lord Belhaven in Parliament, November 1706.

When I consider the affair of a union between the two Nations, I find my mind crowded with a variety of melancholy thoughts.

I think I see a free and independent kingdom losing a power to manage their own affairs by themselves, without the assistance and counsel of any other. I think I see the royal boroughs wormed out of all the branches of their old trade. I think I see the valiant and gallant soldiery either sent to learn the plantation-trade abroad; or at home petitioning for a small pension; while their old regiments are broken, the common soldiers left to beg, and the youngest English corps kept standing. I think I see the honest industrious craftsman loaded with new taxes, drinking water in place of ale. I think I see the laborious ploughman, with his corn spoiling upon his hands, for want of sale. I think I see our mariners delivering up their ships to their Dutch partners; and earning their bread as underlings in the royal English Navy.

Source D: from W. Ferguson, *Scotland's Relations with England: A Survey to 1707* (1977).

The Treaty's easy passage through the English Parliament showed that, quite apart from masterly management, there was no great opposition to it there. Of all the remarkable changes of the time this was the most remarkable. At the beginning of Anne's reign there had been strong aversion in England to the idea of union with Scotland, but by 1707 it was English insistence that made union possible. There is no mystery about what caused this change of attitude – it was brought about by fears for the security of England. A disgruntled Scotland raised the spectre of French intervention and of attack from the north.

Source E: from a letter written by the Earl of Mar to the Earl of Leven, 1708.

The Queen called a Cabinet Council last night, where she was pleased to call the Dukes of Queensberry and Montrose, the Earl of Loudon, Seafield and myself. We gave an account there of what orders the Queen had sent to Scotland, since the news of the invasion. It is expected that the Council will seize the horses and arms of those they think disloyal, and will also be giving their advice and instructions for securing the money, in the Mint and Bank, in case of a hostile landing. It was told to us that since both Houses had advised the Queen to arrest such persons as she had cause to suspect, and are now discussing a Bill for the suspending of Habeas Corpus Acts, it was appropriate that suspected people in Scotland should be arrested.

[END OF SOURCES FOR THE TREATY OF UNION, 1689-1740]

3: THE TREATY OF UNION, 1689–1740

Answer all of the following questions.

1. How far does **Source A** illustrate the problems arising from a shared monarchy?
   Use the source and recalled knowledge.

   Marks

   10

2. To what extent do **Sources B** and **C** agree about the advantages of a union with England?
   Compare the content overall and in detail.

   5

3. How fully does **Source D** identify the reasons for the passing of the Treaty of Union?
   Use the source and recalled knowledge

   10

4. How useful is **Source E** as evidence of political problems following the Union?
   In reaching a conclusion you should refer to:
   * *the origin and possible purpose of the source;*
   * *the content of the source;*
   * *recalled knowledge.*

   5

   (30)

[END OF QUESTIONS ON THE TREATY OF UNION, 1689–1740]

4: MIGRATION AND EMPIRE, 1830–1939

Study the sources below and answer the questions which follow.

Source A: from T M Devine, *The Scottish Nation, 1700-2000* (2006).

It is clear that many of the crafts were being undermined by urban competition in the second half of the nineteenth century. Already by the 1850s, the technology of power looms was destroying the textile economy in numerous villages in Perth, Fife and Angus and promoting large-scale migration as a result. The development of a network of branch railway lines enabled cheap factory goods to penetrate far into the rural areas and so threatened the traditional markets for tailors, shoemakers and other tradesmen. The displacement of craftsmen and their families from the smaller country towns and villages became a familiar feature of the rural exodus by the end of the nineteenth century and before. While some trades vanished completely, others, such as the blacksmiths, continued to thrive as long as the horse economy survived. However, in large part, migration from the land before the 1940s has to be explained in terms of the changing attitudes of the farm labour force itself.

Source B: from an account by a Roman Catholic priest in Glasgow about his Irish parishioners in the 1930s.

Religion was virtually the only security they had 'cause they hadn't much of the world's goods and they found comfort and strength in their religion. Also they found security in that they could go to the local priest and he was there to assist them, often doing things that we now take for granted-like writing letters, getting houses, jobs and so on. The priest also fought their battles for social equality. Generally, the Irish immigrants could be found in those jobs which the native Scots were unwilling to undertake – the unskilled, lowest paid work such as portering and working in sugar-houses. The Church also gave the immigrants an opportunity for meeting their fellow countrymen and this was a source of help to them because they were able to rely on each other. In short, the Irish immigrants were strangers in a foreign land and subject to discrimination and persecution in the workplace. This discrimination left immigrants isolated and outwith the main areas of Scottish society.

Source C: from *The Catholic Irish in Scotland: In Search of Identity* by Tom Gallagher, quoted in *Irish Immigrants and Scottish Society in the Nineteenth and Twentieth Centuries*, edited by T M Devine (1991).

The Irish invasion in the nineteenth century may have provided a new focal point for Scottish identity from which the Irish were excluded. The immigrant Irish brought with them significant numbers who followed the Catholic religion that was essential for the maintenance of their cultural identity. In Glasgow, the Irish dominated the unskilled labour market for generations, finding work as casual construction or dock labourers, coal hewers and as sweated labour in textiles. They were an indispensable mobile workforce whose contribution to the prosperity of the 'Second City of the Empire' went largely unappreciated by contemporaries. The Catholic clergy usually proved insistent upon preserving a community insulated from the surrounding society. It was essential to counteract influences that could weaken the solidarity of the Catholic community and Church activists began to create a wide variety of organisations which were designed to absorb the energies of parishioners. These bodies had distinct religious, recreational, charitable and social functions and it was felt immigrants had no need to go further afield to look for companionship. Thus, a self-enclosed world was created which gave dignity and hope to the people.

Source D: from Jan-Andrew Henderson, *The Emperor's New Kilt* (2000).

Evidence of Scotland's former influence is found all over the globe and often the lone Scottish entrepreneur has had a profound effect on his adopted country while remaining unknown in his homeland. In India, Scots were chiefly responsible for the development of tea plantations and the state education system was shaped by a Scotsman named Mountstuart Elphinstone, while Samuel Laing was India's first finance minister. However, two countries more than any other have been moulded by the Scots: Canada and Australia. Though numbering only one fifteenth of the population, Scots dominated the government and controlled the fur trade, the educational institutions and the banks. In Quebec, the ruling government body was so dominated by Scots that it was called the 'Scotch Party'. Australia saw similar manipulation by Scots, John Macarthur introducing the Merino sheep and considered to be the founder of Australia's sheep industry.

Source E: from an interview given by Mrs Aitken, a Glasgow resident, talking about Jewish settlement in the Gorbals in the early twentieth century, quoted in *The Complete Odyssey, Voices from Scotland's Recent Past*, edited by Billy Kay (1996).

It was nearly all Jewish shops and Jewish firms in the Gorbals. There was Fogel's at the corner of Hospital Street and Cleland Street; there was the Jewish bakery at the corner of Dunmore Street. Gleicken, the tailors were there and the Ashers as well. The Gerbers, the Woolfsons, them that had all the jewellers, the shops in the Trongate, they came from there. There were small cabinet-making businesses and upholstery work right up Cumberland Street. They could get their customers everything. They all opened little shops, just doing alterations and repairs to suits and everything. People always helped each other out. Everyone knew someone who would give credit if times were hard. It was a great place the Gorbals!

[*END OF SOURCES FOR MIGRATION AND EMPIRE, 1830–1939*]

4: MIGRATION AND EMPIRE, 1830–1939

Answer all of the following questions.   *Marks*

1. How far does **Source A** illustrate the reasons for internal migration by Scots during the period 1830s to 1930s?
    Use the source and recalled knowledge.   **10**

2. To what extent do **Sources B** and **C** agree about the assimilation of Irish immigrants into Scottish society?
    Compare the content overall and in detail.   **5**

3. How fully does **Source D** illustrate the impact of Scots emigrants on the British Empire?
    Use the source and recalled knowledge   **10**

4. How useful is **Source E** as evidence of the contribution of immigrants to Scottish society?
    In reaching a conclusion you should refer to:
    *   *the origin and possible purpose of the source;*
    *   *the content of the source;*
    *   *recalled knowledge.*   **5**

                                                                                     (30)

[END OF QUESTIONS ON MIGRATION AND EMPIRE, 1830–1939]

5: SCOTLAND AND THE IMPACT OF THE GREAT WAR, 1914–1928

Study the sources below and then answer the questions which follow.

Source A: from Jack Alexander, *McCrae's Battalion: The Story of the 16th Royal Scots*, (2003).

On the evening of 16 June 1916 McCrae's went into the front line near Dernacourt, three miles south of Albert. The trenches here were even poorer than the last. The dug-outs were overcrowded and the atmosphere stifling. They were greeted with heavy shelling which lasted until dawn and continued through the following day. Donald McLean was killed by a rifle grenade as he settled down to lunch. John Miller, a 25-year-old from Portobello, also died in the bombardment. He was with his brother, Tommy, at the time. They had volunteered together at Tynecastle during the victory over Hibs and both claimed a place in the Hearts Company. The following morning Willie Brydie, an apprentice engineer from Merchiston was sniped during 'stand to'.

Source B: by William H Marwick, from Edinburgh, quoted in Ian MacDougall, *Voices from War: Personal recollections of war in our century by Scottish men and women* (1995).

I felt much in sympathy with the Union of Democratic Control and joined the Edinburgh branch. Opposition to the war at first seemed negligible. But there were those who expressed their doubts about it from the start and they and others like-minded had formed the Union of Democratic Control. It was not specifically anti-war. It included not only pacifists but some who actually served in the war. Then there were those who were definitely opposed to the war on what would be called ideological grounds. They held it was a capitalist war in which the working class had no share and no business to take part. Then there were those who objected on religious grounds. The Quakers opposed all war as being against Christianity and members of other churches took the same position. Then there were those who objected on various other grounds. So it was a very mixed lot.

Source C: by J P M Millar, from Edinburgh, quoted in Ian MacDougall, *Voices from War: Personal recollections of war in our century by Scottish men and women* (1995).

When the war broke out in 1914 I became convinced that socialists had no business getting involved in this struggle. I therefore became one of the miscellaneous band called conscientious objectors, of which the Quakers were the best known. When I made up my mind that I shouldn't take part in the war I wrote to Thomas Johnston, editor of Forward and suggested that those of us who weren't prepared to take part in the war should make preparations for the fact that the government would no doubt in time introduce conscription. He replied that he didn't think conscription would ever be introduced in Britain. But conscription did come and one result of that was the formation of the No-Conscription Fellowship. I founded the Edinburgh branch of the Fellowship and became its secretary. Its membership consisted not only of men of military age, but of women and of men too old for military service.

Source D: from Michael Lynch, *Scotland: A New History* (1991).

The failure of Scottish industry in the 1920s and 30s has been interpreted as largely the product of a weakness of management. It is perhaps the lost generation which lies at the root of it. In 1913 the unemployment rate in Scotland stood at only 1·8 per cent, whereas in London it was 8·7 per cent. By 1923, the positions had been reversed, with 14·3 percent out of work in Scotland compared with 11.6 per cent in the United Kingdom as a whole. It was, however, a different kind of unemployment from the short, irregular lay-offs which had marked the years before 1914: it was long-term and affected the skilled more than the unskilled. The huge demand for labour in wartime manufacturing produced pressures which varied from one industry to another. In engineering the gap in earnings between skilled and unskilled reduced, but elsewhere, and especially in the shipyards and the mines the wage gap continued.

Source E: from Willie Gallacher, *Revolt on the Clyde* (1936).

The 'tuppence an hour' strike was over. We were back once more in the factories. But the strike had made a deep political change. Any hope the war-makers might have had of spreading the war fever throughout the Clyde was now gone for ever. The workers knew their enemies, and that they were not across the North Sea. Revolutionary agitators, under McLean's tuition, were increasing in number day by day, and were warmly cheered at mass meetings wherever they went. It became increasingly difficult for the 'patriots' to get a hearing. From the very beginning the Socialists of Glasgow took a firm stand against the war. This was evidenced when Ben Tillett came to fulfil an engagement with the Clarion Scouts. The meeting was in the Pavilion Theatre. Ben shrieked his undying hatred of the Germans, but the audience of Socialists hooted him off the platform.

[END OF SOURCES FOR SCOTLAND AND THE IMPACT
OF THE GREAT WAR, 1914–1928]

5: SCOTLAND AND THE IMPACT OF THE GREAT WAR, 1914–1928

Answer all of the following questions.

Marks

1. How far does **Source A** illustrate the experience of Scots on the Western Front?
   Use the source and recalled knowledge.

   10

2. To what extent do **Sources B** and **C** agree about conscientious objection to the war in Scotland?
   Compare the content overall and in detail.

   5

3. How fully does **Source D** show the impact of the war on the Scottish economy between 1914 and 1928?
   Use the source and recalled knowledge

   10

4. How useful is **Source E** as evidence of the growth of radicalism in politics in Scotland?
   In reaching a conclusion you should refer to:
   • *the origin and possible purpose of the source;*
   • *the content of the source;*
   • *recalled knowledge.*

   5

   (30)

*[END OF QUESTIONS ON SCOTLAND AND THE IMPACT
OF THE GREAT WAR, 1914–1928]*

[END OF SPECIMEN QUESTION PAPER]

[BLANK PAGE]

X259/301

NATIONAL QUALIFICATIONS 2011	FRIDAY, 20 MAY 9.00 AM – 10.20 AM	**HISTORY HIGHER** Paper 1

Candidates should answer **two** questions, **one** from Historical Study: British History and **one** from Historical Study: European and World History.

All questions are worth 20 marks.

Marks may be deducted for bad spelling and bad punctuation, and for writing that is difficult to read.

[BLANK PAGE]

HISTORICAL STUDY: BRITISH HISTORY

Answer ONE question. Each question is worth 20 marks.

Church, State and Feudal Society

1. "The nobility received all of the benefits from the feudal structure while the peasants received none." How valid is this view of medieval society?

2. "Despite its problems the Papacy maintained its authority in Scotland and England." How valid is this view?

3. How far can it be argued that David I of Scotland and Henry II of England successfully established centralised feudal monarchies?

The Century of Revolutions 1603–1702

4. "Religion was the most important cause of the challenge to the authority of James I in England." How true is this assessment?

5. To what extent did religious issues bring about the English Civil War?

6. How important were the actions of James II in causing the Revolution of 1688–1689?

The Atlantic Slave Trade

7. To what extent were Britain's military victories in the wars of the eighteenth century the main reason for the development of the Atlantic Slave Trade?

8. "Fear of slave resistance and revolt determined how slaves were treated." How valid is this view?

9. To what extent was hostile propaganda the major obstacle to the abolition of the slave trade?

Britain 1851–1951

10. How important was the role of pressure groups in Britain becoming more democratic between 1851 and 1928?

11. "Changing attitudes in British society towards women was the major reason why some women received the vote in 1918." How accurate is this view?

12. "The Liberals failed to deal with the real problems facing the British people." How valid is this view of the Liberals' social reforms from 1906 to 1914?

[Turn over

Britain and Ireland 1900–1985

13. "The response of Unionists to the Home Rule Bill was the main reason for the growth of tension in Ireland up to 1914." How valid is this view?

14. How important was British conduct during the Anglo-Irish War in preventing a peace settlement in Ireland between 1918 and 1921?

15. How important were political differences between the Protestant and Catholic communities in contributing to the developing crisis in Northern Ireland up to 1968?

HISTORICAL STUDY: EUROPEAN AND WORLD

Answer ONE question. Each question is worth 20 marks.

The Crusades, 1071–1204

16. "The Pope's desire to channel the military power of the knightly class was the main reason for calling the First Crusade." How valid is this view?

17. "The success of the Crusaders was due to divisions amongst the Muslim states." How valid is this view of the First Crusade?

18. To what extent can it be argued that Richard I was a greater military leader than Saladin?

The American Revolution 1763–1787

19. "Disagreement over the frontier was the key issue between Britain and the colonies by 1763." To what extent is this true?

20. How far were the views of Edmund Burke typical of British opinion towards the conflict with the American colonists in the period between 1763 and 1781?

21. How important was French intervention to colonial victory in the American War of Independence?

The French Revolution, to 1799

22. To what extent did the Third Estate have the greatest cause for complaint under the Ancien Regime?

23. To what extent was Louis XVI responsible for the failure of constitutional monarchy in 1792?

24. "The constitution of 1795 was the main reason for Napoleon's coup of 1799." How valid is this view?

Germany 1815–1939

25. How important were cultural factors in the growth of national feeling in Germany between 1815 and 1850?

26. To what extent was resentment towards Prussia among the German states the main obstacle to German unification by 1850?

27. How important were economic factors in the rise to power of the Nazi Party between 1919 and 1933?

[Turn over

Italy 1815–1939

28. How important was the role of Mazzini in the growth of Italian nationalism between 1815 and 1850?

29. How important was the influence of Austria in preventing the unification of Italy between 1815 and 1850?

30. To what extent did Mussolini achieve power by 1925 as a result of the weaknesses of Italian governments?

Russia 1881–1921

31. How secure was the Tsar's hold on power in the years before 1905?

32. To what extent was the power of the Tsarist state weakened in the years between 1905 and 1914?

33. How important was Bolshevik propaganda in the success of the 1917 October revolution?

USA 1918–1968

34. To what extent was racism the main reason for changing attitudes towards immigration in the 1920s?

35. "The weakness of the US banking system was the main reason for causing the Great Depression of the 1930s." How accurate is this statement?

36. How important was the emergence of effective organisations to the development of the Civil Rights campaigns after 1945?

Appeasement and the Road to War, to 1939

37. To what extent does disappointment over the terms of the Peace Settlements of 1919 explain the aggressive nature of fascist foreign policies in the 1930s?

38. To what extent does British public opinion explain the policy of appeasement between 1936 and 1938?

39. "Munich was a triumph for British foreign policy." How valid is this view?

The Cold War 1945–1989

40. How important were ideological differences between east and west in the emergence of the Cold War up to 1955?

41. "The Cuban Crisis of 1962 was a direct consequence of the domestic pressures on Khrushchev." How accurate is this view?

42. How important was the danger of Mutually Assured Destruction in forcing the superpowers into attempts to manage the Cold War?

[END OF QUESTION PAPER]

[BLANK PAGE]

X259/302

NATIONAL	FRIDAY, 20 MAY	HISTORY
QUALIFICATIONS	10.40 AM – 12.05 PM	HIGHER
2011		Paper 2

Answer questions on only **one** Special Topic.

Take particular care to show clearly the Special Topic chosen. On the **front** of the answer book, **in the top right-hand corner**, write the number of the Special Topic.

You are expected to use background knowledge appropriately in answering source-based questions.

Marks may be deducted for bad spelling and bad punctuation, and for writing that is difficult to read.

Some sources have been adapted.

SPECIAL TOPIC 1: THE WARS OF INDEPENDENCE, 1286–1328

Study the sources below and answer the questions which follow.

Source A: from a letter by Bishop William Fraser to Edward I, November 1290.

Your ambassadors and the Scottish ambassadors who had been sent to you and also some nobles of the Kingdom of Scotland met at Perth. But a sad rumour echoed among the people that our lady was dead and because of this the kingdom of Scotland is troubled and the community perplexed. When the rumour was heard and published, Sir Robert Bruce, who previously did not intend to come to the meeting, came with a large retinue to confer with some who were there. We do not yet know what he intends to do or how he intends to act. Because of that there is a fear of a general war and a large-scale slaughter unless the Most High, through your active involvement and good offices, administer a quick cure.

Source B: from Richard Oram, *Kings and Queens of Scotland* (2006).

Balliol certainly now assumed the bearing of king, yet he remained aware that he would have to impress the feudal lord of his lands in England if he wanted to secure the Kingdom of Scotland. On St Andrew's day 1292, John was inaugurated as King of Scots on the Stone of Destiny at Scone. Yet the ceremony was overseen by Edward's officials rather than the traditional Scottish earls and churchmen. Worse, within a matter of two months, John—again summoned to Northern England—crumbled under the demand that he renew his homage to Edward as Scotland's overlord. It was this regime that undoubtedly prepared John for further confrontations with Edward I over appeals from Scottish courts that the English king insisted he answered for at Westminster.

Source C: from a contemporary English chronicle.

A certain Scot, by name William Wallace was an outcast from pity, a robber, a sacrilegious man, a man who burnt alive boys in schools and churches in great numbers. Wallace had collected an army of Scots in the battle of Falkirk against the King of England, and had seen that he could not resist the powerful army of the King, and so fled himself from the battle, leaving his people to be slain by the sword. This man, after his innumerable wickednesses, was at last taken prisoner by the King's servants and brought to London, as the King ordained that he should be formally tried. He was put to a most cruel, but amply deserved, death. His head was fixed on a stake and set on London Bridge. His four quarters thus divided, were sent to the four quarters of Scotland. Behold the end of a merciless man whom his mercilessness brought to this end.

Source D: from Alan Macquarrie, *Kingship and Nation* (2004).

William Wallace was probably the son of the laird of Elderslie who had not signed the Ragman Rolls, and was consequently outlawed by the English justiciar. He escaped capture by the English garrison of Lanark with the help of his mistress, who was killed in the process. In revenge, Wallace killed the Sheriff of Lanark and set himself up as head of a band of outlaws. The Battle of Falkirk was a victory for the English mounted knights and the Welsh archers, who wore down the schiltrons by repeated cavalry charges and discharges of arrows. Wallace escaped and rescued the survivors as best he could. He remained at liberty until betrayed by Sir John Stewart of Mentieth. After his trial he was dragged for miles at the tail of a horse to Smithfield where he was put to death by being strangled, and dismembered.

Source E: from Michael Brown, *Wars of Independence, 1214–1371* (2004).

The letters, including the Declaration of Arbroath, were designed to present a united communal front by the Scottish church and people in support of King Robert. The events of 1320 would reveal the limits to this unity. The association of several lords with the letters to Pope John overlay deep distaste for Bruce's kingship which those letters championed. Such distaste was fuelled by a possible revival of the claims of the house of Balliol, in the person of King John's son Edward Balliol. In late 1318 Edward Balliol returned to England and entered service with those Scots who had refused to enter Bruce's allegiance. His presence was highly significant. Inside Scotland were many nobles with ties of sympathy and kinship to Balliol and the Disinherited.

The conspirators were linked together by their consistent opposition to Bruce before Bannockburn and by their kinship to the fallen house of Comyn. Their leaders were Agnes Comyn, countess of Strathearn and her nephew William Soules. Soules had recovered his lands and office as royal butler, yet was clearly unhappy with Robert's lordship.

[*END OF SOURCES FOR THE WARS OF INDEPENDENCE, 1286–1328*]

SPECIAL TOPIC 1: THE WARS OF INDEPENDENCE, 1286–1328

Marks

Answer *all* of the following questions.

1. How useful is **Source A** as evidence of why the Scots asked Edward to resolve the succession crisis in Scotland?
    In reaching a conclusion you should refer to:
    *   *the origin and possible purpose of the source;*
    *   *the content of the source;*
    *   *recalled knowledge.*   5

2. How fully does **Source B** illustrate the relationship between John Balliol and Edward I?
    Use the source and recalled knowledge.   10

3. To what extent do **Sources C** and **D** agree about the career of William Wallace?
    Compare the content overall and in detail.   5

4. How far does **Source E** show the opposition of many Scots to Robert Bruce?
    Use the source and recalled knowledge.   10

                                                                                                        (30)

[*END OF QUESTIONS ON THE WARS OF INDEPENDENCE, 1286–1328*]

SPECIAL TOPIC 2: THE AGE OF REFORMATION, 1542–1603

Study the sources below and then answer the questions which follow.

Source A: from a contemporary *History of the Scottish Reformation* by John Knox.

Shortly after these things, that cruel tyrant and unmerciful hypocrite, falsely called Archbishop of St Andrews, apprehended that Blessed Martyr of Christ Jesus, Walter Myln, a man of old age, who most cruelly and most unjustly he put to death by fire in St. Andrews, on 28th April, 1558. Which did so highly offend the hearts of the godly, that immediately after his death, a new strength of purpose developed among the whole people. In the meantime the town of Perth embraced The Truth. This provoked the Queen Regent to a new fury; in which she willed the Lord Ruthven, Provost of that town, to suppress all Protestant religion there. On 2nd of May 1559, arrived John Knox from France, who, lodging only two nights in Edinburgh, went to Dundee, where he earnestly asked the brethren of Perth, "That he might be permitted to assist them, and to preach the reformed faith amongst them." This was granted to him; therefore he departed to Perth with them; where he began to preach.

Source B: from Jenny Wormald, *Mary Queen of Scots* (1988).

At about 2am on 10th February 1567, the house was blown up. Darnley escaped into the garden, where his body was found: he had been smothered by, it was suspected, the Douglas kinsmen of the Earl of Morton. Mary should have been in strict mourning, instead she attended a wedding the day after Darnley's murder. She allowed Darnley's father Lennox to accuse Bothwell of the murder and bring him to trial. It was a farce. Whoever else was involved, it is significant that no one doubted the principal conspirator was Bothwell. On 15th May she married Bothwell, a Protestant. Mary had always insisted on her right to her personal Catholicism, whatever happened to anyone else in Scotland, and had created considerable problems by doing so. The end was now very near.

Source C: from the records of the General Assembly of the Kirk of Scotland, 1597.

Meeting at Perth, according to his Majesty's request, and concerning the articles proposed by the King. The brethren, after long conference and mature deliberation agree as follows: The Assembly ordains that no minister shall criticise his Majesty's laws but should seek remedy from his Presbytery, Synod or General Assembly which will present his complaints to his Majesty and report on his Majesty's answer. No man's name should be rebuked from the pulpit, unless his fault be well known and in public. Every Presbytery should watch that each minister's doctrine is agreeable with God's word. No meetings should be held by ministers without his Majesty's knowledge and consent, apart from the Kirk Session, Presbytery and Synod meetings. In all principal towns ministers should not be chosen without the consent of their own flock and his Majesty.

Source D: from Gordon Donaldson, *Scotland James V to James VII*, History of Scotland, (1965).

A general assembly met in February at Perth and not, as the previous assembly had appointed, in April at St Andrews. This set the pattern for the years to come. It was hard to raise objections if the king chose to bring forward the date of the assembly, but when his right to do this was admitted it was equally hard to challenge his right to postpone an assembly. It was equally hard to challenge the king's power to name the place of meeting, and year by year he showed a plain reluctance to have an assembly either in Edinburgh or St Andrews, and had preference for towns more easily accessible to ministers from the more traditional north. The assembly of 1597 conceded that ministers should not be appointed in the chief towns without the consent of the king, and passed various measures curbing the freedom of ministers in the course of their sermons, to attack the laws, to censure individuals and comment on politics.

Source E: from Ian Whyte, *Scotland's Society and Economy in Transition 1500–1760*, (1997).

It became the business of the church to regulate the lives of everyone, sometimes to an obsessive and unhealthy degree. The most important instruments of community control developed by the new church were the Kirk Sessions. These aimed to regulate morals and manners of the inhabitants to promote a godly society. People were presumed guilty until proven innocent so a sizable proportion of the population of the community might expect to appear before the session at some point. In St Andrews between 1560 and 1600 about 1,000 cases of sexual misconduct were dealt with in a town whose population can only have been around 4,000. Elders usually had defined areas of the parish to keep under observation, acting as a kind of moral police force. Their powers within their community were sweeping. Accompanied by a witness, elders could enter people's houses.

[END OF SOURCES FOR THE AGE OF REFORMATION, 1542–1603]

SPECIAL TOPIC 2: THE AGE OF REFORMATION, 1542–1603

Marks

Answer *all* of the following questions.

1. How useful is **Source A** as evidence of the growth of Protestantism in Scotland before the Reformation of 1560?
   In reaching a conclusion you should refer to:
   * *the origin and possible purpose of the source;*
   * *the content of the source;*
   * *recalled knowledge.*   **5**

2. How fully does **Source B** explain why Mary, Queen of Scots lost her throne?
   Use the source and recalled knowledge.   **10**

3. To what extent do **Sources C** and **D** agree about James VI's attempts to control the Kirk?
   Compare the sources overall and in detail.   **5**

4. How far does **Source E** explain the social impact of the Reformation on Scotland, to 1603?
   Use the source and recalled knowledge.   **10**

                                                                                    (30)

[END OF QUESTIONS ON THE AGE OF REFORMATION, 1542–1603]

SPECIAL TOPIC 3: THE TREATY OF UNION, 1689–1740

Study the sources below and then answer the questions which follow.

Source A: from a speech by John Dalrymple, Earl of Stair, in Parliament, 1706.

We followed the example of other nations and formed the Company of Scotland to trade with the West Indies. We built ships and planned a colony on the isthmus of Darien. What we lacked were not men or arms, or courage, but the one thing most needful: we lacked the friendly co-operation of England. The pitiful outcome of that enterprise is too sad a story to be told again. Suffice it to say that the English did not treat us as partners or friends or fellow subjects of a British king. They treated us as pirates and enemy aliens. We were exposed to the hostile rivalry of Spain, encouraged by England. Our colony was sacked. We suffered every cruelty an enemy can inflict.

Source B: from Daniel Defoe, *History of the Union* (1709).

Many members of Parliament knew that the standing of Scotland in the British Parliament would not be that of a kingdom, but of a province of England. Also, they knew that Cornwall would send almost as many members to Parliament as the whole of Scotland, and this was an example of Scotland's subjection. This was a general complaint, but was very widespread. The people cried out that they were Scotsmen and they would remain Scotsmen. They condemned the word "British" as fit only for the Welsh, who had already been made the subjects of the English. Scotland had always had a famous name in foreign courts, and had enjoyed privileges and honours there for many years, bought with the blood of their ancestors. The common people went about the streets crying "no union", and called those negotiators traitors, and threatened them to their faces.

Source C: from T. M. Devine, *The Scottish Nation: 1700–2007* (2006).

The "New Party", soon to be known by the exotic name of "Squadrone Volante", had emerged out of the Country Party in 1704. As events were to prove, this group of around two dozen members was to have a key role in the outcome of the union vote. Crucial in carrying the treaty as a whole was Article XV, which dealt with the "Equivalent". This was an attractive inducement to the Squadrone Volante, the small party whose support the Court Party had to retain in order to achieve ultimate success, so finely balanced was the overall position in Parliament. Some of the Equivalent was to be used to compensate the investors in the ill-fated Darien Company. Among the most significant of these were members of the Squadrone. The formidable political management machine of the Court Party contrasted with the disarray of the parliamentary opposition.

Source D: from Christopher A. Whately, *The Scots and the Union* (2007).

With around twenty-five Squadrone MPs, the government could carry the union, and did. Squadrone votes proved critical in securing approval for several of the articles which, had they been defeated, would have brought the union process to a shuddering halt. In part the Court's success was achieved by political management, which was to spur court-minded MPs into attending and voting for a cause many were at best sympathetic to, and only in a few cases seriously enthusiastic about. There were MPs however who voted consistently for the articles without benefiting at all from the Equivalent—eight of these were associated with the Squadrone. If the purpose of the Equivalent had been to bribe MPs, the outcome was disappointing. Support for union depended on much more than material gain.

Source E: from Michael Lynch, *Scotland: A New History* (1992).

Most historians would agree that economic benefits did not materialise before the 1740s. The more limited the questions about the economic effects of 1707, the firmer the answers are likely to be. The free trade area which opened up after 1707 brought prosperity to only a few Scots. The most obvious symbol of economic success in mid-eighteenth century Scotland were the Glasgow tobacco lords, who around 1750 controlled almost half of Scotland's imports. Yet the enterprising Scots of the immediate post-1707 generation were often the smugglers or black marketers. The worst forecast of the swamping of Scottish manufacturing did not happen, but manufacturing industries found at best only sluggish demand for their products in the new English market and British colonies. In agriculture, the most important sector of the Scottish economy, the effects of union were insignificant.

[END OF SOURCES FOR THE TREATY OF UNION, 1689–1740]

SPECIAL TOPIC 3: THE TREATY OF UNION, 1689–1740

Marks

Answer *all* of the following questions.

1. How useful is **Source A** as evidence of worsening relations between Scotland and England between 1690 and 1705?
    In reaching a conclusion you should refer to:
    *   *the origin and possible purpose of the source;*
    *   *the content of the source;*
    *   *recalled knowledge.*

    5

2. How fully does **Source B** illustrate the arguments for and against the Treaty of Union?
    Use the source and recalled knowledge.

    10

3. To what extent do **Sources C** and **D** agree about the reasons for the passing of the Treaty of Union?
    Compare the sources overall and in detail.

    5

4. How far does **Source E** explain the economic effects of the Union up to 1740?
    Use the source and recalled knowledge.

    10

    (30)

[END OF QUESTIONS ON THE TREATY OF UNION, 1689–1740]

SPECIAL TOPIC 4: MIGRATION AND EMPIRE, 1830–1939

Study the sources below and then answer the questions which follow.

Source A: from Angus Nicholson, Canada's Special Immigration Agent in the Highlands of Scotland, 1875.

All the competing Emigration Agencies formerly reported on, are still at work as actively as ever. The New Zealand and Australian authorities are particularly alert, the streets of every town and village being always well ornamented with their bills and posters offering free passages and other inducements to emigrants. Not only so, but nearly all newspapers being subsidised by means of their advertisements, are doing their full share in the same direction. It has to be noted that a considerable number of potential recruits have been diverted from Canada to New Zealand as a result of the latter's offer of free passages. It is extremely difficult for us to attract emigrants when these territories are offering free passages while we expect the emigrants to pay their own fares to Canada.

Source B: from Martin J Mitchell, *Irish Catholics in the West of Scotland*, in his "New Perspectives on the Irish in Scotland" (2008).

The prevailing view about Catholic Irish in nineteenth-century Scotland is that they were despised by the bulk of the native population, and as a result formed separate and isolated communities in the towns in which they settled in significant numbers. Yet, there is considerable evidence that members of Catholic Irish communities were involved—often in significant numbers—in strikes, trade unions and trade union campaigns. Moreover, this participation was both welcomed and sought by Scottish workers. Some historians have highlighted sectarian riots and disturbances in Scotland in the nineteenth century as proof that there was considerable Protestant working class hostility towards the Catholic Irish community. However, if these incidents are looked at more closely, most of the incidents did not involve Scottish workers, but were instead "Orange" and "Green" disturbances involving Protestant Irish and Catholic Irish immigrants. The available evidence states or suggests that most Scottish workers were not participants—they remained aloof and let the two immigrant groups continue their old battles.

Source C: from Jock Phillips and Terry Hearn, *Settlers–New Zealand Immigrants from England, Ireland and Scotland, 1800–1945* (2008).

The vast majority of Scots who emigrated to New Zealand came from around Edinburgh or Glasgow, playing important roles in the country's economic development. [...] Not surprisingly, the Dunedin entrepreneurs, like the clothing magnates John Ross and Robert Glendinning, or the Burt Brothers who established a nationwide plumbing firm, were Scottish. The *Dictionary of New Zealand Biography* database suggests that Scots were also slightly over-represented among those noted for their contribution to education and rather more strongly among those involved in science and health. Otago saw the first New Zealand high school for girls open in 1871 thanks to the daughter of an iron-merchant from Angus. The first headmistress was another Scot. The Scottish education system of 1872 was the model for New Zealand's 1877 Education Act and the fact that Otago had for a long time the only medical school in the country, and the strong links that school established with Edinburgh, helps to explain the continuing impact of Scots-born people in both the health and scientific fields.

Source D: from James Adam, *Twenty-Five Years of an Emigrant's Life in the South of New Zealand,* (1876).

A gentleman who thirteen years ago was a draper's assistant in Scotland now owns the finest retail business in Dunedin, employs fifty hands and pays £250 weekly in wages. The enterprise of the Dunedin merchants has done much for the commerce and prosperity of Otago. The Scot has certainly made his mark on this land, not only in commerce but also in the field of education, setting up schools throughout the area. Several of the Scots' descendants have also become doctors, administering to the health of the local population in a most efficient manner. In 1862, another born Scot from Edinburgh, arrived in Dunedin to conduct a geological survey of Otago and three years later he was appointed to found the Geological Survey of New Zealand, managing New Zealand's premier scientific society. It must be stated, however, that not all of the emigrants have made their presence a wholly welcome one in this land. Thankfully, this type of immigrant is far from common-place.

Source E: from J. D. Mackie, *A History of Scotland* (1978).

In almost every way Scotsmen were deriving benefits from the British Empire. It enabled some firms and individuals to make great fortunes; above all it offered opportunities of employment to the sons of the growing Scottish middle-class. This fact can be conveniently illustrated by reference to the jute trade of east-central Scotland, centred on Dundee. The raw material came from abroad: jute came almost exclusively from the Indian province of Bengal. The textile manufactured from this imported good was subsequently exported all over the world. Sacking from Dundee was used in great quantities, from Argentina to Canada. In the same way the heavy industries of Scotland exported a high proportion of their products. Canadian grain might well be taken in sacks made in Dundee, by locomotives manufactured in Springburn near Glasgow, to be loaded onto ships built on the Clyde.

[*END OF SOURCES FOR MIGRATION AND EMPIRE, 1830–1939*]

SPECIAL TOPIC 4: MIGRATION AND EMPIRE, 1830–1939

Marks

Answer *all* of the following questions.

1. How useful is **Source A** as evidence of the reasons for Scottish migration and emigration?
   In reaching a conclusion you should refer to:
   - *the origin and possible purpose of the source;*
   - *the content of the source;*
   - *recalled knowledge.*

   5

2. How fully does **Source B** illustrate the experience of immigrants in Scotland?
   Use the source and recalled knowledge.

   10

3. To what extent do **Sources C** and **D** agree about the contribution of Scots to the economic growth and development of the Empire?
   Compare the sources overall and in detail.

   5

4. How far does **Source E** show the importance of Empire to Scotland's development?
   Use the source and recalled knowledge.

   10

   (30)

[*END OF QUESTIONS ON MIGRATION AND EMPIRE, 1830–1939*]

SPECIAL TOPIC 5: THE IMPACT OF THE GREAT WAR, 1914–1928

Study the sources below and then answer the questions which follow.

Source A: from the diary of Private Thomas McCall, Cameron Highlanders describing the attack at Loos, September, 1915.

The soldier lying next to me gave a shout, saying, "My God! I'm done for". His mate next to him asked where he was shot. He drew himself back and lifted his wounded pal's kilt, then gave a laugh, saying, "Jock, ye'll no die. Yer only shot through the fleshy part of the leg!" We moved on towards the village of Loos, where machine guns were raking the streets and bayonet-fighting was going on with Jerry (slang for Germans). Prisoners were being marshalled in batches to be sent under guard down the line. I came to a little restaurant. By the noise going on inside I thought they were killing pigs. I went inside and opened a door where blood was running out from underneath. I saw some Highlanders busy, having it out with Jerry with the bayonet.

Source B: from Nicholas Morgan, *In War's Wake,* (1984).

During the four years of the war, recruitment to the armed forces from Scotland came to nearly a quarter of the adult male population, a higher percentage than any other country in the UK. Scottish forces suffered disproportionately higher losses than their English counterparts. Wartime, in particular, revolutionised the position of women in the economy, but women's war-work, whether unskilled tasks such as shell-filling or the more skilled jobs, was intended to be temporary. In 1918 women demonstrated in Glasgow, protesting against their enforced removal from the workplace. The slaughter remained to haunt a nation. Grey granite war memorials sprang up in cities, towns and especially villages throughout the country, where lists of names often paid testimony to rural communities that were never to recapture the strength of their pre-war years.

Source C: from Trevor Royle, *The Flowers of the Forest: Scotland and the First World War* (2006).

The Clyde in 1913 launched 750,000 tons of shipping but by the end of the 1920s the Clyde was launching merely 56,000 tons of shipping, and 69 per cent of insured workers in the Scottish shipbuilding trade were unemployed. In 1913 Scotland manufactured about one fifth of the U.K.'s steel output and employed 140,000 miners but 20 years later the coal industry was finding work for only 80,000 hands and producing a third less coal. In 1913 Scottish unemployment was well below 10% but in the 1920s it never fell below 10%. The Dundee jute trade was deeply depressed and the Borders woollen industry for the greater part of the year was on part-time working. In the late 1920s the value of Scottish farming was falling while it was still rising in England, and in the fishing industry the numbers of those employed and the value of the catch were both steadily dropping.

Source D: from Edwin Muir, *Scottish Journey* (1935).

By 1928 the story in Scotland was one of general economic decline. Between 1921 and 1923 shipbuilding on the Clyde dropped from 500,000 tons to 170,000 mainly as a result of cancellations but the Clyde was already beginning to pay for the artificial boom which had rescued it during the war years. On January 5 the unthinkable happened when the last ship to be built at Beardmore's left the Clyde and the shipyard at Dalmuir was put up for sale. Coal production suffered as a result of falling international markets, especially in Eastern Europe, and the same fate for the same reason hit the fishing industry. Jute production in Dundee was adversely affected by declining orders, shrinking markets and workers' strikes. In 1921 a census carried out by the Board of Agriculture showed the number of male farm workers had fallen a great deal. According to the Board's findings the decline was not restricted to any particular part of the country but was widespread throughout Scotland. Soon machine age farming would change the face of farming forever.

Source E: from T. M Devine, *The Scottish Nation 1700–2007* (2006).

The emergence of Red Clydeside and the Labour breakthrough was only one part of the realignment of Scottish politics after the war. The most decisive feature was the complete collapse of Liberalism as an effective electoral force. At the end of 1916 Lloyd George had split the party and by the election of 1918 Liberalism was in disarray. Among the working classes the Labour Party was most likely to benefit from Liberal misfortunes. The Rent Strike had greatly increased the prestige and influence of the ILP. While the Liberal government denounced strikers as unpatriotic, the ILP supported the workers' grievances over prices and rents. Labour also excelled in organisation. The focus was constantly on local issues of housing, rents and jobs. Labour gained the lion's share of the new post 1918 electorate. The reward came in 1924 when Labour became the biggest party in Scotland, sending 29 MPs to parliament.

[*END OF SOURCES FOR THE IMPACT OF THE GREAT WAR, 1914–1928*]

SPECIAL TOPIC 5: THE IMPACT OF THE GREAT WAR, 1914–1928

Marks

Answer *all* of the following questions.

1. How useful is **Source A** as evidence of the experience of Scots on the Western Front?
   In reaching a conclusion you should refer to:
   - *the origin and possible purpose of the source;*
   - *the content of the source;*
   - *recalled knowledge.*   5

2. How fully does **Source B** show the impact of war on Scottish society?
   Use the source and recalled knowledge.   10

3. To what extent do **Sources C** and **D** agree about the economic effect of the war on Scotland?
   Compare the sources overall and in detail.   5

4. How far does **Source E** explain the reasons for the growth of radicalism in politics in Scotland?
   Use the source and recalled knowledge.   10

                                                                                          (30)

[*END OF QUESTIONS ON THE IMPACT OF THE GREAT WAR, 1914–1928*]

[*END OF QUESTION PAPER*]

[BLANK PAGE]

2012

[BLANK PAGE]

X259/12/01

NATIONAL QUALIFICATIONS 2012	FRIDAY, 25 MAY 9.00 AM – 10.20 AM	HISTORY HIGHER Paper 1

Candidates should answer **two** questions, **one** from Historical Study: British History and **one** from Historical Study: European and World History.

All questions are worth 20 marks.

Marks may be deducted for bad spelling and bad punctuation, and for writing that is difficult to read.

[BLANK PAGE]

HISTORICAL STUDY: BRITISH HISTORY

Answer ONE question. Each question is worth 20 marks.

Church, State and Feudal Society

1. To what extent was the contribution of the Church to society in medieval Scotland and England confined to religion?

2. How successful were David I of Scotland and Henry II of England's attempts to increase royal authority?

3. How important was the growth of towns in causing the decline of feudal society?

The Century of Revolutions 1603–1702

4. How effective was Charles I's rule in Scotland between 1625 and 1642?

5. How important were religious issues in causing the Revolution of 1688 to 1689?

6. "Financial reform was the most significant change brought about by the Revolution Settlement." How valid is this view?

The Atlantic Slave Trade

7. To what extent was the slave trade the major factor in the development of the British economy in the eighteenth century?

8. "The slave trade was too important to the British economy to allow it to be abolished." How valid is this view?

9. How significant was the campaign organised by the Anti-Slavery Society in bringing about the abolition of the slave trade?

Britain 1851–1951

10. "Britain was still far from being a democratic country by 1928." How valid is this view?

11. To what extent did the Liberal reforms of 1906 to 1914 make a significant improvement to the lives of the British people?

12. "The Labour Government of 1945 to 1951 met the needs of the people 'from the cradle to the grave'." How valid is this view?

[Turn over

Britain and Ireland 1900–1985

13. How far did World War One change political attitudes towards British rule in Ireland?

14. How important were economic issues in contributing to the developing crisis in Northern Ireland up to 1968?

15. How important were the religious and communal differences between both communities in preventing peace in Ireland between 1968 and 1985?

HISTORICAL STUDY: EUROPEAN AND WORLD

Answer ONE question. Each question is worth 20 marks.

The Crusades, 1071–1204

16. How important were religious factors in the decision of Europeans to go on crusade?

17. "While Richard was a greater military leader, Saladin was a better diplomat." How valid is this view?

18. How far had the crusading ideal declined by the Fourth Crusade in 1204?

The American Revolution 1763–1787

19. How important was the rejection of the Olive Branch petition in the colonists' declaration of independence in 1776?

20. How important was the colonists' advantage of fighting on home ground in their eventual victory in the American Revolution?

21. "The American Constitution of 1787 was an answer to the problems highlighted by the experience of British rule." How accurate is this view?

The French Revolution, to 1799

22. To what extent did revolution break out in France in 1789 as a result of the economic crisis of 1788 to 1789?

23. To what extent did the increasing intervention of the army in politics bring about Napoleon's coup of 1799, which created the Consulate?

24. "The Bourgeoisie gained most from the French Revolution." How valid is this view?

Germany 1815–1939

25. How strong was nationalism in Germany by 1850?

26. To what extent were the weaknesses of the Weimar Republic the major reason for the rise of the Nazi Party between 1919 and 1933?

27. "Through their economic policies the Nazis gave the people what they wanted." How valid is this as a reason for the Nazis maintaining power between 1933 and 1939?

[Turn over

Italy 1815–1939

28. How successful were supporters of Italian nationalism up to 1850?

29. How accurate is it to argue that the appeal of fascism was the main reason why Mussolini came to power in Italy by 1925?

30. How important was the use of fear and intimidation in maintaining Fascist control over Italy between 1922 and 1939?

Russia 1881–1921

31. How important was working-class discontent in causing the 1905 revolution in Russia?

32. To what extent did the Bolsheviks gain power due to the weaknesses of the Provisional Government?

33. How important was the use of terror by the Reds in allowing them to win the Civil War?

USA 1918–1968

34. How far can it be argued that the activities of the Ku Klux Klan was the most important obstacle to the achievement of Civil Rights for black people up to 1941?

35. How important was the emergence of effective black leaders in the growing demand for Civil Rights between 1945 and 1968?

36. To what extent did the Civil Rights campaigns of the 1950s and 1960s result in significant improvements in the lives of black Americans?

Appeasement and the Road to War, to 1939

37. To what extent did fascist powers use diplomacy to achieve their aims?

38. "A reasonable settlement under the circumstances." How valid is this view of the Munich agreement of 1938?

39. To what extent did the occupation of Czechoslovakia in March 1939 lead to the outbreak of World War Two six months later?

The Cold War 1945–1989

40. How effectively did the Soviet Union control Eastern Europe up to 1961?

41. To what extent were the Superpowers' attempts to manage the Cold War between 1962 and 1985 prompted by the economic cost of the arms race?

42. How important was the role of Gorbachev in ending the Cold War?

[END OF QUESTION PAPER]

[BLANK PAGE]

X259/12/02

NATIONAL QUALIFICATIONS 2012	FRIDAY, 25 MAY 10.40 AM – 12.05 PM	**HISTORY HIGHER** Paper 2

Answer questions on only **one** Special Topic.

Take particular care to show clearly the Special Topic chosen. On the **front** of the answer book, **in the top right-hand corner**, write the number of the Special Topic.

You are expected to use background knowledge appropriately in answering source-based questions.

Marks may be deducted for bad spelling and bad punctuation, and for writing that is difficult to read.

Some sources have been adapted.

SPECIAL TOPIC 1: THE WARS OF INDEPENDENCE, 1286–1328

Study the sources below and answer the questions which follow.

Source A: from the Treaty of Birgham (1290).

Having considered the peace and tranquillity of both kingdoms and in doing so mutual friendship should continue between our peoples for all time, we have granted in the name of our lord (Edward I) that the rights and liberties and customs of Scotland shall be wholly preserved. We promise that the kingdom of Scotland shall remain separate and divided from the kingdom of England by rightful boundaries and borders as has been observed up to now and that it shall be free and independent.

We grant that no tenant-in-chief of the king of Scotland shall be forced to go outside the kingdom to do homage or fealty or to pay relief for his lands. No parliament shall be held outwith the kingdom and borders of Scotland on matters concerning that kingdom or its borders or the position of those that live in the kingdom. No one of the kingdom of Scotland shall be held to answer outwith that kingdom for any agreement entered into, or for any crime committed, or in any other cause contrary to the laws and customs of that kingdom.

Source B: from GWS Barrow, *Robert Bruce* (1988).

The whole course of the negotiations which culminated in the marriage agreement, called the Treaty of Birgham, shows the guardians above all anxious to do nothing that might impair the "rights" or the integrity of Scotland.

The Treaty of Birgham was the high-watermark of the endeavour by the Guardians and the community. The treaty envisaged two feudal kingdoms, England and Scotland ruled separately though in harmony by a king and queen. The Scottish kingdom was to remain, as the Scots had demanded, free and without subjugation. Elections to the clergy in Scotland were to be free of external interference and tenants-in-chief of the Scots Crown need do homage for their lands in Scotland only, persons in Scotland who had been accused of a crime or sued at law should not have to answer in a court outside their country.

The treaty has been praised as a document of wise statesmanship and patriotism, but it was also something else. It was essentially a cautious, protective document.

Source C: from the Chronicle of Walter of Guisborough, 1296.

All that day and the next our king was expecting the burgesses of Berwick to come to his peace but they would not accept the peace which he offered. Twenty-four English warships attacked Berwick but were driven back. When these things were told to our king who was still in the field where everyone could see the smoke rising high from the ships, the king ordered them to sound the bugles and enter the city. When the city was taken they killed more than 8,000 of the enemy. On the same day the men of strength who were in the castle garrison surrendered. The king kept their captain Lord William Douglas until the end of the war. He allowed two hundred men who were with him to go free carrying their arms having first taken an oath from them that they would never lift a hand against him or the kingdom of the English.

Source D: from A.F. Murison, *Sir William Wallace* (2000).

The remnants of the Scots army drew from Falkirk towards the north, burning the town and castle of Stirling as they passed. So far Edward pursued them. Having repaired the castle and garrisoned it with Northumbrians, he is said to have harried St Andrews and St Johnston. He then passed through Selkirk Forrest to the west where he found that Bruce had burned Ayr Castle and retired to Carrick, but Edward could not pursue for lack of food. Continuing his journey through Annandale, Edward took and burned Loch Maben castle. At Carlisle he held a parliament and distributed lands in Scotland to his officers.

Shortly after their retreat from Falkirk, perhaps at Scots Water, or at a meeting in St Johnston, Wallace is said to have resigned voluntarily the office of Guardian of Scotland. The Scots writers at the time stated that this step was necessary because of the impossibility of maintaining the independence of his country in co-operation with the jealous nobles.

Source E: from Richard Oram, *The Kings and Queens of Scotland* (2006).

Robert was quick to capitalise on Bannockburn. Not only was he able to recover his queen and daughter from captivity in exchange for English prisoners, but also at parliament in November he overcame his remaining Scottish opponents and took their lands in Scotland. This gave him extensive resources with which to reward his supporters and subjects in order to secure their loyalty. Robert also intensified his attacks on northern England both in search for cash and to force Edward II to recognise Bruce's kingship of a free Scotland. The bleeding of northern England in 1314–1315 really did little to pressure Edward II.

By 1323 Bruce attempted to secure peace for war-weary Scotland, even negotiating a peace not with Edward II but his lieutenants in northern England. Yet faced with the English King's refusal to give up Scotland, Robert had to settle for a long uneasy truce in 1323. Robert did not withdraw from politics, but worked hard to ensure a relatively stable inheritance for his son. A new mutual defence agreed with France in 1326 was part of this, but a full peace, between England and an independent Scotland, was still his ultimate goal.

[*END OF SOURCES FOR THE WARS OF INDEPENDENCE, 1286–1328*]

SPECIAL TOPIC 1: THE WARS OF INDEPENDENCE, 1286–1328

Marks

Answer *all* of the following questions.

1.   To what extent do **Sources A** and **B** agree about the Scots' attempts to protect their independence after the death of Alexander III?
Compare the sources overall and in detail.   **5**

2.   How useful is **Source C** as evidence of the subjugation of the Scots by Edward I in 1296?
In reaching a conclusion you should refer to:
  • *the origin and possible purpose of the source;*
  • *the content of the source;*
  • *recalled knowledge.*   **5**

3.   How far does **Source D** show the changing military balance between Scotland and England, 1298–1301?
Use the source and recalled knowledge.   **10**

4.   How fully does **Source E** explain the reasons for the ultimate success of Bruce in maintaining Scotland's independence?
Use the source and recalled knowledge.   **10**

(30)

[*END OF QUESTIONS ON THE WARS OF INDEPENDENCE, 1286–1328*]

SPECIAL TOPIC 2: THE AGE OF REFORMATION, 1542–1603

Study the sources below and answer the questions which follow.

Source A: from *The Treaty of Edinburgh*, 1560.

At Edinburgh on 6 July 1560 the following terms are agreed between France and England. All military forces of each party shall withdraw from the realm of Scotland, and all warlike operations in England, Ireland and Wales shall entirely cease. And since the realms of England and Ireland belong by right to Queen Elizabeth, no other is allowed to call, write, name or have himself called, written or named king or queen of England or Ireland. Nor is anyone to use the signs and arms of those kingdoms. It is therefore agreed that the most Christian King Francis and Queen Mary shall abstain from using or carrying the said title or arms of the kingdom of England or Ireland. And King Francis and Queen Mary will fulfil all those things which were granted by their representatives to the nobility and people of Scotland provided that the nobility and people of Scotland fulfil and observe what was contained in those conventions and articles.

Source B: from Rosalind K. Marshall, *John Knox* (2000).

Mary of Guise died shortly after midnight on 11 June 1560. Elizabeth I had already sent William Cecil to Newcastle to negotiate with French envoys and he now moved to Edinburgh. A truce was arranged between England and France and the Treaty of Edinburgh was signed on 6 July. The principal clause stated that all foreign soldiers were to withdraw from Scotland. Francis II and Mary, Queen of Scots, would henceforth abstain from displaying the English arms with those of Scotland. Since the Scots had spontaneously and freely professed and acknowledged their obedience and loyalty towards their most Christian king and queen, Francis and Mary would fulfil all their obligations in the treaty. Everything relating to religion would be referred to the Scots Parliament, and after the treaty had been signed John Knox held a great service of thanksgiving in St Giles.

Source C: from Sir James Melville, *The Murder of Riccio*, 9 March 1566.

David Riccio obtained the position of secretary to Mary, and got her Majesty's attention, which caused him to be so envied and hated that some of the nobility would ignore him. I told him that it was thought that most of the business of the country passed through his hands, and advised him, when the nobility were present, to give them their place. However, the King, Darnley, probably gave his consent too easily to the slaughter of seigneur Riccio, which the Lords of Morton, Ruthven, Lindsay and others had devised, so that they could be masters of the court and hold the parliament. When the murderers entered, seigneur Riccio clutched the Queen and cried for mercy; but George Douglas drew out the King's dagger and struck him with it. He gave screams and cries and was roughly removed from the Queen, who could not get him safe, neither by threat or entreaty. He was forcibly dragged out of the room and slain and her Majesty was kept captive.

Source D: from Jenny Wormald ed., *Scotland: A History*, (2005).

The King's tolerance of Catholic earls had long been resented by the Kirk. When local feuding between the Catholic Earl of Huntly and the Protestant Earl of Moray led to the latter's murder, the incident was used by the Kirk to gain concessions in the Golden Act. Yet despite the Golden Act, James never conceded the principle of royal supremacy over the Kirk. He would make increasingly successful efforts to tighten royal control over the general assembly and re-establish the authority of bishops. Following the crisis years of the 1590s, James published his works on kingship, reflecting on the necessity of obedience to his divinely ordained authority and on the challenges of managing an unruly Kirk and powerful nobility. These suggest a monarch deeply frustrated by his subjects' lack of respect for the crown's authority, and show his determination to civilise his kingdom by bringing Scotland's remote localities under more direct royal control.

Source E: from Ian B. Cowan, *The Scottish Reformation* (1982).

The way the partnership between Kirk and society worked in post-Reformation Scotland was very different from the pre-Reformation era. The most striking aspect of this new relationship was a new religious fervour demonstrated by an unwavering support for Presbyterian beliefs. In some respects the role of the church in society had been greatly reduced because secular forces undertook duties that had previously been the preserve of the Catholic Church. The right of a congregation to choose its own minister was asserted in the Second Book of Discipline. The place of music in the services of the Kirk and in the life of the people was to suffer as a result of the Reformation. The character of the Kirk was established in the immediate post-Reformation era when political and economic circumstances forced the victorious reformers to adopt a compassionate attitude towards the representatives of the old faith. In this respect the Scottish Reformation was to produce little of the intolerance that characterised the Reformation in England and on the continent.

[*END OF SOURCES FOR THE AGE OF REFORMATION, 1542–1603*]

SPECIAL TOPIC 2: THE AGE OF REFORMATION, 1542–1603

Marks

Answer *all* of the following questions.

1. To what extent do **Sources A** and **B** agree about the changes brought in by the Treaty of Edinburgh in 1560?
   Compare the sources overall and in detail.   **5**

2. How useful is **Source C** in explaining Mary's difficulties in ruling Scotland?
   In reaching a conclusion you should refer to:
   - *the origin and possible purpose of the source;*
   - *the content of the source;*
   - *recalled knowledge.*   **5**

3. How far does **Source D** illustrate the efforts of James VI to control the Kirk?
   Use the source and recalled knowledge.   **10**

4. How fully does **Source E** explain the impact of the Reformation on Scotland?
   Use the source and recalled knowledge.   **10**

   (30)

[*END OF QUESTIONS ON THE AGE OF REFORMATION, 1542–1603*]

SPECIAL TOPIC 3: THE TREATY OF UNION, 1689–1740

Study the sources below and answer the questions which follow.

Source A: from Christopher A. Whatley, *The Scots and the Union* (2006).

In the 1690s Scotland was tipped over the edge of an economic abyss that was to have profound political consequences for the nation's history. Factors included a series of harvest failures and the effects of England's war with Scotland's ally France, particularly the damaging loss of French trade. The erection of protective tariffs by countries overseas blocked the export of certain Scottish goods. Finally, there was the disaster of Darien, Scotland's ambitious scheme to establish a colony in South America. As it happened, the outcome—eventually—was incorporating union with England, but the decade of crisis might equally have produced a very different result.

Source B: from Daniel Defoe, *History of the Union* (1709).

Since the Union of the Crowns in 1603, and in a hundred years of joint monarchy with England, the Scots had been very sensitive to the sinking economic condition of their nation. Also, they were aware of the visible damage both to trade and to the wealth of the inhabitants of the country. This was plainly owing to the loss of Scottish ministers' presence at Court in London, the disadvantages of tariffs and the influence the English had over their kings. It was just as plain that one way for the Scots to restore themselves was in terms of incorporating union and alliance with England. There would be advantages for Scottish commerce of free access to English and empire markets. Without incorporating union, the Scottish economy would remain unstable. It was either union, or a return back to their separate self-existing state.

Source C: is from a petition from Stirling Town Council to the Scottish Parliament, 18 November 1706.

We have considered the great affair of Union of Scotland and England as contained in the articles of the treaty. We desire true and continued peace and friendship with our neighbours in England. However, we judge it our duty to the nation and parliament, with all due respect to parliament, to state that this treaty will prove ruinous to our manufacturing industry, since the new freedom of trade will never balance the new insupportable burden of taxation. The treaty will deprive us, and the rest of the royal burghs in this nation, of our fundamental right of being represented in the legislative power. Thus, an ancient nation, so long and gloriously defended by patriots, will be suppressed as our dear parliament is extinguished and we are brought under a burden which we will never be able to bear, with fatal consequences which we tremble to think about.

Source D: is from Douglas Watt, *The Price of Scotland: Darien, Union and the Wealth of Nations* (2007).

It was anticipated that there would be little opposition to the treaty in the English Parliament, so it made sense to secure its passage in Scotland first. The Scottish Parliament opened on 3 October in a tense Edinburgh. The tactics of the opposition were to disrupt and delay proceedings and hope for a popular uprising against the treaty. Riots rocked Edinburgh and Glasgow in November and December. Anti-union petitions flooded into parliament. However, the opposition was divided and poorly led by the unpredictable Duke of Hamilton. He may have been bribed by the Court party. At a crucial point, when there were plans to withdraw from parliament, he called off with the excuse of toothache and then, on his return to parliament, he refused to participate in the walkout. An armed rising by Cameronians and Jacobites turned into a fiasco as its leaders backed down when they were paid off by Queensberry. This attempt proved that the political opposition to union were not willing to engage in violence to support the continued existence of the Scottish Parliament.

Source E: is from Paul Henderson Scott, *The Union of 1707* (2006).

One irony of the Union is that it did not in the end extinguish Scotland as a nation; it retained its own distinctive identity, attitudes and ideas, and its traditions were so strong that they were not easily eradicated. The consequences of the Treaty in this respect were not as harmful as they might have been, although it did exert a strong Anglicising influence. Nevertheless, the guarantees to the Scottish legal system in the Treaty and to the Church in the Act of Security for the Kirk had more influence on Scotland than the distant British Parliament. English and Scottish historians have concluded that the continuation of the Scottish systems of education and local government were a significant achievement of Union.

[*END OF SOURCES FOR THE TREATY OF UNION, 1689–1740*]

SPECIAL TOPIC 3: THE TREATY OF UNION, 1689–1740

Marks

Answer *all* of the following questions.

1. To what extent do **Sources A** and **B** agree about worsening relations between Scotland and England between 1690 and 1705?
    Compare the sources overall and in detail. **5**

2. How useful is **Source C** as evidence of attitudes towards the union in Scotland?
    In reaching a conclusion you should refer to:
    *   *the origin and possible purpose of the source;*
    *   *the content of the source;*
    *   *recalled knowledge.* **5**

3. How far does **Source D** explain the passage of the Treaty of Union through the Scottish Parliament?
    Use the source and recalled knowledge. **10**

4. How fully does **Source E** explain the effects of Union up to 1740?
    Use the source and recalled knowledge. **10**

    (30)

[*END OF QUESTIONS ON THE TREATY OF UNION, 1689–1740*]

SPECIAL TOPIC 4: MIGRATION AND EMPIRE, 1830–1939

Study the sources below and answer the questions which follow.

Source A: from the Quarterly Journal of Agriculture 1832–1834.

I have not the slightest hesitation in declaring, that it appears to me as plain as the sun at noonday, that a farmer in Scotland, occupying a farm that does not pay him, distressed as he must be, struggling from morning to night with mental anxiety and worry pressing upon his mind and yet after all quite unable to support his family or better their circumstances—I say that a farmer continuing to remain in Scotland even when unemployed while so much land lies in Canada to occupy, acts the part of an insane person. In a short time there will be no cheap land to be procured about these parts. The best way for my brothers to lay out their money here in Canada is in buying land which is every year rising in value.

Source B: from the *Scotsman*, 20 February 1923, "Emigration boom in the Hebrides".

Great interest is being taken in the scheme of the Ontario government to emigrate young men and women between 18 and 23 to Canada. The Ontario agent finds that he could treble the number he is authorised to enlist owing no doubt to the depressed state of trade in Lewis, the lack of employment generally and the inability of the farmers to satisfy the hunger of the families. Immediately on landing, employment will be found for farmers and the women can find employment in domestic work. The pay is good as experienced men can at the very start earn £5 to £6 per month. The men also have the prospect of becoming owners of their own farms once again.

Source C: adapted from *New Arrivals* by Tony Jaconelli in *Our Glasgow Story*.

On New Year's day 1921, I trailed along holding on to my younger brother, Michael. Our father, Domenico, carried Biagio. My oldest brother, Giacomo, brought up the rear. We had left our warm village in Italy to join Domenico's brother in some place called Scotland. School was a nightmare for me but Giacomo, a name that was quickly shortened to Jack, revelled in school life. He was a quick learner and always able to take care of himself. A few times I found myself surrounded by classmates chanting at me because I was a foreigner. Jack scattered them and they stopped bothering me completely. Our family moved house a few times in an effort to improve our lot. Domenico took a job in the largely Italian trade of terrazzo tile workers and most of my brothers followed him into the trade. Meanwhile my grasp of the Glasgow dialect improved daily. Within a couple of years I lost all trace of my mother tongue and developed a strong, guttural Glasgow accent. In no time at all I was a complete Glaswegian.

Source D: from Ian Donnachie, *Success in the "Lucky" Country* (1988).

There were many fields of Scottish achievement in Australia. Scots were early and successful pioneers in sheep farming and the wool trade, which became big business, centred in places such as Melbourne and Adelaide. Scots also invested heavily in mining, at first in coal and later in copper, silver and gold. The Gold Rush of the 1850s brought to Australia a considerable number of Scottish miners, many of whom stayed after the initial gold fever died down and prospered. Shipping and trade were other areas of enterprise in which Scots excelled. Two later shipping firms were both fiercely Scottish, McIllwraith McEachan and Burns Philp. The profits of Burns Philp were built on the northern Queensland sugar boom of the 1880s in which Scots played a large part in creating the profitable business. Politics and government was another sphere in which the Scots made a sustained contribution to Australian life.

Source E: from ed. T.M. Devine, *Irish Immigrants and Scottish Society in the Nineteenth and Twentieth Centuries* (1991).

The immigration of the Irish into Scotland forms one of the most significant themes of modern Scottish history. The movement of the Irish changed the population balance of several lowland towns but especially Glasgow, Greenock, Dundee, Paisley and Airdrie, among others. Scotland's industrialisation was made easier because employers had access to a huge reservoir of Irish labour which was not only cheap but, was ready and willing to move anywhere and do anything to find work. The huge construction schemes of the nineteenth-century cities and the roads, railways, canals, docks and harbours that supported Scotland's industrial revolution depended ultimately on this vast labour supply. To local Scots, the Irish arrivals seemed to be overwhelmingly poor, diseased, mainly Catholic and recognisably alien. In short, the Irish were seen as a dangerous threat to the Scottish way of life. The Irish presence is also vital to an understanding of Scottish culture as the Catholic Irish and their descendants have played such an influential role in the evolution and shaping of Scottish society ranging from literature to music and on to football.

[*END OF SOURCES FOR MIGRATION AND EMPIRE, 1830–1939*]

SPECIAL TOPIC 4: MIGRATION AND EMPIRE, 1830–1939

Answer *all* of the following questions.

Marks

1. To what extent do **Sources A** and **B** agree about the reasons for Scottish migration to Canada?
   Compare the sources overall and in detail.   **5**

2. How useful is **Source C** as evidence of the assimilation of immigrants into Scottish society?
   In reaching a conclusion you should refer to:
   * *the origin and possible purpose of the source;*
   * *the content of the source;*
   * *recalled knowledge.*   **5**

3. How far does **Source D** show the contribution of Scots to the economic growth and development of the Empire?
   Use the source and recalled knowledge.   **10**

4. How fully does **Source E** explain the effects of migration and Empire on Scottish society?
   Use the source and recalled knowledge.   **10**

                                                                                              (30)

[*END OF QUESTIONS ON MIGRATION AND EMPIRE, 1830–1939*]

SPECIAL TOPIC 5: THE IMPACT OF THE GREAT WAR, 1914–1928

Study the sources below and answer the questions which follow.

Source A: by John Jackson, *Private 12768: Memoir of a Tommy* (2004) writing about the Battle of Loos.

The situation at Hill 70 was serious. A third time the order was given to attack that awful hillside, but the enemy with his reserves at hand, were too many for us and again we fell back, truly we were holding to the motto of the regiment "A Cameron never can yield". We numbered at this stage less than 100 and for all we knew might be all that was left of 6th Cameron Highlanders. As the evening drew on we made a fourth and final attempt to win and hold the ridge. This time we meant to do or die. To the sound of the pipes and led by our brave old colonel, bareheaded and with no other weapon than his walking stick, we made for the top of Hill 70 through murderous rifle and machine gun fire, while shells crashed all around us. We made the top but now we were desperate for the promised reinforcements but no help could we see.

Source B: by Philip Gibbs, official British wartime correspondent on the Western Front for the *Daily Chronicle*, writing about the Battle of Loos.

By seven-forty the two assaulting brigades of the 15th Division had left the trenches and were in the open. Shriller than the scream of shells above them was the skirl of pipes, going with them. The orders of the Scottish troops, which I saw, were to go "all out," and to press onto Hill 70, with the absolute assurance that all the ground they gained would be held behind them by supporting troops. With the promise of reinforcements to follow, they trudged on to Hill 70. For a time there was a kind of Bank Holiday crowd on Hill 70. The German machine gunners, knowing that the redoubt on the crest was still held by their men, initially dared not fire. Then the quiet of Hill 70 was broken by the beginning of a new bombardment from German guns. "Dig in," said the officers. "We must hold on at all costs until the reinforcements come up." None came and they were forced to withdraw.

Source C: from *The Glasgow Herald,* 29th October 1915.

The first attempt to put into force the eviction notices which have been issued against Glasgow tenants who are participating in the "Rent Strikes" was made yesterday afternoon in Merryland Street, Govan. The householder is a woman who has not been making her rent payments. As has been the custom since the beginning of the movement against increased rents, a demonstration of the "strikers" was held at the time when the eviction notice became operative. While Mrs Barbour of the Glasgow Women's Housing Association was addressing those who had assembled, two sheriff officers arrived and endeavoured to gain admission to the house. As soon as it was known that it was proposed to evict the tenant the demonstrators determined to resist. Most of them were women, and they attacked the officers and their assistants with peasmeal, flour, and whiting. A woman was arrested on a charge of assaulting one of the officers.

Source D: from Clive H. Lee *The Scottish Economy and the First World War* (Scotland and the Great War edited by C.M.M. MacDonald and E.W. McFarland 1999).

Many of the changes caused by the war were temporary such as the readjustment of agricultural production to improve self-sufficiency and the boom in the jute industry. When normal trade was resumed in the 1920s, the massively weakened position of British manufacturers in export markets became apparent. As a consequence of the war, Scottish and British industry lost its international competitiveness. The war certainly shifted the balance of international trade against Scottish shipbuilders by increasing world-wide capacity which hit the industry after the war. Also, Scottish textile manufacturers were never able to regain the Asian markets, especially India, as the war allowed competitors to move in. But the war also demonstrated the fragility of the Scottish heavy industry base and the growing need for imported raw materials.

Source E: from W. Hamish Fraser, *Scottish Popular Politics From Radicalism to Labour* (2000).

The war years also showed that support for Scottish Home Rule had not really declined. The policy of the Scottish Trade Union Congress was to call on the Parliamentary Labour Party to support "the enactment of a Scottish Home Rule Bill". The same spirit of nationalism forced Arthur Henderson and the Labour leadership in London, much against their better judgement, to allow a separate Scottish Council of Labour with a considerable amount of self-government. At the same time, the war undermined even further the organisation of Scottish Liberalism, but also much of its moral authority. The more radical elements were disenchanted by Lloyd George's political tactics and by his aggressive determination to accept nothing less than unconditional surrender. Liberalism was thrown into disarray while the ILP was able to emerge as the natural successor to advanced liberal radicalism.

[*END OF SOURCES FOR THE IMPACT OF THE GREAT WAR, 1914–1928*]

SPECIAL TOPIC 5: THE IMPACT OF THE GREAT WAR, 1914–1928

Marks

Answer *all* of the following questions.

1. To what extent do **Sources A** and **B** agree about the experience of Scots on the Western Front?
   Compare the sources overall and in detail.   **5**

2. How useful is **Source C** as evidence of the impact of the war on Scottish women?
   In reaching a conclusion you should refer to:
   • *the origin and possible purpose of the source;*
   • *the content of the source;*
   • *recalled knowledge.*   **5**

3. How far does **Source D** illustrate the economic difficulties faced by Scotland after 1918?
   Use the source and recalled knowledge.   **10**

4. How fully does **Source E** describe the impact of the war on political developments in Scotland?
   Use the source and recalled knowledge.   **10**

                                                                                                    (30)

[*END OF QUESTIONS ON THE IMPACT OF THE GREAT WAR, 1914–1928*]

[*END OF QUESTION PAPER*]

[BLANK PAGE]

HIGHER | ANSWER SECTION

SQA HIGHER HISTORY
SPECIMEN QUESTION PAPER, 2011 & 2012

HIGHER HISTORY PAPER 1
SQP

1. Each question is marked out of 20.

2. In Paper 1 candidates will be rewarded according to:

   (a) **Knowledge and Understanding – 6 marks are allocated for** the relevant knowledge they use to address the question. Marks will be awarded for each accurate, full point they make; these points may be further developed, as in the following example, relating to the effectiveness of the Liberal Reforms:

   Old age pensions *(0 marks for stating this)* **were given to all people over 70** *(1 mark)*; **married couples received 7/6 and single people 5s** *(a second mark for knowledge).* **This provision was not enough to live on, but old people were able to help pay their families if they lived with them** *(no further mark for knowledge, but an argument which would receive credit under the category Argument and Evaluation).*

   (b) **Argument/Evaluation – 10 marks are allocated for** the quality of thought revealed in their answers by the arguments and evaluation demonstrated. This should be taken as including the extent to which the candidate:

   - gives an answer which is relevant to the question and relates explicitly to the question's terms;
   - argues a case;
   - makes the various distinctions required by the question;
   - responds to all the elements in the question, and to any isolated factor in particular;
   - explains, analyses, debates and assesses rather than simply describes or narrates;
   - answers with clarity and fluency and in language appropriate to historical writing at this level.

   (c) **Structure – 4 marks are allocated for** the appropriateness of the organisation of the answer, according to the degree to which the response

   - establishes the context of the question and the relevant factors to be considered in the introduction
   - demonstrates a development of the issue
   - responds to the question in the form of a balanced conclusion based on the evidence and arguments deployed.

3. The following descriptions provide additional guidance on the marks awarded to essays displaying various characteristics.

KNOWLEDGE – Up to 6 marks can be awarded for substantive points and points further developed which are relevant and accurate.

STRUCTURE – Up to 4 marks can be awarded if:

The introduction clearly sets the issue in its wider context, indicates relevant factors and demonstrates a solid line of argument.

There is a coherent development directly focused on the question.

The conclusion is balanced, summarising the arguments and coming to an overall judgement directly related to the question.

ARGUMENT – Up to 10 marks can be awarded if:

The evidence is integrated into a sustained analysis.

The argument is sustained and balanced, with some awareness of alternative interpretations and/or historical debate.

Historical Study: British History

Church, State and Feudal Society

1. The candidate assesses the extent to which the life of peasants was 'poor, brutal and without hope', using evidence and arguments such as:

Arguments for poor, brutal and hopeless lifestyle

Place in society

- The feudal term of villein or serf indicated a peasant who was not free to leave his home farm or village. They were bought and sold along with the land and were expected to work at least 3 days a week in the lord's lands without recompense and hand over the best of their produce in exchange for the rent of their farmland.

Work

- Peasants, or villains, tended to work hard, mostly in the agricultural sector. All the work had to be done by hand and this resulted in long hours of backbreaking work.
- Not all peasants received the same amount of good farming land, and often it was the case that land was rotated amongst the peasants. This dissuaded them from attempts to improve the land; many did not put in the extra effort when next year their neighbour would reap the benefit.

Lifestyle

- Accommodation was often very poor, especially for the lower strata of peasant society. Many peasants lived in poorly constructed one-bedroom dwellings, which they shared with their animals. A single hearth provided all the heat, lighting and cooking facilities.
- Firewood was at a premium; peasants were forced to pay a penny to their lord for the right to pick up fallen wood for the fires.
- Food was basic and, in times of famine, starvation was a real threat.

Arguments against such a brutal existence

Place in society

- Peasants played an important part of feudal society, beyond the need for a productive class working in agriculture. It was expected that peasants would run their own day-to-day lives without the need for the feudal lord's presence. Local reeves and bailiffs, appointed by the peasants or the lord himself, would act in his stead.
- Villeins had to organise themselves through the local manor court. The court dealt with sharing the land, fined those that broke the rules, and even brought murderers to trial.

Work

- While work was hard the manor court ensured that everyone had a fair share of the good land to grow their crops. During bad times there were systems in place to share out food so that no one in the village went hungry.
- As the 12th century progressed famine became rare in England, since the manor system pulled in isolated communities and helped create new more viable villages throughout the kingdom.

- Improvements in agricultural equipment and the use of ploughs drawn by horses instead of oxen speeded up the work and reduced the hours required in the field.

Lifestyle

- Archaeological evidence points to homes occupied by small nuclear families, some with upper rooms that indicate a level of privacy previously thought impossible.
- Evidence of leisure activities included cards, chess pieces, musical instruments and even a football. Peasants were no longer bound to their lord's land as they once were.

Social mobility

- Some peasants famously left behind their humble beginnings, proving that social mobility was possible in the 13th and 14th centuries. William of Wykeham became bishop of Winchester.

2. The candidate assesses the political role of the Church with its religious role within society, using evidence and arguments such as:

Arguments that the church's role was political

Investiture contest

- Political argument between the Church and State as to who had the right to appoint senior clergy members. Such offices came with large grants of land in England and often held considerable political and military significance.
- Monarchs did not wish the papacy to choose political undesirables for such an important position eg William the Lion and the argument over the Bishop of St Andrews in 1180.

Position within Feudal Structure

- Within the feudal system bishops and abbots were seen as other large landowners with the rights to raise troops in time of need eg Bishop of Durham led the English forces that defeated David I at the Battle of the Standard in 1138.

Administrative role

- The Church provided the majority of clerks for the state government. They were needed to keep records, write charters, laws, keep accounts etc.

Divine authority

- The development of canon law during this period was a direct threat to the growth of the monarchies. The papacy argued that all power of kings was invested through them during their coronation by God through the church.
- Monarchs argued that the power was given directly to them by God. As such, the papal position was that kings were subservient to popes. The papacy continued to argue their position and used papal sanctions such as excommunication and the interdict to bring monarchs to heel.

Arguments that the church's role was religious

Belief in Christianity

- This was dominant within society; it provided people with an understanding of the world and how it worked. The Church held the key to this understanding and the promise of salvation and eternal life after death. Through the power of the sacrament the church effectively held the keys to heaven.

Church services

- The importance of marriage, funerals and christenings brought people closer to attaining their passage to heaven.

Relics and saints

- Significance of relics and saints as a means to communicate with God and beg divine favour or protection.

Importance of the pilgrimage

- Pilgrimage, including the Crusade, to holy centres was an important part of medieval life.

The role of the Regular Church

- Monasteries were seen as 'Prayer Factories' and used to intercede with God for the ordinary lay population.

3. The candidate evaluates the importance of their desire to modernise the economy as a cause of monarchy's increasing central authority during the 12th century, using evidence and arguments such as:

Arguments that the economy was the most significant reason for the development of a more central form of government

Growing cost of warfare

- Throughout the 12th century kings found it increasingly more expensive to raise the funds to build castles or raise feudal armies.

Civil war in England

- Constant warfare during the period of civil war in England drained the treasury.
- During the time of upheaval between Stephen and Matilda, barons and sheriffs had become increasingly lax in paying their taxes. Sheriffs kept the taxes collected in their region for themselves, or only a small amount found its way into the royal treasury.

Under-developed economy in Scotland

- Prior to David I, revenue was mostly limited to the incomes from royal demesnes. The lack of royal burghs limited international trade and early medieval Scottish kings lacked the financial resources to tackle the Mormaers directly without the Community of the Realm backing them.

Other factors promoting the need to develop central authority

Law and order

- Throughout England and Scotland the justice system was liable to change depending on which lord held sway over that part of the land. Money often bought justice and archaic trial by ordeal or combat was still common.
- Royal justice was usually reserved for more serious crimes. Issues of land, an important aspect of justice, were often poorly judged or unfairly settled.

Growth of the nobility

- In both England and Scotland the power of the monarchy was threatened by the growth in power of the nobility.

Nobles in England

- During the time of the Civil War the barons had increased in stature and political importance due to both sides vying for their support. As a result barons built castles without royal permission, increased the numbers of knights beyond limits agreed by their charters, acquired land illegally and many hired large armies of Flemish mercenaries.

Nobles in Scotland

- The Mormaers in Scotland were semi-independent and held almost autonomous power over large tracts of Scotland. The Earls of Moray had a long tradition of independence, even going so far as to usurp the crown during the reign of Macbeth. The common army of Scotland was summoned by the Mormaers not the king, and was directly under their control.

Introduction of feudalism into Scotland

- David I's introduction allowed him to increase the number of loyal barons and create a new feudal court.

The Century of Revolutions 1603-1702

4. The candidate evaluates the importance of finance within the wider context of other factors contributing to the challenge to authority, using evidence and arguments such as:

Finance

* James I wanted to exist financially independent of Parliament. He manipulated the statute books to re-impose anachronistic laws which were designed merely to raise revenue. Fiscal devices such as monopolies and wardships were unpopular. The king alienated his natural allies in the House of Lords by selling honours and titles and appearing to devalue the status of the aristocracy. His increases in customs duties led to the Bates Case in 1606 which James I won, although Parliament declared the duties illegal in 1610.

Other factors

Religion

* James I had a lifelong hatred of Puritanism. Puritans existed in large numbers in the House of Commons and were demanding church reform. The king feared moves towards Presbyterianism and rejected the Millenary Petition at the Hampton Court Conference of 1604, saying 'no bishops, no king'. He vowed to maintain an Episcopalian Church of England.
* He relaxed the Recusancy Laws against Roman Catholics, which revealed that there were more Roman Catholics than many in the House of Commons had feared. The Gunpowder Plot of 1605 increased tension and turned many against Roman Catholics. Parliament was horrified that the king allowed his son to marry a Roman Catholic French princess and allow her to celebrate mass privately at court.

Politics

* Parliament had been encouraged since the days of Henry VIII to make policy, and therefore its members felt they could criticise the Crown freely. However, James I asserted the Divine Right of Kings as he claimed he had been accustomed to this in Scotland, which made his status as a foreigner more unattractive to the English Parliament.
* The House of Commons opposed him to an extent which affected the stability of the nation. The king conceded defeat in the Goodwin Case which gave Parliament fresh impetus to challenge him further. James I attempted to curtail Parliamentary freedom of speech by imprisoning outspoken MPs in the Tower of London when Parliament was dissolved.

Law

* James I attempted to control the court system by appointing judges who would favour the Crown. Parliament saw this as unfair and objected to the abuse of power. The king imposed martial law in towns where troops were preparing to embark on foreign campaigns. Parliament opposed this. The king billeted troops in the homes of civilians in order to enforce the law.

5. The candidate assesses the extent of the success with which Charles I imposed his authority on Scotland, using evidence and arguments such as:

Political challenge

* Charles I caused political resentment as a result of his policies which took power and land from Scottish nobles, as well as his decision not to visit Scotland until 1633, when he was crowned there. After this he appointed bishops rather than nobles to the Scottish Privy Council, including John Spottiswoode as Chancellor, the first non-secular official in this position since the Reformation.
* Charles I gave increasing power to bishops, which undermined the status of the Scottish nobility. The Stuart notion of the Divine Right of Kings was chiefly brought to an end by the Scots' opposition to Charles I's attempts to impose his will on the Scottish people.

Religious policy

* Charles I introduced William Laud, the Archbishop of Canterbury, to Scotland in 1633, and Laud proceeded to oversee Anglican practice in Scottish churches, which was resented by many. The king approved of a unification of the churches without consulting the Privy Council. The 1635 Book of Canons declared that the monarch had authority over the Church of Scotland and introduced a new Service Book which was a Scottish bishops' variation of the English Prayer Book. On 23 July 1637 it was read at St. Giles Cathedral by the Dean, John Hanna, who subsequently had a stool thrown at him by a serving woman, Jenny Geddes. In the chaos that ensued, the Bishop of Edinburgh was shouted down by the crowd in support of Geddes. Across Scotland people declared their opposition to the Service Book, placing Charles I's Privy Council in a difficult position, caught between the king and his opponents.

The Covenanters

* In Scotland the Covenanting movement challenged Charles I over his religious policies and was also politically active. Covenanters wanted to preserve Presbyterianism in Scotland. The National Covenant of 1638 was designed to promote a church free from monarchical meddling.
* Charles I's failure to suppress the Covenanters contributed to the outbreak of the War of the Three Kingdoms, during which the English Parliament's treaty of alliance with the Scottish Covenanters, the Solemn League and Covenant of 1643, was a key feature of the positive change in the fortunes of the king's enemies.

First Bishops' War

* The first Bishops' War took place in 1639. Charles I could not raise enough money to fight the war effectively, and was forced to agree to a truce in June as part of the Pacification of Berwick. As well as conceding military failure, this also gave the Scots religious freedoms. Charles I's inability to put down the Scots brought an end to his Eleven Years' Tyranny, as he recalled Parliament in 1640 to request revenue to continue his war with Scotland. This Short Parliament lasted one month as the king dissolved it rather than debate his role during the Eleven Years Tyranny as a condition of Parliament's granting of funds.

Second Bishops' War

* The second Bishops' War was a continuation of the first, but ended in equal humiliation for Charles I in the Treaty of Ripon of October 1640, which cost England the price that the Scottish Parliament had to pay for its forces. Again, defeat by the Scots forced the king to recall Parliament, this time after being advised to do so by a grouping of peers known as the Magnum Concilium. The Long Parliament was to last longer than the previous one, but still represented a downturn in the king's fortunes, as the Civil War shortly followed.

6. The candidate evaluates the importance of Cromwell's dependence on the army within the wider context of other issues that contributed to the lack of acceptable government found between 1649 and 1659, using evidence and arguments such as:

Role of the Army

* Army officers formed the Council of State with the Rump Parliament. Extremists in the army opposed too great an involvement of Parliament in governing the country.

- The creation of a military dictatorship from 1653 drew comparisons with the Stuart monarchs' martial law, as did the formation of the first Protectorate in September 1654 and the drawing up of military districts under the governance of major-generals during the second Protectorate from October 1656.
- Parliamentarians resented the influence of the army on constitutional affairs throughout the Interregnum.

Other factors

Cromwell's dominance
- Cromwell dominated politics and was in a unique position to influence the direction of the country. However he was a contrary character who espoused democratic principles but acted in a dictatorial manner, as he knew an elected government would contain his enemies and could lead to independence for Scotland and Ireland. His roots were in Parliament but his rise to the rank of general during the Civil War meant that he favoured the military during the Interregnum.
- He was naturally conservative, but many of his policies were ahead of his time, such as relief for the poor and the insane during the Barebones Parliament. Cromwell was a Puritan but passed progressive reforms, such as civil marriages, which horrified many.
- He was too preoccupied with foreign matters early on in the Interregnum, relied too heavily on the army, ignored Parliamentary concerns, and suffered from the absence of a monarch to act as a check on his actions such as passing unpopular legislation.

Foreign matters
- Faced with possible invasion, Cromwell was forced to fight several battles to control Scotland.
- He had to put down rebellions in Ireland by Royalists and Catholics brutally, which caused further resentment and hostility.
- War was waged on Holland to enforce the Navigation Acts. In the mid-1650s war with Spain caused increased taxes.
- Distractions caused by foreign affairs may have led to social issues such as coal shortages in the winter of 1652-3 not being addressed appropriately and therefore increasing instability in England.

Parliament
- The Rump Parliament consisted of MPs who had failed to avert Civil War in 1642 and who now had to address the same problems in 1649. Puritans amongst them were keen on church reform and viewed this as their priority. Parliament was opposed to the role of the army, and wanted to have a greater say in drawing up the constitution.
- Quarrels between MPs and army officers were a feature of the Interregnum. Parliament stood in the way of toleration and thus prevented religious wounds healing.

Absence of monarchy
- After Charles I's execution in 1649, the Council of State abolished the monarchy and declared a Republic, or Commonwealth. Previously problems could be tackled by monarch and Parliament. However, now there was no check on Parliamentary power.
- In Scotland, Charles II was crowned king and some of his supporters wanted him to ascend the throne in England also. Without a king, Cromwell ruled on his own for two different periods during the Interregnum, drawing comparisons with Charles I's 11-year tyranny.

Unpopular legislation
- The Treason Law and Censorship Law were introduced in 1649. In 1650 the Oath of Allegiance was imposed for all men over 18. He abolished the High Court in 1654 which caused a backlog of 23,000 cases.
- The Barebones Parliament was accused of introducing too many reforms in too short a space of time. The constitution was drawn up solely by army officers which drew further criticism. Roman Catholics and Anglicans were excluded from voting by the First Protectorate, which also introduced strict Moral Codes that curtailed popular forms of entertainment and enforced the Sabbath.
- The Commission of Triers and Committee of Ejectors, which oversaw the appointment of clergymen and schoolmasters, proved unpopular with the church.
- A 10% land tax was resented by the aristocracy. Taxation in general increased to fund wars with Spain.
- Cromwell's approval of his son Richard as his successor led many to feel that Cromwell viewed himself as a monarchical figure.

Surrounded by enemies
- Royalists accused Cromwell of regicide; army extremists pushed for greater martial authority.
- Presbyterians impatiently demanded church reforms.

Inexperience
- The Barebones Parliament consisted of many well-intentioned but inexperienced figures who proved incapable of using power effectively.

Doomed from the start
- All of the pre-Civil War problems such as religious, political, legal and economic issues, plus additional foreign policy issues, meant that Cromwell was always going to encounter difficulties.

The Atlantic Slave Trade

7. The candidate evaluates the reasons for the development of the slave trade, with reference to the need for labour, using evidence and arguments such as:

Need for labour
- Huge profits were to be made from trade in tropical crops such as sugar cane; this created demand for labour to work on plantations in the colonies.
- Tropical crops such as sugar cane required a large labour force to plant, look after, harvest and process in harsh, unpleasant conditions.
- High death rate among native populations due to lack of resistance to diseases brought by European traders and colonists and ill-treatment at the hands of colonists created labour shortage in the West Indies.
- The failure to find alternative sources of labour: few colonists were willing to work on plantations as manual labour; there was a limit to the number of British criminals who could be sent as forced labour; limited number and timespan of indentured servants.

The legal position
- The status of slaves as property was long established. It took a series of court cases from the 1770s that dealt with the rights of former slaves within the British Isles to challenge the legality of slavery and the slave trade eg Granville Sharp's resolute campaign to prove the illegality of slavery in England that culminated in Lord Mansfield's decision in the Somerset case.

Military factors
- The Seven Years War was in many ways an imperial war fought between Britain, France and Spain and many of the most important battles of the Seven Years War were fought at sea to win control of valuable overseas colonies; Britain emerged from the war as the leading European imperial power, having made large territorial gains in North America

and the Caribbean, as well as India. Slave labour was necessary to exploit these gains.

Racial factors
- Facing a labour shortage colonists turned to the labour system developed in Spain, Portugal, and the Atlantic islands ie the use of enslaved Africans; entrenched racism among merchants and landowners meant that enslaving African captives was accepted by colonists; the unequal relationship that was created as a consequence of the enslavement of Africans was justified by the ideology of racism - the belief that Africans were inferior to Europeans; many Europeans claimed that African captives would be executed in Africa if the slave trade was abolished; many colonists believed that African slaves benefited from being in the care of enlightened Europeans rather than African despots.

Religious factors
- The Church of England had links to slavery through the United Society for the Propagation of the Gospel missionary organisations which had plantations and owned slaves; the Church of England supported the laws not to educate enslaved Africans; some Bible passages such as the Curse of Ham from Genesis were used to justify slavery; other Bible passages such as Exodus were banned in British colonies because they could be interpreted as being hostile to slavery.

Importance of slave trade to British economy
- Financial, commercial, legal and insurance institutions emerged to support the activities of the slave traders; slave traders became bankers, plantation owners became MPs, stately homes were built on the proceeds of the slave trade and many new businesses were financed by profits made from slave trading.

8. The candidate assesses the importance of the slave trade in the British economy in the 18th century, using evidence and arguments such as:

Evidence that the Slave Trade was important
- Importance of the slave trade in the development of the economy: financial, commercial, legal and insurance institutions emerged to support the activities of the slave traders; slave traders became bankers and many new businesses were financed by profits made from slave trading.
- The slave trade played an important role in providing British industry with access to raw materials and this contributed to the increased production of manufactured goods.
- Ports such as London, Bristol and Liverpool prospered as a direct result of involvement in the slave trade; other ports such as Glasgow profited from trade with the colonies; thousands of jobs were created in Britain supplying goods and services to slave traders.
- The slave trade was important to the economic prosperity and well-being of the colonies.
- The slave trade was an important training ground for British seamen, providing experienced crews for the merchant marine and the Royal Navy. However, the high death rate, particularly from disease, meant that the trade could be considered as a graveyard for seamen.
- Wealth generated by the slave trade meant that domestic taxes could be kept low.
- Argument that the slave trade was the vital factor in Britain's industrialisation was put forward in Williams' Capitalism and Slavery thesis.

Evidence that other factors were important
- Changes in agriculture: these created an agricultural surplus which:
  - fed an expanding population
  - produced a labour force in the towns for use in factories

  - created a financial surplus for investment in industry and infrastructure.
- Technological innovation: development of water and steam power; new machinery; transport changes.
- Mineral and energy resources, particularly iron and coal.
- Political stability.
- Much of the profits of slavery were dissipated in conspicuous consumption eg landed estates.

9. The candidate assesses the impact of the slave trade on African societies, using evidence and arguments such as:

Negative effects
- Africans could become slaves as punishment for a crime, as payment for a family debt, or most commonly of all, by being captured as prisoners of war; with the arrival of European and American ships offering trading goods in exchange for captives, Africans had an added incentive to enslave each other, often by abducting unfortunate victims.
- Rich and powerful Africans were able to demand a variety of consumer goods and in some places even gold for captives, who may have been acquired through warfare or by other means, initially without massive disruption to African societies.
- By the end of 17th century European demand for African captives, particularly for the sugar plantations in the Americas, became so great that they could only be acquired through initiating raiding and warfare; large areas of Africa were devastated and societies disintegrated.
- Some societies preyed on others to obtain captives in exchange for European firearms, in the belief that if they did not acquire firearms in this way to protect themselves, they would be attacked and captured by their rivals and enemies who did possess such weapons.
- Europeans seldom ventured inland to capture the millions of people who were transported from Africa as captives; in the areas where slavery was not practised, such as among the Xhosa people of southern Africa, European slave ship captains were unable to buy African captives.
- West Africa was impoverished by its relationship with Europe while the human and other resources that were taken from Africa contributed to the economic development and wealth of Europe and the European colonies in the New World; the transatlantic trade also created the conditions for the subsequent colonial conquest of Africa by the European powers.
- It is estimated that around 10 million people were transported from Africa over the eighteenth century. This was a huge drain on the most productive and economically active sections of the population and this led to economic dislocation and falls in production of food and other goods.

Positive effects
- African slave sellers grew wealthy by selling African captives to European traders on the coast; they were able to deal on equal terms with European traders who built 'factories' on the West African coast to house captives before selling them onto the slave ship captains who in turn transported the captives to the colonies of the New World.
- On the African side, the slave trade was generally the business of rulers or wealthy and powerful merchants, concerned with their own selfish or narrow interests, rather than those of the continent; at that time, there was no concept of being African; identity and loyalty were based on kinship or membership of a specific kingdom or society, rather than to the African continent.
- Growth of states whose basis was the slave trade, notably Dahomey.

Britain 1851-1951

10. The candidate assesses the extent to which the growth of democracy in Britain after 1860 was due to social and economic change, using evidence and arguments such as:

Social and economic change

• The industrial revolution changed where people lived, how they worked, and how they felt about their position in society.
• Middle classes – wealth creators – argued they should have more of a say in running the country.
• Development of basic education and cheap popular newspapers raised working class political awareness.
• Spread of railways helped create national political identity. People were more aware of issues.
• Less fear of revolutionary "mob" – the skilled working class was more educated and respectable, as is shown in support for the North in the American Civil War by elements of the artisan class; an argument for extending the vote in 1867.
• The skilled working class was vital to the economic success of Britain.
• Increasing urbanisation led to pressure for redistribution of parliamentary seats – 1867, 1885, 1918.
• Impact of the Great War on the key issue of votes for women; realisation of the economic role of women in wartime was a factor in passing the 1918 Act – fears of a revival of militant women's campaign.

Changing ideology and attitudes

• Political reform was no longer seen as a threat cf struggles for liberty in Europe and USA. Britain was usually supportive of this and therefore it was difficult to argue against democratic progress at home.
• American Civil War – influence of Lincoln's Gettysburg Address.

Political advantage

• Politicians often believed they could gain political advantages from passing reforms eg the 1867 Reform Act was passed by the Conservatives after being in opposition for many years – arguably trying to win votes.
• Liberal party also tried to gain political advantage. John Bright argued for secret ballot, to free working class electorate from fear of retaliation by bosses and landlords.
• Corrupt and Illegal Practices Act – it is possible to argue that it was a pragmatic move by the Liberals. By limiting the amount spent on elections, they might reduce advantages held by the wealthier Conservatives.
• Reforms of 1880s – it could be argued that they served as a distraction from foreign policy problems facing the Liberal government; Redistribution of Seats Act – Liberals hoped for political advantage from urban voters now being more fairly represented.

Popular pressure

• Impact of campaigns by Reform League and Reform Union in 1866-67 – large demonstrations.
• Dangers of withholding the franchise from working classes – alarm at Hyde Park riots of July 1866. Less evidence of popular pressure in 1884 Reform Act.
• Impact of campaigns by women's movements up to 1914 – clear historical debate on this; effects of Suffragette campaign; government concern at a revived campaign after war was arguably a factor in the decision to grant votes to women aged 30 and over in 1918.

11. The candidate assesses the extent to which Britain had become democratic by 1928, using evidence and arguments such as:

The vote

• In 1867 most skilled working class men in towns got the vote. In 1884 many more men in the countryside were given the vote. In 1918 most men over 21 and some women over 30 gained the vote. Finally in 1928 all men and women over 21 were given the vote.

Fairness

• Secret Ballot 1872, Corrupt and Illegal Practices Act 1883 and the re-distribution of seats in 1867, 1885 and 1918 all helped created a fairer system of voting. The effectiveness of these varied; they were less effective in areas where the electorate was small, or where a landowner or employer was dominant in an area eg Norwich.

Choice

• Although the working class electorate increased by 1880s there was no national party to express their interests. The Liberals and Conservatives promoted middle, even upper, class capitalist values. The spread of socialist ideas and trade unionism led to the creation of the prototype Labour Party – the LRC – by 1900 thereby offering a wider choice to the electorate.

Access to information

• Education – in the later 19th Century there was a great increase in literacy and hence access to information on which to base choice. Also railways spread information nationally and were important in the growth of democracy.

National Party Organisation

• As the size of the electorate grew individual political parties had to make sure their 'message' got across to electorate eg development of National Liberal Federation, Conservative Central Office, Primrose League.

Power of Lords

• From 1911 the Lords could only delay bills from the House of Commons for two years rather than veto them. They had no control over money bills.

Widening opportunity to become MP

• The property qualification to be MP was abolished in 1858. Payment for MPs began in 1911 enabling working class men to sit.
• By 1928 Parliament was much more fully representative of the British people but points still to be resolved included:
  – undemocratic anomalies – plural votes and the university constituencies – were not abolished until 1948
  – in 1949 the two year delaying power of the House of Lords was reduced to only one year but the power of House of Lords (not reformed until 1990s) in law making still continues
  – voting system still first past the post in UK.

12. The candidate evaluates concern about the extent of poverty in Britain in influencing the Liberal Government's decision to introduce social reforms in 1906-1914, using evidence and arguments such as:

Background

• Change in attitude from 19th Century ideas of Laissez-Faire – growing arguments that the state should have a definite role for the well-being of its citizens.

Concerns about poverty

• Reports of Charles Booth and Seebohm Rowntree – clear evidence that, no matter how hard poorer people tried, they could not lift themselves out of poverty. Reports showed that poverty had definite causes – low pay, unemployment, sickness, old age – cures for this were beyond the individual efforts of poor. People were usually poor through no fault of their own.
• Concept of the "deserving poor" – those who were poor through no fault of their own – this idea took root and was an important theme running through the Liberal reforms.

Other Influences on the government

- National security – South African War – rejection of almost 25% of volunteers on fitness grounds. Figure even higher from volunteers from cities – Government seriously alarmed about this. Politicians were concerned whether Britain could protect its Empire or even survive against a stronger enemy if the nation's "fighting stock" of young men was so unhealthy.
- National efficiency – By 1900, Britain was no longer the strongest industrial nation – facing serious competition from new industrial countries like Germany. It was argued that, if the health and educational standards of British workers got worse, then Britain's status as a leading industrial power would be threatened. In addition, Germany had introduced a system of welfare benefits and old age pensions in the 1880s. View that Britain could do likewise.
- Political advantage – Some historians argue that political advantage was a key factor in motivating the Liberals to introduce social reforms. The majority of working men were now voters – and the new Labour Party was actively competing for their votes. Argument that the Liberals were concerned about retaining traditional working class support.
- New Liberalism – "Old" Liberalism believed that poverty was due to personal defects but, as the realisation grew that poverty itself imposed restrictions on choices available to individuals, a new definition of Liberalism developed. "New" Liberals argued that state intervention was necessary to liberate people from social problems over which they had no control.

Britain and Ireland 1900-1985

13. The candidate evaluates the importance of the growth of Irish Nationalism as a factor in increasing tension in Ireland before 1914, using evidence and arguments such as:

The growth of Irish Nationalism: The Irish cultural revival and re-emergence of Irish

Republicanism

- In 1884 the Gaelic Athletic Association was set up 'for the preservation and cultivation of our national pastimes' and games like Gaelic football and hurling became very popular. In 1883 the Gaelic League was also set up whose aim it was to revive, and preserve the Irish language and Gaelic literature.
- Setting up of Sinn Fein (Ourselves Alone) by Arthur Griffith in 1904 to boycott all things British and for the Irish to set up their own parliament in Ireland, which Griffith thought would force the British Government to collapse. The Irish Republican Brotherhood was revived with Thomas Clarke recruiting young men in Dublin for the movement. These two groups both wanted an Ireland separate from Britain and both were willing to use force.

Other factors changing British Politics and Ireland

- After 1910 the Liberals needed the support of the Irish Nationalists as they would not have a majority otherwise; as a price for this support they passed the three Home Rule bills, but the House of Lords, dominated by Conservatives, were opposed to Home Rule and wanted to maintain the Union. The first two bills were rejected.
- With the support of John Redmond the leader of the Nationalists a Bill was passed to reduce the power of the House of Lords, which was dominated by Conservatives, from being able to block a Bill to only being able to hold up the passing of a Bill for two years. As a result the Home Rule Bill for Ireland, which was previously blocked by the House of Lords, could now be passed.
- The possibility of the Home Rule Bill being passed eventually led to the Curragh Mutiny; the government could no longer rely on British troops in Ireland carrying out its policies.

Distinctive economic and religious features of the Northern Counties

- Ulster was mainly Protestant and feared that a government led by Dublin would see the imposition of laws on Northern Ireland based on the Catholic faith. This they were opposed to. Ulster was worried they would lose the economic benefits they enjoyed from being part of the British Empire, such as markets for the linen and shipbuilding industries.

The Unionist response to the Home Rule Bill

- Setting up of the Ulster Volunteer Force (UVF): Signing of the Solemn League and Covenant in Belfast at Town Hall; to the world's press, 250,000 Ulstermen pledged themselves to use 'all means necessary' to defeat Home Rule. The role of Carson and Craig. Sir Edward Carson's theatrical political performances caught the public imagination and brought the case of the Unionists to the nation. Orange and Ulster Unionist groups were revived.

Nationalist reactions

- The Irish Volunteer Force (IVF) was set up: Members from the Gaelic League, the Gaelic Athletic Association, Sinn Fein and the IRB all joined hoping to use the IVF for their own purposes. By May 1914 it had 80,000 members.
- In 1913, a third private army, the Irish Citizen Army, was set up, under the leadership of James Connolly, a socialist. It had two clear aims: to gain independence for Ireland and set up a socialist republic for the working class of all religions to work together to improve their lives. Minority opinions took different views: support for an Irish Republic from groups like the Irish Republican Brotherhood – Connolly's views; supporters of a workers republic – Griffith; or Sinn Fein – Pearse and his supporters. These were very much minority views at this time.

14. The candidate assesses the extent to which the First World War changed the political situation in Ireland, using evidence and arguments such as:

Irish Attitudes to World War I at its outset

- Initially the war brought prosperity to Ireland – manufacturing and farming benefited; low unemployment.
- Propaganda – powerful Germany invading helpless and small (Catholic) Belgium.
- Ulster was very supportive of Britain to ensure favourable treatment at the end of the war.
- Nationalists and Redmond backed the war to get Home Rule, urging Irishmen to enlist. The Irish press gave support to the war effort. Irish Volunteers gave support to help Home Rule be passed after the war. Recruitment was successful in the south as almost ¼ million men joined up.

The Nationalist Movement

- Opposition to war was very much a minority in 1914; Sinn Fein and Arthur Griffith (not powerful at this time); also Pearse, Connolly and their supporters as well as a section of the Irish Volunteers.

The Easter Rebellion, 1916

- Timing influenced by the war – 'England's difficulty is Ireland's opportunity'. Pearse saw the need for a blood sacrifice to galvanise Irish opinion. Rebels raised the Tricolour above the captured GPO with 'Proclamation of the Irish Republic'. The buildings occupied were of little strategic importance, but symbolism was more important. There was strong criticism of the Rising at the time by the public, politicians, churchmen, as well as press for unnecessary death and destruction: 450 dead, 2,500 wounded, cost £2½ million.

Changing Attitudes Towards British Rule after 1916

- There was initial hostility from the majority of Irish people to the Rising of a small group of rebels; majority of people supported Redmond and the Nationalist Party. Strong hostility of Dubliners towards the rebels resulted from the destruction of the city centre.
- Public hostility to the rebels was squandered – secret courts martial, execution of leaders over 10 days as well as imprisonment without trial and at least one execution without a trial. These political developments meant a growth of sympathy and compassion for rebels replacing condemnation of the Rising. The rebels were seen as martyrs and Republican support surged upwards. Sinn Fein was wrongly blamed for the Rising and saw a subsequent rise in support for them.

Anti-Conscription Campaign

- Many Irish opposed conscription and this pushed people in protest towards Sinn Fein who openly opposed it. This caused the Nationalists to withdraw from Westminster. Sinn Fein and the Nationalists organised a campaign: general strike on April 23rd; the Catholic Church and the Mayor of Dublin drew up the National Pledge, opposing conscription (De Valera drew up the Pledge). The conscription was not extended to Ireland for which Sinn Fein was given credit. Conscription campaign drove Sinn Fein underground where they became more tightly organised.

Decline of Nationalist Party

- The Irish Convention failed to reach agreement, which weakened the position of the Nationalists. This led to a feeling that the British could not be trusted and the Nationalists could not deliver. Three by-election wins for Sinn Fein gave the impression that they, not the Nationalists, spoke for the people.
- In March 1918 Redmond died; his influence had been waning as, unlike Carson, he was not included in the new cabinet. Many Irish shifted away from the Nationalists as they felt Sinn Fein was doing more for Ireland.

Rise of Sinn Fein

- Collins and De Valera provided improved leadership for Sinn Fein. Michael Collins built up the IRB and Irish Volunteers when in prison. Rebel prisoners from Frongoch continued their struggle on being freed. Opposition grew to Britain, due to martial law, house searches, raids, control of press, arrest of 'suspects' without trial, and vigorous implementation of Defence of the Realm Act. Thomas Ashe's funeral became propaganda for Sinn Fein. The Catholic Church and the business community came over to the side of Sinn Fein. Victory of Sinn Fein in 1918 election.

Entrenchment of Unionism in the North

- Unionists' 'blood sacrifice' on the Western Front – expectation that this would be recognised in any post-war settlement. The rise of Sinn Fein was viewed with increasing alarm, as was the participation of the Catholic Church in wartime politics eg the National Pledge.

15. The candidate evaluates the importance of the differences between De Valera and Collins as a factor in causing the Civil War in Ireland, using evidence and arguments such as:

Divisions in Attitudes in the Republican Movement over the treaty

- Collins supported the treaty; Ireland had an elected Government. De Valera opposed it and felt it should be resisted even if it meant Civil War. Sean MacEntee opposed the treaty as did Liam Lynch and Sinn Fein who wanted an independent Ireland.

- The treaty was accepted by 64 votes to 57 by the Dail Eireann on 7th January, 1922. De Valera voted against the treaty and resigned as President, to be replaced by Griffith and Collins became Head of the Irish Free Government.
- Collins and De Valera tried to reach a compromise to avoid war but none was reached. Some of the IRA units supported the treaty, whilst others opposed it. Some of the anti-treaty IRA took over some important buildings in Dublin, eg Four Courts. The murder of Sir Henry Wilson (security adviser for the Northern Ireland government) forced Michael Collins to call on the official IRA to attack the 'Irregular IRA'.

Issue of Partition

- The Government of Ireland Act split Ireland in two, with six counties in the North and 26 in the South.
- One third of the Ulster population was Catholic and wanted to be united with the South. The IRA refused to recognise the new Parliament and kept up its violence. Sectarian violence increased in Ulster. Roles of the Ulster Special Constabulary, Special Powers Act and the Local Government Emergency Powers Act. In the South, the Government of Ireland Act was ignored; Sinn Fein won 124 seats unopposed.
- In Northern Ireland, the Unionists won 40 of the 52 seats available. The twenty six counties in the south had a separate parliament in Dublin.
- Partition was a highly emotive issue, and it alone would have caused discord.

Dominion Status

- Under this agreement Ireland became a Dominion of the British Empire, rather than being completely independent from Britain. Under Dominion Status the new Irish State had three important things to adhere to:
  - the elected representatives of the people to take an oath of allegiance to the British Crown
  - the Crown was represented by a Governor General
  - appeals in certain legal cases could be taken to the Privy Council in London.

This aspect of the treaty was repugnant to many Irish people, not just Republicans.

Historical Study: European and World History

The Crusades, 1071-1204

1. The candidate evaluates the importance of fear about the expansion of Islam as a reason for the calling of the First Crusade, using evidence and arguments such as:

Fear over the expansion of Islam

- Pope Urban used the fear of Islamic expansion in his famous speech at Clermont in 1095. He pointed to the successful Reconquista in Spain. El Cid had only captured Valencia from the Moors in 1094.
- He pointed to the threat of the Turks to Byzantium, a topic that was already talked about across Europe. He claimed that the loss of Anatolia had 'devastated the Kingdom of God.'
- He detailed claims of Turkish activities such as torture, human sacrifice and desecration.

Other factors

The development of Christianity

- The new style of pope, influenced and trained at the monastery of the Cluny, heralded a shift in the emphasis of Christianity. No longer were popes to be subservient to the monarchs or warlords of Europe.
- Popes now actually challenged kings and demanded the right to appoint priests, bishops and cardinals as they saw fit. This

led to the development of the Investiture Contest and this power struggle directly affected Urban, possibly influencing his decision.

The Great Schism
- The papacy was anxious to re-join the two halves of the Christian church. Since the Great Schism of 1054, where the Pope of Rome and Patriarch of Constantinople excommunicated each other, it had been the goal of every pope to become head of the Greek Orthodox Church. Now the Crusade seemed to offer Pope Urban the opportunity to achieve this.

Development of Mediterranean trade
- The development of trade within the Mediterranean Sea had been in the hands of ambitious cities in Italy, notably Venice, but also Pisa and Genoa. By 1095 Venice had bound its future to Byzantium.
- Their preferential trade agreements with Constantinople for silk, spices and other luxury goods meant that they were keen to see Byzantium saved from the expansion of the Turks.

Threat to Byzantium
- The Seljuk Turks had been threatening the Empire for decades. There was fear in Europe that if Byzantium was allowed to fall then the expansion of this new aggressive Islamic group into central Europe would be inevitable.
- Alexius was seen as a bulwark against this eventuality and his letter asking for help was taken very seriously.

Development of feudalism
- The introduction of Norman feudalism across Western Europe had created the knightly class. Their dedication to learning the arts of war had created a culture based around the skills of fighting. Even the tournaments had come to be seen as integral part of the culture and as entertainment.
- However, to use their skills in anger was a sin. Pope Urban had long considered how he could turn the nature of the Western knights to a less aggressive, less damaging activity.
- The Church had already successfully introduced the Peace of God, an agreement that non-combatants would be spared in any conflict. Urban saw the Crusade as a way to channel this aggression in a way that would be of benefit to Christianity.

2. The candidate evaluates the importance of the desire to acquire territory as a reason for the popularity of the crusading movement, using evidence and arguments such as:

Acquisition of Territory
- Many of the great magnates on this expedition had intentions to acquire new estates for themselves. The motives of many of the leaders of the Prince's Crusade have been put down to this.
- Bohemond and Baldwin in particular showed little zeal in carrying on with the Crusade once they had acquired Antioch and Edessa respectively.

Other factors

Religion
- It is generally believed that the Remission of Sins offered by Pope Urban was an attractive solution to the dilemma of knights. Salvation was a constant worry for those who trained to kill. Urban had successfully sold the need to protect Christianity from the Muslim threat and the general desire to re-establish the pilgrimage routes to the holy lands contributed to the growing belief that it was important to save Christ from this threat.
- The mass appeal of the People's Crusade can only be explained by the belief that they were doing good and helping God.

- Of the leaders of the Princes' Crusade, Raymond of Toulouse is often held up as an example of a knight riding to the defence of the Holy Lands. This is a rather simplistic idea and his decision to take Tripoli in 1100 casts a shadow over this interpretation of his motives.

Peer pressure
- The pressure put on knights by their families to take the cross was at time severe. Wives tended to be keenly aware of the politics at court and had a role in influencing the decisions of some.
- Stephen of Blois had married Adela, daughter of William I of England. It would have been unthinkable for such a notable knight not to go on the Crusade.

Love of fighting vs. fear of sin
- The Crusade provided the solution to the problem of knights and their need for salvation. Killing was only wrong if one killed Christians. Urban indicated that the killing of a Muslim was a just act, and the equivalent to prayer or penance.
- This, and the promise of remission of current sins, was a great relief to those knights worried about their eternal soul. Tancred's biographer wrote about both his worry over this dilemma and his relief at Urban's suggestion.
- In later Crusades many of the religious aspects of the Crusade are adopted and modified by the growing idea of chivalric codes.

Desire for adventure
- For some, the humdrum existence of 11th century Europe could be replaced by the excitement of the Crusade. Pilgrimages had always been seen as important, and the idea of this as an armed pilgrimage was very appealing. It offered a way out for many serfs from their lives in bondage, or perhaps a chance to see the Holy Lands.

Threat of famine
- Many were forced to leave because of the lack of available farmland in an already overcrowded Europe.
- Several famines have also been suggested as a possible motive. It was popularly believed that the Holy Lands were lands of plenty.

3. The candidate evaluates the importance of the Christian defeat at Hattin as a cause of the fall of Jerusalem, using evidence and arguments such as:

Importance of Hattin
- King Guy led the armies of Jerusalem to save Count Tiberius's wife as Saladin's forces had surrounded her castle. Tiberius himself had a few worries about the safety of his wife. His fortress could have withstood a siege. Saladin's forces lacked the required siege engines to make a successful attack. Additionally, Saladin could not keep his disparate forces in the field for any length of time. Tiberius' advice to Guy was to hold his forces back to protect Jerusalem.
- However, figures such as Reynald persuaded Guy that to leave the Countess of Tripoli besieged would be un-chivalric and that Guy would lose support if he did not ride out.
- The army could find little water to sustain them in the desert. Their only option was to make for Hattin and the oasis there. This was an obvious trap; Saladin surrounded them with burning brushwood and dry grass. Trapped on the Horns of Hattin the Christian army were suffering from the sun and lack of water.
- Eventually they were forced to attack before they lacked the strength to do so. The Christian horses were too weak for a prolonged struggle and their infantry were surrounded by Saladin's horse archers and cut off.

- Saladin ordered the slaughter of all members of the militant orders, but Guy and many of his followers were allowed to surrender and enter captivity.
- Without the army to protect the kingdom even the massive fortifications could not stand against Saladin's forces.

Other factors

Infighting within Jerusalem
- Two factions struggled for power within Baldwin IV's court, those of Guy de Lusignan and Baldwin's close advisor Raymond III of Tripoli. In 1180 Guy married Sibylla, Baldwin's sister. Guy tended to favour an aggressive policy.
- The activities of Reynald of Chatillon helped to destabilise the fragile peace treaty between Baldwin IV and Saladin.

Death of Baldwin IV
- Baldwin died in March 1185, taking his strategy of non-aggression towards Saladin with him. He was replaced for a short time by his nephew, Baldwin V. However a short power struggle after the boy's death in August let Guy de Lusignan assume the throne, abetted by Sibylla.

Influence of the Templars
- The Knights Templar, unlike the Hospitallers, were firmly in the camp of the 'hawks' (warmongers). They wanted nothing more than to carry on with the crusading ideal and rid the Holy Lands of the Muslims. Treaties and compromise were unacceptable to them.

Lack of resources within Jerusalem
- Even the combined armies of the Crusader States were not strong enough to successfully win a war, especially in the long run. It is arguable that it was inevitable for the Crusader States to fall to a united Islamic state.

Unification of Islamic forces under Saladin
- Saladin had managed to successfully unite the Muslims of Syria and Egypt behind his leadership. This effectively surrounded Jerusalem and left them with a very weak military position.
- Saladin successfully used the idea of a religious war against the Christians to hold the separate Islamic groups together.

Saladin's internal problems
- Saladin himself had his critics within the Muslim ranks, saying he was more interested in maintaining his position than defeating the Christians. It was seen by many that his stance on the Kingdom of Jerusalem was weak. After Guy assumed the throne and Reynald continued his attacks the pressure on Saladin to respond grew. This encouraged him to act aggressively.

The American Revolution 1763-1787
4. The candidate assesses the threat of colonial resentment towards the Navigation Acts to British control of the American colonies using evidence and arguments such as:

Navigation Acts
- Passed in 1650s, these stated that colonists could only sell their goods to the British, could only buy goods from the British and could only use British shipping. The Royal Navy enforced the Acts by patrolling the east coast of the colonies for rogue Dutch, French or Spanish ships.
- However, the acts gave colonists a guaranteed market. During the Whig Ascendancy in mid-1700s many colonists were able to ignore the Acts as the Royal Navy was unable to enforce them strictly.

Old colonial system
- Britain treated colonies merely as a source of revenue, and plundered valuables from America. Those in New England and the Middle Colonies objected to being used as a dumping ground for British goods. Wealthy Southern plantation owners objected to members of the British government attempting to control them. Frontiersmen were frustrated at British attempts to prevent them from going beyond the Frontier. However, being part of the Empire meant protection from the British Army against the French and Indians.

Political differences
- The colonies were more politically advanced than Britain, each having its own elected Assembly which passed local laws and raised local taxes, and so they resented the lack of representation in the British Parliament which sought to control their lives. However, the British Empire provided an order to the existence of the colonies. Britain acted out the role of Mother Country. Britain appointed a governor for each colony, whose payment by the colony ensured an element of control for the colonists over the governor.

George III
- When George III ascended the throne in 1760 he oversaw a re-imposition of British rule over the colonies. This was seen as tantamount to foreign invasion by many colonists who had acted in an independent spirit during the Whig Ascendancy. Colonies had their own militia and did not feel the British Army was required in America.
- George III aimed to ensure the security of the colonies by maintaining a British military presence and together with Parliament planned an economic strategy to raise money from the colonists to pay for this.

The Seven Years War
- The war highlighted the status of the colonies as territories to be fought over by imperial powers. Britain, France and Spain all viewed America as a potential possession. The British fought the Seven Years War which prevented the colonies being ruled by France.
- Victory in 1763, and the acquisition of Canada, should have made British rule more secure, but the removal of the French threat meant that many colonists saw less need for British protection.

Neglect by Britain
- During the Whig Ascendancy, colonist assemblies had assumed powers which should have been exercised by governors, and they resented Parliament's attempts to reverse this trend.

Land claims
- Quarrels arose after individual colonists and land companies unwittingly violated treaties agreed between Britain and Native American tribes.

5. The candidate evaluates the importance of the issues over taxation as a reason for the colonists' move towards independence, using evidence and arguments such as:

Disputes over taxation

Stamp Act
- This first form of taxation on the colonies, in 1765, was objected to by colonists because they were not represented in the British Parliament which imposed these taxes. 'No taxation without representation' became a familiar protest during this time. The act stated that an official stamp had to be bought to go on any printed matter, and colonists subsequently refused to pay for this. They stated that they already paid financial dues to the British through the Navigation Acts and other restrictions and that they had their own militia and did not need to pay for the British Army to protect them. However, the British said that taxation would contribute to the costs of the Seven Years War and also pay

for the continued presence of the British Army in America to protect the colonies.

The Declaratory Act
- This stated in 1766 that Britain had the right to maintain a tax on the colonists at all times.

Townshend Duties
- After the Stamp Act was repealed in 1766, these Duties, which were on glass, tea, paper and lead, were imposed in 1767. Colonists challenged the right of Parliament to impose duties that seemed designed purely to raise revenue. However, the British insisted that the duties be paid in order to defray the costs of acting as Mother Country to protect the colonies.

Tea duties
- George III insisted that although some taxes had been repealed, a tax should remain on tea from 1770 in order to maintain the British right to tax the colonists. Later reductions in this tax led to colonist suspicions that the British were attempting to get the colonists to buy cheap tea in order to coerce them into accepting British taxation.
- The Boston Tea Party in December 1773 was an expression of some colonists' frustrations at British policy towards them. However, the British denied that alterations to tea import duties were designed to get the East India Company out of financial trouble and were in fact a concession to colonist objections to taxation.

Other factors

Proclamation of 1763
- The Proclamation forbade anyone from going beyond the Frontier. Bold adventurers amongst the colonists were thus kept within the jurisdiction of the British authorities. However, Empire Loyalists maintained that the Proclamation offered greater protection to the colonists from potential hostility from the French or Native Americans in the period after the Seven Years War.

Re-imposition of the Navigation Acts
- After 1763 these were enforced by the Royal Navy after over 40 years of the colonists being able to disregard them during the Whig Ascendancy.

British intransigence
- Britain retained an uncompromising attitude in the face of continued colonist protest and pleas for compromise.

Rejection of Olive Branch Petition/Role of George III
- George III rejected the colonists' last attempt at compromise. The 2nd Continental Congress had written an appeal to the king pledging its allegiance to the crown and bitterness towards Parliament, yet the appeal fell on deaf ears as George III declared the colonists to be in rebellion. Many colonists started to consider independence as the only means of changing their relationship with Britain. However, the petition was an expression of loyalty to George III which masked many colonists' intentions to declare greater autonomy for themselves, regardless of the king's reaction.

Parliamentary ignorance
- In America there was a perception that both Houses of Parliament wilfully dismissed the spirit and determination of the colonists to establish constitutional union with Britain.

Influence of Thomas Paine
- The republican pamphlet 'Common Sense' was published in January 1776 and sold 100,000 copies.

Punishment of Massachusetts
- This was the British response to the Boston Tea Party, in a series of acts starting in March 1774, known to the colonists as the Intolerable Acts – closing the port of Boston, altering the constitution of the legislature of Massachusetts, billeting British troops in colonial homes, and suspending trial by jury in the colony. Other colonists acted in sympathy with Massachusetts and showed unity at the First Continental Congress in September 1774. However, the British spoke of the punishments as the Coercive Acts, which were an attempt to get the colonists to see that acts of hostility towards Britain would not be tolerated.

Boston Massacre
- The Massacre occurred in 1775. Although five working-class men died, including one black man, the reports of five middle-class white men dying caused outrage amongst politically-minded colonists. The Committees of Correspondence meant that news of the Massacre spread quickly around the 13 colonies.
- The acquittal of the British soldiers led many colonists to fear for their personal liberty and to believe that they would one day be enslaved by the British. However the Massacre was an incident which animated people mainly in the New England area, something which later caused George III to voice his belief that problems in America were 'localised'.

6. The candidate assesses the view that the American War of Independence was a global conflict, using evidence and arguments such as:

Franco-American Alliance
- France entered the war and took the conflict to Europe. Britain was forced to re-assign its military resources to defend itself and the Empire. The French contribution to the colonists' cause took many forms – men, ammunition, training, supplies, and uniforms, fighting Britain around the world. However, France was not persuaded until February 1778 to make its alliance with America, by which time the Continental Army was already starting to make progress in the war in the colonies.

Dutch and Spanish entry
- When the Dutch and the Spanish entered the war, Britain's navy was stretched even further and it became increasingly difficult to focus on the war in the colonies. European nations now competed for parts of Britain's empire around the world. However, the war between Britain and the colonists on land was not directly affected greatly by the Dutch and Spanish involvement.

Armed League of Neutrality
- This grouping of Russia, Sweden and Denmark gave extra cause for concern to Britain, as they were willing to fire on any Royal Navy ships which interfered with their merchant fleets. However, the League was not actively involved in the war, merely endeavouring to protect its own shipping.

Control of the sea
- The battle for control of the sea drew massively on the resources of all countries involved and significantly drained Britain's finances. However, the war at sea continued after the surrender at Yorktown, and the British recognised the Treaty of Versailles despite regaining control of the sea, suggesting the war on land was more significant to the outcome for the colonists.

German mercenaries
- Britain used over 7000 of these in the colonies.

Changing views in Britain
- With the increasing European involvement, some Parliamentarians questioned Britain's ability to win a prolonged war.

Canadian aspect

- The colonists had appealed unsuccessfully for Canadian support, which meant the British were not distracted by concerns about possible rebellion in Canada.

7. The candidate evaluates the grievances of the Bourgeoisie as a challenge to the Ancien Regime, using evidence and arguments such as:

The grievances of the Bourgeoisie

- The bourgeoisie—often individually wealthy, this social group nonetheless resented the privileges and exemptions enjoyed by the First and Second Estates. Although they had displayed their talents in business, the law and in education members of the bourgeoisie were denied access to political power and suffered higher tax burdens than their social "superiors". Businessmen were particularly bitter about trade barriers, different regional weights and measures and restrictive trade and working practices which inhibited the free inter-flow of trade and industrial expansion. Intellectually astute, they had taken on board the ideas of the Philosophes which had called for a more rational, fair and equal society where privileges, exemptions and restrictive practices would be ended. It is hardly surprising that the bourgeoisie were at the head of revolutionary political, social and economic change during 1788 and 1789.

The role of the rest of the Third Estate

- The Peasantry—the peasants laboured under a hugely unfair burden of taxation. Their grievances were compounded by the failure of the grain harvest in 1789. This hit agricultural incomes and the economic crisis peaked at the point when the political future of France was being decided in the newly-formed National Assembly (June). The ending of feudalism (August 1789) also had much to do with peasant discontent reaching its peak during the "Great Fair" in the countryside in July.
- The urban workers—the economic crisis in agriculture hit manufacturing in 1789 when rising bread prices cut the demand for manufactured goods. Lay-offs and falling incomes intensified revolutionary fervour in the great cities such as Paris. Overall, the greatest threat to the Ancien Regime came from the bourgeoisie but the influence of other social groups cannot be ignored.

The role of the Clergy

- The Clergy was split into the Upper and Lower Clergy. The Upper Clergy were almost wholly exempt from the payment of taxes and were tenacious in holding onto the privilege. The Catholic Church owned 10% of land in France and extracted tax (the tithe) from the peasantry in order to fund the Church's operations.
- The Lower Clergy often sympathised with the peasants in their parishes who suffered under an enormous burden of taxation relative to income and this precipitated tensions within the hierarchy of the Church. It also explains why some of the clergy were prepared to lead protests against the Ancien Regime on behalf of their parishioners—eg in drawing up Cahiers des Doleances in preparation for the meeting of the Estates-General in 1789. The Cahiers revealed a catalogue of discontent and provided a platform from which an attack on the privilege, venality and exemption from taxation rife in the Ancien Regime—privileges and exemptions enjoyed by the Upper Clergy—could be launched.
- Moreover, attempts to increase government income through a Land Tax levied on the Church and the Nobility were met by bitter opposition in the Assembly of Notables among whose number the Upper Clergy were prominent. This precipitated a financial crisis and the convocation in 1788 of the Estates-General. This decision led directly to the attack on privilege which culminated in the collapse of the Ancien Regime in 1789 with the establishment of the National Assembly in June, the end of feudalism in early August and the Declaration of the Rights of Man in late August.

The role of the Nobility

- Like the Clergy, the Nobility were almost wholly exempt from taxation. As a result they, too, have to accept a considerable degree of culpability for the Revolution. As with the Clergy, the Nobility was split—between the traditional Nobles of the Sword and the more recently ennobled Nobles of the Robe. The former gained access—often through birth rather than merit—to the highest and most lucrative offices of the state, Church and Army. The "old" nobility sought to protect these privileges against the "new" nobility—and, indeed, the bourgeoisie. Clearly this precipitated tension and a desire for change.
- Many of the leaders of the movement which sought revolutionary change in 1788 and 1789 were drawn from the ranks of the lesser nobility. Their intellect, organisation and education made them formidable opponents on the Ancien Regime—often in alliance with the numerically larger bourgeoisie. It is also worth noting that the Assembly of Notables bitter opponents of reform) counted many of the traditional nobility among their number.

8. The candidate evaluates the degree to which financial problems brought about the collapse of the Ancien Regime, using evidence and arguments such as:

Role of financial problems

Cost of 18th Century wars

- These placed an huge burden on State finances. The cost of the Seven Years War (1756-63) and France's financing of the American War of Independence (1776-83) had added considerably to the debt incurred by the wars fought by Louis XIV earlier in the century.
- Much of this was financed by loans so that by the 1780s about half of France's national income was going on payment of debt. (It should be noted, though, that despite criticism of the profligacy of the Royal Court it accounted for only c. 5% of State spending.)

There were severe problems in servicing this debt

- The nobility and the clergy were almost wholly exempt from the payment of taxes. Attempts to raise taxation revenue from these social groups were opposed at every turn. When short-term loans to finance the American wars had to be repaid from 1786 onwards there could be no more large-scale borrowing since investors were losing faith in the State's ability to re-pay.
- Anticipated tax revenues were projected to fall making matters worse. There had to be changes to the system of taxation if the Regime was to survive.

Attempts to introduce tax reforms in the late 1780s brought matters to a head

- Taxation had to be extended to the previously exempt nobility and clergy since the rest of society (the Third Estate) could bear no further burden of taxation. Finance Minister Calonne's attempts to introduce a Land tax foundered on the opposition of the nobles and the Assembly of Notables in 1787.
- The king's dismissal of Calonne ended any hopes of significant tax reform. The king was forced, in 1788, to re-call the Estates-General in the following year. This marked the beginning of the end for the Ancien Regime.

Other factors

Social divisions

- There were tensions between traditional nobility (of the sword) and the newly ennobled nobility (of the robe) wherein the 'old' sought to hold onto their control of key positions of the State, the Army and the Church, much to the annoyance of the 'new'.
- The bourgeoisie had grown considerably in number during the 18th Century but had little or no influence on State policy-making, yet they were expected to contribute to taxation whereas the nobility and clergy were not.
- The church hierarchy were resented by the lower clergy; parish priests often sided with the peasants in their locality but the upper clergy viewed peasants with contempt and merely as a source of taxation.
- The peasantry were becoming increasingly discontented with the disproportionate burden of taxation which fell on them.
- The urban workers endured exploitation by bourgeois masters and suffered through restrictions on trade.

The Philosophes

- While not advocates of Revolution, these 18th century philosophers had challenged many of the social, political and economic assumptions of the Ancien Regime and their ideas fostered principles of social, political and economic liberty which increasingly undermined it.

The American War of Independence

- Apart from contributing to the massive financial problems of the Regime, the American wars reinforced principles of 'no taxation without representation' and liberty from centralised authority – ideas which many of the lower nobility and bourgeoisie embraced in the years before 1789.

Economic Crisis of 1788/9

- Peasant unrest intensified as a result of bad harvests and severe grain shortages also caused disquiet in the major cities such as Paris. This increased the pressure on the Monarchy and the system of Government generally.

Political crisis of 1788/9

- The convocation of the Estates-General brought social divisions between First, Second and Third Estates to a head. Cahiers des Doleances revealed deep disquiet over a range of inequalities such as feudal dues and the unfairness of the taxation system and put immense pressure on the Ancien Regime.

9. The candidate evaluates the degree to which Robespierre alone can be blamed for the Reign of Terror in France during 1793-94 by using evidence and arguments such as:

Role of Robespierre

Robespierre's justification of terror as an instrument of the 'general will'

- Robespierre believed that the 'general will' of the sovereign people both created and sanctioned policy-making within the nation. The will of the people could only prevail within a Republic. Any individual who sought to oppose this was, by implication, guilty of treason against the nation itself. In such circumstances death – the ultimate weapon of Terror – was entirely appropriate. Hence Robespierre's belief that 'terror is virtue' – that to create and maintain a 'virtuous' nation which enshrined the revolutionary principles of liberty and equality, it was necessary to expunge any counter-revolutionary activity violently.

Robespierre and the Committee of Public Safety (created April 1793)

- Robespierre became a member of the Committee in July 1793 and came to control its operations. Until his own execution in July 1794, the Committee became the main instrument for the application of terror in defence of Robespierre's ideal of a 'Republic of Virtue'. During this period Robespierre sanctioned the use of terror against:
  - the monarchy and émigré opponents of the Republic e.g. Marie Antoinette executed
  - provincial counter-revolutionaries particularly in the Vendée
  - Hebertists, whose anti-Christian stance Robespierre found both distasteful and dangerous
  - Dantonists who challenged the authority of Robespierre and who were therefore (since Robespierre's government represented the 'general will') guilty of treason.
- With the imposition of the infamous Law of 22nd Prairial (June 1794), Robespierre was given virtually unlimited powers to eliminate opponents of his Republic of Virtue and during the period of the Great Terror in June and July 1794, over 1500 were executed.
- Had Robespierre lived beyond Thermidor there is no doubt the death toll would have risen even higher. However, while Robespierre must bear responsibility for the intensification of the Terror during 1793-1794, the use of terror as an instrument of state policy was by no means confined to Robespierre.

Other factors

The defence of the revolution after the execution of Louis XVI (January 1793)

- The Convention's major concerns at the start of 1793 were two-fold: to eliminate counter-revolutionary activity which intensified, particularly in the provinces after Louis' execution and to execute the war against the Republic's émigré and foreign opponents as ruthlessly and as effectively as possible. At this point the Convention was still controlled by the relatively moderate Girondins.
- However, the Convention sanctioned a range of counter-revolutionary legislation such as:
  - the creation of the Committee of Public Safety; The Committee of General Security
  - Revolutionary tribunals to try opponents of the Republic and impose the death penalty if required and Surveillance Committees established in local areas to identify counter-revolutionary activity.
- Thus, most agree that most of the essential institutions of the Terror were actually in place before the Jacobins – and Robespierre – came to power. The moderates in the Convention had set up the structure of the Terror by the spring of 1793.

Terror as the 'order of the day' (September 1793)

- It was pressure from mass demonstrations in Paris which intimidated the Convention into adopting terror as 'the order of the day' i.e. a method of government control. This was more to do with the exigencies of the foreign and civil wars which were threatening the Republic at this point than with Robespierre's philosophising over the nature of the Republic and the role of terror within it.

The impact of the war

- The external dangers France faced radicalised the revolution. It occasioned a witch hunt for enemies within. The war led to the concept of the 'nation in crisis'. This had to be enforced, violently if necessary.

10. The candidate evaluates the importance of economic factors as against other reasons for the growth of German nationalism, using evidence and arguments such as:

Economic factors

- Urbanisation and industrialisation of the German states –

political fragmentation – can be argued to be the most important obstacle to German economic development. Middle-class businessmen called for a more united market to enable them to compete with foreign countries.

- Prussian economic expansion – Prussia's gain of territory on the River Rhine after 1815 (drift in power away from Austria and towards Prussia as the latter began to build on the rich resources such as coal and iron deposits) meant it had good reason to reach an agreement with neighbours to ensure relatively free travel of goods and people between its lands in the east and the west. Businessmen complained that tax burdens were holding back economic development – Prussia created a large free-trade area within Prussia herself – aided the needs of businessmen.
- Zollverein – the 'mighty lever' of German unification. By 1836, 25 of the 39 German states had joined this economic free-trade area (Austria excluded).
- Railway/road development – post-1830s the development of railways/roads ended isolation of German states from each other. This enabled the transport and exploitation of German natural resources. Economic co-operation between German states encouraged those seeking a political solution to the issue of German unity.

Political factors
- Ideas of the French Revolution – these appealed to the middle classes in the German states.
- Impact of Napoleonic wars – many Germans argued that Napoleon/ France had been able to conquer German states pre-1815 due to their division as separate, autonomous territories. German princes had stirred national feeling to help raise armies to drive out the French, aiding the sense of a common German identity with common goals.
- 1848 Revolutions in Germany – raised consciousness greatly even though they failed.

Cultural factors – 'Romanticism'
- Main unifying force was language – 25 million Germans spoke the same language and shared the same culture and literature.
  - Writers and thinkers (e.g. Heine, Fichte, Goethe, Brothers Grimm, Schiller, Hegel) encouraged the growth of a German consciousness.
  - Post-1815 nationalist feelings first expressed in universities. Growth of *Burschenschaften* pre-1815 dedicated to driving French from German soil – zealous but lacking a clear idea of how best to accomplish the task.
  - The Hambacherfest and student demonstrations – little accomplished by the students.
- Early 19th century was a time of great change in all European states and it has been suggested that the political changes of the time can only be explained by an understanding of the social and economic developments of the time.

11. The candidate assesses the extent of the growth of German nationalism by 1850, using evidence and arguments such as:

Evidence that nationalists made significant progress
- *Vormarz* period – evidence suggests that workers were starting to take a real interest in politics and philosophy, but only in relatively small numbers.
- Cultural nationalism – work of poets, musicians, writers and their effects on Germans. The impact was largely on educated Germans and not everyone was interested in such ideas – not considered vital to the everyday lives of the ordinary people.
- 1840 – French scare to German states. Ordinary Germans now roused to the defence of the fatherland. Not confined to educated classes. Spread of nationalist philosophy to large

numbers of ordinary Germans shown. Enhanced reputation of Prussia among German nationalists.
- Economic nationalism – middle class businessmen pushing the case for a more united Germany in order to be able to compete with foreign countries. Benefits evidenced by the Zollverein to German states. Arguments that 'economic' nationalism was the forerunner to political nationalism

Evidence that nationalists had not made significant progress
- Growth of the *Burschenschaften* – dedicated to seeing the French driven from German soil. Nationalist enthusiasm tended to be of the romantic type, with no clear idea of how their aim could be achieved. Much of the debate in these societies was theoretical in nature and probably above the comprehension of the mass of ordinary Germans.
- Political nationalism – virtually non-existent between 1820 and 1848. Suppressed by the Karlsbad Decrees and the Six Acts. Work/success of Metternich in suppressing such a philosophy.
- Work of the German Confederation and the rulers of the autonomous German states to suppress nationalism.
- Troppau Congress – decision taken by the representatives of Austria, Prussia and Russia to suppress any liberal or nationalist uprisings that would threaten the absolute power of monarchs; huge blow to nationalists within the German states.
- German *Bund* – remained little more than a talking shop. Austrian domination of the *Confederation* and the *Bund* stifled political change.
- 1848 Revolutions and the Frankfurt Parliament; no agreement was reached on a gross – or a kleindeutsch solution. German rulers regained authority. Divided aims of revolutionaries. Self-interest of the rulers of the German states led to their opposition to Frankfurt Parliament. Frederick William of Prussia backed down in face of Austrian pressure at Olmutz and the humiliation of Prussia: German nationalism was arguably a spent force.

12. The candidate evaluates the importance of Bismarck's leadership as against the other factors in the unification of Germany, using evidence and arguments such as:

Bismarck's foreign policy 1863-1871
- Bismarck's aim was to increase the power of Prussia by whatever means necessary.
- Bismarck and his 'realpolitik'/diplomacy in the '3 wars' against Denmark, Austria and France.
- Bismarck took the initiative, as opposed to Austria, in the war against Denmark; his 'solution' to the Schleswig-Holstein question.
- Bismarck's skilful manipulation of events leading up to the war with Austria in 1866 plus his establishment of friendships with potential allies of Austria beforehand.
- Bismarck's wisdom in the Treaty of Prague, 1866.
- Bismarck's manipulation of the Ems Telegram to instigate a war with France in 1870.
- Bismarck's exploitation of the weaknesses of European statesmen/rulers e.g. Napoleon III; mistakes made by Bismarck's adversaries.
- Bismarck's skill in isolating his intended targets (diplomatically).
- Arguments about the role of Bismarck:
  - 'Bismarck did not fashion German unity alone. He exploited powerful forces which already existed...' (Williamson)
  - '...it was he (Bismarck) who created the conditions which rendered possible the creation of a Great Germany.' (Hitler)

– 'Bismarck's admirers often exaggerate the extent of the obstacles in his path.' (Medlicott)

Other factors

Military factors

- Significance of military reforms of Moltke and Roon – creation of modern powerful army which Bismarck used.
- The decline in Austrian power and influence – economically and militarily – during the 1850s particularly.
- Distraction to Austria of commitments in Italy.

Economic factors

- Growth in Prussian economic power – development of railways, transport links, roads, for example; importance of the Rhineland and the Saarland to Prussian economic development. Able to finance and equip Prussian army.
- The Zollverein – the Prussian-dominated free-trade area; the significance to German political unification - the 'mighty lever of German unification.'

Political factors

- Influence of Napoleon Bonaparte – reduction of number of German states; growth of a national consciousness.
- The 1848 revolutions in German states – importance of Frankfurt Parliament/decisions taken regarding a unified Germany; Prussia was a potential leader; Austria was excluded from Germany ('kleindeutschland')
- The Nationalverein – aim was the creation of a united Germany; composed of intelligent and economically important section of German society – businessmen; identified Prussia as leader of a united Germany.

Cultural factors

- Growth of German cultural nationalism/Romantic Movement – Burschenschaften, writers, music, for example, leading to an increased German national consciousness among the educated classes.

Italy 1815-1939

13. The candidate evaluates the importance of economic factors to the growth of national feeling, using evidence and arguments such as:

Economic factors

- Economic factors were not important directly. Wealth lay in land (landowners were often reactionary) and trade (where the educated bourgeoisie were more receptive to ideas of liberalism and nationalism).

Cultural factors

- The Risorgimento was inspired by Italy's past. Poets such as Leopardi glorified and exaggerated past achievements kindling nationalist desires. Poets and novelists like Pellico inspired anti-Austrian feelings amongst intellectuals as did operas such as Verdi's 'Nabucco' and Rossini's 'William Tell.'
- There was no national 'Italian' language – regional dialects were like separate languages. Alfieri inspired 'Italian' language based on Tuscan. The poet and novelist Manzoni wrote in 'Italian'. Philosophers spread ideas of nationalism in their books and periodicals.
- Moderate nationalists such as Gioberti and Balbo advocated the creation of a federal state with the individual rulers remaining but joining together under a president for foreign affairs and trade. Gioberti's 'On the moral and civil primacy of the Italians' advocated the Pope as president whilst Balbo, in his book 'On the hopes of Italy', saw the King of Piedmont/Sardinia in the role.
- Radical nationalist Mazzini not only inspired dreams of a united, democratic Italian republic through his written works, but also formed an activist movement 'Young Italy' whose aim was to make these dreams a reality.

Other factors

Effects of the French Revolution

- 'Italian' intellectuals had initially been inspired by the French Revolution with its national flag, national song, national language, national holiday and emphasis on citizenship.

Role of Bonaparte

- Napoleon Bonaparte's conquest inspired feelings of nationalism – he reduced the number of states to three; revived the name 'Italy'; brought in a single system of weights and measures; improved communications; helped trade inspiring desire for at least a customs union. Napoleon's occupation was hated – conscription, taxes, looting of art – led to realisation that, individually, the Italian states were weak.

Resentment of Austrian Rule

- After the Vienna settlement in 1815, hatred of foreign control centred on Austria. The Hapsburg Emperor directly controlled Lombardy and Venetia; his relatives controlled Parma, Modena, Tuscany. Austria had strong ties to the Papacy and had alliances with other rulers. Conscription, censorship, the use of spies and the policy of promotion in the police, civil service and army only for German speakers was resented.
- Austrian army presence within towns like Milan and the heavily garrisoned Quadrilateral fortresses ensured that 'Italians' could never forget that they were under foreign control and this inspired a growing desire for the creation of a national state.

Role of Nationalist Societies

- The growth of secret societies, particularly the Carbonari, led to revolts in 1820, 1821 and 1831. Also the 'Young Italy' society and their revolts in the 1830s.

Role of Pio Nono

- The election of a new, seemingly reformist Pope, Pius IX, in 1846 inspired feelings of nationalism particularly amongst businessmen and traders as he wished to form a customs union.

14. The candidate assesses the extent of the growth of nationalism by 1850 using evidence and arguments such as:

The Risorgimento

- Modern Italians highlight the importance of the Risorgimento as part of their gradual evolution as a nation. This is seen through the appearance of patriotic literature such as novelists, poets and philosophers including Pellico, Leopardi, Gioberti, Balbo and Mazzini. These inspired intellectuals and students, but did not reach the vast majority of the population who were illiterate (90% in some areas).

Cultural aspects

- Operas by Verdi and Rossini inspired anti-Austrian feelings rather than desire for a national state.

Language

- The use of Tuscan as a 'national' language by Alfieri and Manzoni spread ideas of nationalism but was restricted to intellectuals.
- Regional dialects remained the norm; these were like separate languages making communication difficult.

Geography

- Geographical difficulties (mountains and islands) hindered the spread of nationalist ideas. Napoleon Bonaparte had built roads and encouraged closer trading but restoration monarchs opposed road/railway building, re-established customs duties and imposed travel restrictions on their populations making communication amongst nationalists difficult.

The Italian States

- Individual rulers were opposed to nationalism and encouraged regionalism. They used censorship, police, spies and help from the Austrian army to crush revolts (in 1820s, 1830s and 1840s).

Secret Societies

- Membership of secret societies grew. They were willing to revolt and die for their beliefs; however, they lacked clear aims, organisation, leadership, and resources and operated in localised cells. Some Carbonari were nationalist but others favoured liberalism.
- There was a growing desire for the creation of a national state amongst students but this was a narrow group. Membership of 'Young Italy' was estimated by Mazzini at 50,000. This is now seen by historians as exaggerated.

Nationalist divisions

- Differences divided the nationalist movement curtailing growth. Moderate nationalists (Gioberti and Balbo) wanted a federal state, but had different ideas on who should preside over this. Gioberti's hopes ended in 1848 when Pope Pius IX denounced nationalism. Balbo's ended with the Austrian defeat of the 'nationalist army' led by Piedmontese King Charles Albert in 1848/49.
- Mazzini inspired radical nationalists but his dreams of a united, democratic Italian republic were idealistic and too extreme for most. His dreams were shattered with the failure of the masses to rise in support of the Roman Republic in 1849 and its defeat by French troops.

The 1848/49 revolutions

- The 1848/49 revolutions showed that nationalist leaders would not work together – Charles Albert hated Mazzini and would not support republican ideas. He himself was suspected of being rather less nationalist and more intent on expanding his own kingdom and this lessened his support.

Popular attitudes

- The mass of the population were indifferent to nationalist ideas. 90% of the population of the Italian states worked on the land and were weighed down with poverty/harvest worries/starvation and were indifferent to politics. Peasant and working class membership of the Carbonari for example was virtually unknown. They did revolt during bad times as can be seen in 1848 but their revolts were not nationalist.

15. The candidate evaluates the role of Garibaldi's military leadership in the process of uniting Italy by 1871, using evidence of arguments such as:

Garibaldi

- He was a committed nationalist; he fought in the War of Liberation for Victor Emmanuel. His role was crucial in forcing north/south unification – the role of the 'thousand'; military success in Sicily and Naples; handing his 'conquests' to Victor Emmanuel at Teano. He tried but failed to take Rome.

Other factors

The role of foreign powers

France

- Victor Emmanuel of Piedmont/Cavour realised that foreign help was needed to drive the Austrians from Italy. Crimean War/Paris Peace provided the opportunity for Cavour to remind Britain and France of Italy's 'unhappy' state.

Following the Orsini Plot, Napoleon III held a secret meeting at Plombières, July 1858 with Cavour. The result was a formal treaty in January 1859. Napoleon III promised 200,000 men to fight for Piedmont if Austria attacked. This would prove crucial.

- War of Liberation, 1859 – the two main victories of Magenta and Solferino were French. At Villafranca Austria handed Lombardy to France who gave it to Piedmont. Garibaldi acknowledged the importance of French help. The war inspired rebellions in Tuscany, Parma, Modena, Romagna and demands for union with Piedmont. Napoleon was not happy, but was persuaded to accept by British diplomacy and Cavour's renewed offer of Nice and Savoy.
- Napoleon did not intervene over Garibaldi's expedition. He made a secret agreement accepting Cavour's proposed invasion of the Papal States to stop Garibaldi reaching Rome. This allowed the Piedmontese to defeat the Papal Army, taking The Marches and Umbria. In 1866 Austria handed Venetia to France who gave it to Italy.
- The Italians took Rome after the defeat of Napoleon in 1870.

Attitude of Britain

- Britain was involved in diplomacy over the Duchies. British naval presence helped Garibaldi land at Marsala. Britain refused a joint naval blockade with France to stop Garibaldi crossing the Sea of Messina – crucial for Garibaldi's success.
- Britain was the first power to officially recognise the Kingdom of Italy.

Prussia

- The Italians made a secret agreement to help Prussia in the war against Austria 1866. Prussian war against France gave the Italians the chance to take Rome.

Roles of other individuals

Cavour

- He played a vital role – modernisation of Piedmont; diplomacy before War of Liberation. Provocation of Austria; encouragement of National Society especially in Duchies/Romagna and his handling of the plebiscites. Cavour's diplomacy and manoeuvring over Garibaldi's expedition; the invasion of Papal States forcing unification on Piedmontese terms.

Victor Emmanuel

- As King of Piedmont his retention of the Statuto meant Piedmont became the focus for nationalism. He appointed Cavour. He made anti-Austrian speeches to parliament to antagonise the Austrians. He took Piedmont to war – Crimea, War of Liberation, invasion of the Papal States and war against Austria 1866. He became Italy's first king and his forces took Rome.

16. The candidate assesses the security of the Tsarist regime before 1905, using evidence and arguments such as:

Opposition Groups

- Opposition and revolutionary groups were fairly weak. There were various revolutionary groups like the Social Revolutionaries (supported by peasants seeking land reform), Social Democrats (supported by industrial workers) and Liberals (who wanted a British style parliament). However these groups on their own were not powerful or popular enough to affect change. Moreover these groups were further weakened by the fact they were divided and disorganized – leaders often in prison or in exile.

- ### The "Pillars of Autocracy"
  The features of the Tsarist state which strengthened it, and made it almost impossible for opposition groups to challenge it:

The Church
- Helped to ensure that the people, particularly the peasants, remained loyal to the Tsar. They preached to the peasants that the Tsar had been appointed by God and that they should therefore obey the Tsar. Ensured the peasants were aware of the Fundamental Law.

Fundamental Law
- This stated "To the emperor of all Russia belongs the Supreme and unlimited power. God himself commands that his supreme power be obeyed out of conscience as well as out of fear." This was the basis of the Tsarist state.

The Army
- This was controlled by the officers who were mainly upper class, who were therefore conservative and loyal to the Tsar. They ensured that the population and the peasants in particular were loyal to the Tsar. They crushed any insurgence and were used to enforce order in the country and loyalty to the Tsar.

The Secret Police (Okhrana)
- This was set up to ensure loyalty to the Tsar and weed out opposition to the Tsar. They did this by spying on all people of society irrespective of class. Those showing any sign of opposition to the Tsar were imprisoned or sent in to exile. Large numbers were exiled.

Civil Service
- Mainly employed middle class people therefore ensuring the loyalty of that class. The Civil Service was responsible for enforcing laws on censorship and corruption as well as about meetings which made it very difficult for the revolutionaries to communicate.

Censorship
- This controlled what people were able to read, controlling what University lecturers could say, controlled access to schools, limited books available in libraries.

Russification
- This was the policy of restricting the rights of the national minorities in the Russian Empire by insisting that Russian was the first language. As a result, law and government were conducted throughout the Russian Empire in the Russian language. This maintained the dominance of the Russian culture over that of the minorities. State intervention in religion and education. Treated subjects as potential enemies and inferior to Russians.

Zubatov Unions
- Organised by the police, these were used to divert the attention of the workers away from political change by concentrating on wages and conditions in the factories, thus reducing the chances of the workers being influenced by the revolutionary groups. Unions in 1903 became involved in strikes and so were disbanded due to pressure from employers.

17. The candidate evaluates the significance of military defeat in causing the 1905 revolution, using evidence and arguments such as:

Military Defeat
- The Russo-Japanese War was disastrous for Russia. Defeats by Japan were humiliating and led to discontent in Russia over the Tsar's leadership, the incompetence of the Tsar's government and the state of Russia's armed forces.
- Russian armed forces were unhappy with their poor pay and conditions, the incompetence of their leaders and their defeats which led to low morale. Naval Mutiny in the Black Sea Fleet, Battleship Potemkin, over poor conditions and incompetent leadership worried the Tsar as the mutiny threatened to spread.

Other factors
Economic Problems
- Russia had been experiencing a number of economic problems in the period before 1905. Russia had started the process of industrialisation however its cost meant that Russia used foreign loans and increased taxes to fund it. The working and living conditions in the cities were very poor and this along with long working hours and low pay led to discontent.
- The vast majority of Russians were peasant farmers who lived in poverty and were desperate to own their own land. Many peasants were frustrated at paying redemption payments and at the unwillingness of the government to introduce reforms. An economic slump in Russia hurt the newly created Russian industries and coupled with famine in 1902/1903 led to food shortages. There was an outcry when Russian grain was still being exported to pay for the foreign loans.

Political Problems
- Growing unhappiness with Tsarist autocratic rule. The middle class and the industrial workers were calling for a constitutionally elected government as they were so frustrated at the incompetence of the Tsar's government, especially during the war with Japan. During 1905 workers set up groups called soviets to demand better pay and conditions. The Russian nobility feared a revolution if moderate reforms were not introduced.
- Tsar Nicholas II was seen as being too weak and unable to make good decisions for Russia in a crisis.
- National minorities hated the policy of Russification as it ignored their language, customs and religion and many felt so isolated that the desire for independence intensified.
- As the war with Japan progressed there were a growing number of protests from different parts of Russian society calling for the war to end and the Tsar to share his power.

Events
- Bloody Sunday, January, 1905. Troops fired on the unarmed crowd which led to strikes in all major towns and cities. Terrorist acts followed towards government officials and landowners.
- Peasant violence in the countryside when peasants took over land and burned landowners' estates started after the government threatened to repossess the land of those behind with their redemption payments.

18. The candidate assesses the extent to which the February 1917 revolution was caused by Tsar Nicholas II, using evidence and arguments such as:

Tsar Nicholas II
- The Tsar was seen as a weak ruler as he was so easily influenced by the Tsarina, Rasputin and his Ministers. At times the Tsar appeared to be more interested in his family than in the issues facing Russia. He was stubborn as he ignored advice and warnings from Rodzyanko and he failed to understand the severity of events in February 1917.
- In September 1915 the Tsar took personal control of the armed forces, which left him personally responsible for any defeats. This also meant that he left the Tsarina in charge, which was not welcomed in Russia as she was German and her relationship with Rasputin was viewed with suspicion.
- By February 1917 the Tsar had lost control of the armed forces as well as the support and loyalty of the Russian people, which contributed to the February 1917 revolution.

Other factors

The First World War – military problems
- The war did not go well for the Russian armed forces and they suffered many defeats. Russia also lost control of Poland in 1915, which was a severe blow to Russian pride.
- The Russian army lacked vital resources, including adequate medical care, and this led to high fatality and casualty rates. There were claims of defeats caused by incompetent officers who refused to cooperate with each other as well as communication difficulties. This led to low morale and desertions; the Tsar began to lose control and support of the armed forces. The generals forced his abdication at Pskov.

The First World War – social and economic problems
- The war put a tremendous strain on the already fragile Russian economy. Long term discontent with both peasants and industrial workers. The inadequate transport system was unable to cope with the supply demands of the military as well as the needs of the Russian economy and society. There was a lack of food made worse by the transport problems and the scorched earth policy and as a result in the cities there were long queues and bread riots culminating in the International Women's Day protest in Petrograd.
- The war was costing 17 million roubles a day and Russia had to get loans from Britain and France. Economic problems such as heavy taxes, high inflation and price rises meant that many were living in poverty.
- The people had expected the war to be won by Christmas 1914 so they were war weary by 1917 and suffering from grief, anxiety and low morale. They wanted the war to end but they knew the Tsar would not agree to that and they became so unhappy and frustrated they protested and went on strike which led to the February Revolution as the army sympathised with them and consequently sided with them against the Tsarist system.

The First World War – political problems
- There had been long-term discontent with the Tsar's autocratic rule as he seemed unwilling to share his power despite promises (October Manifesto and Fundamental Laws). The Dumas had limited power and the Tsar dissolved them and changed the franchise.
- War exacerbated existing problems with the Tsar leaving the Tsarina to run the country in his absence. Frustration grew at the incompetence of the Tsar and his ministers, Rasputin's influence and not having a say in how the country was being run and this led to protests and ultimately to the February Revolution.

19. The candidate evaluates the importance of isolationism in explaining changing attitudes towards immigration, using evidence and arguments such as:

Pre-war desire to isolate
- Change in attitude apparent in the 19th century. 1884 Immigration Restriction League.
- 1882 Federal Immigration Act.
- Chinese Exclusion Act.
- 1913 Alien Land Law.

Isolationism and the First World War
- At the beginning of the First World War American public opinion was firmly on the side of neutrality.
- Wanted to keep out of foreign problems and concentrate solely on America.
- President Wilson – America should not become involved in Europe's 'Civil War'.
- Many immigrants during the First World War had sympathies for their mother country.
- Many German immigrants had supported the German side

in the war and society was split when the USA joined the war against Germany.
- Irish Americans were suspected of being anti-British.
- Many citizens felt hostile to anything foreign.
- When the war ended, most Americans wanted a return to isolationism.
- America did not join the League of Nations; many Senators were concerned that if the USA joined, it might soon get dragged into another European War.

Other factors

Social fears
- Immigrants congregated with people from their own culture in ghettos.
- Immigrants blamed for high crime rates in cities – particularly those cities with high levels of immigrants e.g. Sacco and Vanzetti case.

Economic fears
- Trade unions believed that anything they did to improve conditions or wages was wrecked by Italian or Polish workers who were prepared to work longer hours for lower wages.
- 1919 strikes – new immigrants were used as 'strike breakers'. Caused huge resentment and an increase in the desire to stop immigrants coming into the country.

Fear of communism
- Russian revolution in 1917 had established the first Communist state committed to spreading revolution and destroying capitalism.
- 'Red Scare' 1919 and it looked as if revolution was imminent.
- Palmer Raids – August 1919.

Prejudice and racism
- Changing nature of immigrants. Old Immigrants – WASPs mainly from North and West of Europe. New Immigrants – mainly from Southern and Eastern Europe. New immigrants were Catholic or Jewish – worried WASP America.
- New immigrants unfamiliar with democracy – viewed as a threat to the American constitution. New immigrants continued to wear traditional dress and looked out of place.

20. The candidate evaluates the importance of the "separate but equal" decision of the Supreme Court in delaying civil rights reforms, using evidence and arguments such as:

Legal impediments   Supreme Court decisions
- 'Jim Crow Laws' - separate education, transport, toilets etc – passed in Southern states after the Civil War
- 'Separate but Equal' Decision 1896, when Homer Plessey tested their legality
- Attitudes of Presidents e.g. Wilson 'Segregation is not humiliating and is a benefit for you black gentlemen'.

Other Factors

Ku Klux Klan
- Founded in 1860s to prevent former slaves achieving equal rights.
- Suppressed by 1872, but in the 1920s there was a resurgence.
- By 1925 it had three million members, including the police, judges and politicians.
- Secret organisation with powerful members.
- 1923 Hiram Wesley Evans became the Klan's leader.
- Methods horrific: included beatings, torture and lynching. Roosevelt refused to support a federal bill to outlaw lynching in his New Deal in 1930s.
- Activities took place at night – men in white robes, guns, torches, burning crosses.
- March through Washington in 1925.

Lack of political influence

- 1890s: loopholes in the interpretation of the 15th Amendment were exploited so that states could impose voting qualifications.
- 1898 case of Mississippi v Williams – voters must understand the American Constitution.
- Grandfather Clause: impediment to black people voting.
- Most black people in the South were sharecroppers they did not own land and some states identified ownership of property as a voting qualification.
- Therefore black people could not vote, particularly in the South, and could not elect anyone who would oppose the Jim Crow Laws.

Divisions in the black community

- Booker T Washington, accomodationist philosophy, regarded as an 'Uncle Tom' by many.
- In contrast W E B De Bois founded the NAACP – a national organization whose main aim was to oppose discrimination through legal action. 1919 he launched a campaign against lynching, but it failed to attract most black people and was dominated by white people and well off black people.
- Marcus Garvey and Black Pride – he founded the UNIA (Universal Negro Improvement Association) which aimed to get blacks to 'take Africa, organise it, develop it, arm it, and make it the defender of Negroes the world over'.

Discrimination and poverty in the North

- The great Migration.
- Development of urban ghettos: crime, lack of education
- Average black worker was unskilled and poorly paid.
- Excluded from skilled work by trade unions and racially prejudiced employers.

21. The candidate assesses the effectiveness of the increased federal powers under the New Deal in solving the social and economic problems of the 1930s, using evidence and arguments such as:

The New Deal – aims

- Context of the victory of Roosevelt in 1932 presidential election after the inadequate response of Hoover and the Republicans to the Great Depression that followed the Wall Street Crash. Roosevelt and the Democrats took a more interventionist approach to dealing with the economy than the Republicans.
- The New Deal aimed to provide relief for the unemployed, aid recovery of the economy and reform to create a fairer society.

Social problems

- The Second New Deal 1935-1937: reforms to improve living and working conditions for many Americans through acts such as the Social Security Act (1935) providing a state pension scheme for the old, widows, as well as help for the disabled and poor children.
- National Labour Relations Act (1935) gave workers the right to join Trade Unions, etc.
- Ending unpopular prohibition to raise revenue and popular morale!
- Debate on the issue of reform of society: 'confidence' in government and its role in running the economy. It changed expectations in America, protected workers and provided social reform.

Economic problems

- Launch of 'Alphabet Agencies giving relief and recovery in first 100 days of Roosevelt presidency: e.g. Federal Emergency Relief Administration (FERA), Tennessee Valley Authority (TVA), Public Works Administration (PWA) providing relief and work.

- Confidence building measures such as checking banks in 1933 to ensure they were well run and credit worthy.
- Economic prudence by cutting wages of state employees by 15% and spending savings on relief programmes.
- Debate on the economic effects in terms of relief and recovery: they certainly helped in terms of providing basic relief.
- As to recovery, they made a difference, but its role is open to discussion as unemployment continued to be a problem, never running at less than 14% of the working population.
- The importance of rearmament in reducing unemployment and revitalizing the American economy was considerable, particularly after the mini-slump of 1937.

22. The candidate evaluates the relative importance of economic difficulties in explaining the aggressive nature of fascist foreign policies in the 1930s using evidence and arguments such as:

Economic difficulties

- Germany and Italy's post-WW1 economic difficulties – e.g. labour unrest, unemployment, inflation.
- Fascist economic policies in Italy in the 1920s – relative recovery.
- The impact of the world economic crisis 1929-32 on the German and Italian economies, intensified international competition and protectionism.
- Continuing economic problems in the 1930s, e.g. needs of rearmament and domestic consumption.
- Economic imperatives, e.g. need for additional resources, leading to aggressive, expansionist foreign policies, e.g. Italy in Abyssinia, German drive to the east.

Other factors

Legacy of the First World War

- German desire to get revenge for defeat in WW1.
- Determination to revise/overturn Paris Peace Settlement – German resentment of war guilt, reparations, disarmament, lost territory. Italian resentment of failure to gain control of Adriatic.

Imperialism

- Mussolini's 'Roman' ambitions in the Mediterranean and Africa; Hitler's ambitions in Eastern Europe and Russia.

Militarism

- Fascist glorification of war; Prussian/German military traditions.

Ideology

- Pathological hatred of communism, anti-Soviet crusade; contempt for democracy.
- Irredentism, e.g. Hitler's commitment to incorporation of all Germans within Reich.

Leadership

- Extent to which foreign policies driven by Hitler's and Mussolini's own beliefs, personalities, charismatic leadership.

Weakness of opposition

- Failure of the League. Divided response of other powers, e.g. British appeasement, French political divisions, US isolationism, mutual suspicion of Soviet Russia; relative weakness of successor states in East European.
- Example of success of Japan in Manchuria in defiance of League.

23. The candidate assesses the extent to which fascist foreign policy in the 1930s relied on the use of military force by comparison with political, diplomatic, economic and other methods, using evidence and arguments such as:

Military force

- The militaristic nature and image of Fascism/Nazism.
- The speed and scale of rearmament, including conscription.
- The emphasis on air power and the growing threat from the air.
- Italy's naval ambitions in the Mediterranean – 'Mare Nostrum'.
- Italian invasion of Abyssinia – provocation, methods, and relatively poor performance against very poorly equipped enemy.
- German remilitarisation of Rhineland – Hitler's gamble and timing, his generals' opposition, lack of Allied resistance.
- Spanish Civil War – aid to Nationalists, testing weapons and tactics, aerial bombing.
- Anschluss – attempted coup 1934; relations with Schuschnigg; invasion itself relatively botched militarily; popularity of Anschluss in Austria.
- Czechoslovakia – threats of 1938; invasion of March 1939.
- Italian invasion of Albania – relatively easy annexation of a client state.
- Poland – escalating demands; provocation, invasion.
- The extent to which it was the threat of military force which was used rather than military force itself – e.g. Czechoslovakia in 1938; and the extent to which military force itself was effective and/or relied on an element of bluff – e.g. Rhineland.

Other methods

- Diplomacy and the protestation of 'peaceful' intentions and 'reasonable' demands.
- Appeals to sense of international equality and fairness and the righting of past wrongs e.g. Versailles.
- Withdrawal from League and Disarmament Conference.
- Signing of pacts, agreements and alliances:
  - German-Polish Non-Aggression Pact
  - Stresa Front – Italy, France, Britain
  - Anglo-German Naval Agreement
  - Austro-German agreement
  - Rome-Berlin Axis and Anti-Comintern Pact
  - Munich Agreement
  - Nazi-Soviet Non-Aggression Pact.
- Clever timing and exploitation of weaknesses/divisions among potential opponents.
- Use of economic influence and pressure, e.g. on south-eastern European states.

24. The candidate assesses the degree of success of British foreign policy in achieving its aims between 1933 and March 1938, using evidence and arguments such as:

The preservation of peace

- This was Britain's foremost aim, and up to March 1938 (and later), this was achieved.
- Conflicts that did occur (Abyssinia, Spain) were on the periphery of Europe/the Mediterranean.

Relations with Germany

- Rearmament:
  - Hitler was successful in reintroducing conscription and rearming but there were significant economic restraints and by the late 1930s Germany's potential enemies were rearming at a faster rate
  - the growth of the Luftwaffe was a serious reverse for Britain
- The Anglo German Naval Agreement (1935)
  - This successfully limited German naval strength to 35% of British, but this was of lesser concern to Germany.

- Rhineland:
  - Hitler was successful in remilitarising Rhineland – more as a result of bluff, clever timing and French/British weakness than German military strength.
- Anschluss:
  - failure of attempted Nazi coup in 1934 due to Italian opposition, but successful annexation of Austria in 1938 – although invasion itself was chaotic and inefficient from military point of view. This was another fait accompli, but Britain could have done little to prevent it.

Relations with Italy

- Mussolini's plans for a new Roman Empire in the Adriatic, the Mediterranean and North Africa were a blow to British foreign policy in hoping to convert Mussolini into an ally.
- Stresa Front (1935) initially seemed successful.
- Hoare-Laval Pact – public revulsion to Franco-British connivance at Italian aggression led to Hoare's resignation.
- Imposition of limited sanctions on Italy alienated Mussolini, thereby driving him closer to Hitler, yet failing to save Abyssinia.

The Spanish Civil War

- Britain's main aim was to prevent this becoming an international war, and was successful in achieving this.
- The policy of non-intervention was sponsored by Britain; it also guaranteed that Britain would be on good terms with the victors.
- The policy was openly breached by Germany and Italy, and to a lesser extent the Soviet Union. Resolute action did end attacks on merchant shipping in the Mediterranean.

25. The candidate assesses the extent to which the Cold War was caused by America's decision to drop the atom bomb, using evidence and arguments such as:

Impact of the atom bomb and arms race

- Use of atom bombs on Hiroshima and Nagasaki had one aim of impressing the USSR and making them ready to make concessions in Eastern Europe. Stalin refused to be intimidated and in fact it made him even more suspicious of the USA and determined to make the Soviet Union a nuclear power as soon as possible; the development of the arms race.

Other factors

Ideological differences   aims and agendas before 1945

- Impact of 1917 Bolshevik revolution in Russia on relations with the western powers: Soviet withdrawal from WW1, involvement of West with anti-Bolshevik Whites: ideological differences between Communist and Capitalism. WW2: suspicion of USSR by allies because of Nazi-Soviet Pact of 1939. Tensions within the wartime alliance as the defeat of Nazism became clear. Soviet Union felt they had done the bulk of the land fighting and wanted security for the USSR. Stalin determined to hang on to land gained and create a series of sympathetic regimes in Eastern Europe. The USA wanted to create a free trade area composed of democratic states. Exemplification through Yalta Conference: Soviet actions in Poland, Romania, Bulgaria, etc and Allied actions in Western Europe and Greece.

The status of post-war Germany

- The Potsdam Conference and policy over Germany whereby the allied sectors remained free as compared to the Soviet sector which was stripped of assets as reparations. The economic status of Germany: creation of Bizonia in the West. Contrast between the developing capitalist west and centrally controlled east: introduction of Deutsche Mark in the West led to the Berlin Blockade in 1948.

Changing Western policy

- Truman and the policy of containment: British power had been destroyed; decline in their world commitments, specifically in Greece where civil war raged between Communists and Royalists. Fear of similar problems in Italy when allied troops left. Truman acknowledged world dividing into two hostile blocs in his speech to support free peoples and oppose totalitarian regimes – exemplified by the Marshall Plan. Fulton speech by Churchill. Creation of competing military alliances: NATO and Warsaw Pact further polarised the world.

Cold War sealed with a Hot War: Korea

- Stalin encouraged Communist North Korea to invade Capitalist South. This led to American-led UN intervention on behalf of the South, and resultant Chinese intervention. Soviet and American pilots fought each other across Korea. Stalemate along 38th parallel.

26. The candidate assesses the effectiveness of Soviet reaction to demands for political change in Eastern Europe up to 1961, using evidence and arguments such as:

Soviet political change: Nikita Khrushchev

- 1955 emergence of Nikita Khrushchev as leader on death of Stalin. He encouraged criticism of Stalin and seemed to offer hope for greater political and economic freedom across the Eastern European satellite states.
- Speech to 20th Party Congress, Feb 1956: Khrushchev attacked Stalin for promoting a cult of personality and for his use of purges and persecution to reinforce his dictatorship. Policy of de-Stalinisation.
- Development of policy of peaceful co-existence to appeal to the West.
- Development of policy of different roads to Socialism to appeal to satellite states in Eastern Europe who were becoming restless.

Demands for change and reaction: Poland (1956)

- Riots sparked off by economic grievances developed into demands for political change in Poland.
- On the death of Stalinist leader Boleslaw Bierut in 1956 he was replaced by Wladyslaw Gomulka, a former victim of Stalinism, which initially worried the Soviets.
- Poles announced own road to Socialism and introduced extensive reforms.
- Release of political prisoners (and Cardinal Wyszynski, Archbishop of Warsaw), collective farms broken up into private holdings, private shops allowed to open, greater freedom to factory managers.
- Relatively free elections held in 1957 which returned a Communist majority of 18.
- No Soviet intervention despite concerns.
- Gomulka pushed change only so far. Poland remained in the Warsaw Pact as a part of the important 'buffer zone'. Political freedoms were very limited indeed. Poland was a loyal supporter of the Soviet Union until the 1980s and the emergence of the Solidarity movement.

Demands for change and reaction: Hungary (1956)

- Hungarians had similar complaints: lack of political freedom, economic problems and poor standard of living.
- Encouraged by Polish success criticism of Stalinist, Mátyás Rákosi regime grew and he was removed by Khrushchev.
- Popular upsurge of support for change in Budapest led to a new Hungarian government headed by Imre Nagy who promised genuine reform and change.
- Nagy government planned multi-party elections, political freedoms, the withdrawal of Hungary from the Warsaw pact and demands for the withdrawal of Soviet forces.

- Nagy went too far. The Soviet Union could not tolerate this challenge to the political supremacy of the Communist Party and the break up of their carefully constructed buffer zone. They intervened and crushed the rising brutally.
- Successful intervention, but lingering resentment from mass of Hungarian people, though some economic flexibility allowed the new regime of Janos Kadar to improve economic performance and living standards.

Demands for change and reaction: Berlin (1961)

- Problem of Berlin – a divided city in a divided nation.
- Lack of formal boundaries in Berlin allowed East Berliners and East Germans to freely enter the West which they did owing to the lack of political freedom, economic development and poor living standards in the East.
- Many fleeing (2.8 million between 1949 and 1961) were skilled and young, just the people the communist East needed to retain. This was embarrassing for the East as it showed that Communism was not the superior system it was claimed to be.
- Concerns of Ulbricht and Khrushchev: attempts to encourage the Western forces to leave Berlin by bluster and threat from 1958 failed.
- President Kennedy of America spoke about not letting the Communists drive them out of Berlin. Resultant increase in tension could not be allowed to continue.
- Building of barriers: barbed wire, then stone in August 1961, to stem the flood from East to West.
- Success in that it reduced the threat of war and the exodus to the West from the East to a trickle.
- Frustration of many in East Germany. Propaganda gift for the US and its allies.

Reality of Soviet policy

- Soviets would not allow the buffer zone to be broken up.
- Need to ensure survival of Communism was paramount.
- Some economic freedoms were allowed, but at the expense of political freedoms.

27. The candidate assesses how far public protests at home led to the American withdrawal from Vietnam using evidence and arguments such as:

Public opposition in America

- Public opposition supported by the press was probably the main reason for withdrawal. Vietnam a media war, images showed the public the brutality of war e.g. South Viet police chief executing a Viet Cong in Saigon during the Tet Offensive of '68. Such images damaged American claims to be the 'good guys'. Extent of the opposition is debated. Probably a minority in '65, growing by the time of crucial Tet offensive in '68. Oct 1969 largest anti-war protest in US History. Protestors in every major city in America. Opposition of Black power groups. Protest could be violent: May 1970 protest at Kent State University, Ohio led to four students being shot. Unpopularity of the draft. On the other hand, there was pressure for escalation from 'hawks' in America as well.

Other factors

American government and decision making

- USA was a democracy: public pressure and perception mattered. Nixon noted extent of opposition: withdrawal of 60,000 troops in 1969, policy of Vietnamisation. Economic cost of the war: US deficit of $1.6 billion in 1965 increased to $25.3 billion in 1968. Tax increases unpopular. Congress only got involved in limiting money and action in late 60s and early 70s. Divisions within administrations: e.g. LBJ had Rusk advising to continue the struggle in South-East Asia, compared to Senator Fulbright arguing for de-escalation.

North Vietnamese strengths

• A hard peasant life bred determined soldiers. Viet Cong enlisted for years, unlike American troops who signed up for a year. Belief in their cause of Communism also a factor. Great determination: e.g. the Ho Chi Minh trail was kept open despite American bombers continually attacking it. Viet Cong knew the jungle, survived in atrocious conditions, developed effective tactics and were more effective in winning the 'hearts and minds' of civilians than the Americans. Military objectives were realistic: General Giap aimed to break the will of the American Government. Support of Chinese and Soviet aid from 1965 of importance.

South Vietnamese weaknesses

• Corruption and decay of South Vietnamese government, especially in Saigon. Lack of political and social cohesion in South Vietnam led to divisions and turmoil which filtered through to their armed forces.

American military tactics

• Mass bombing had no real effect according to the Jason Study by MIT in 1966, owing to the agricultural nature of North Vietnam and the widespread jungle cover. Tactics on the ground – soldiers brave, but a minority did not believe in the war. Difficulties dealing with the conditions and knowing which Vietnamese were the enemy led to stress and confusion. Short commissions for officers and rotation of troops led to loss of expertise in the field.

HIGHER HISTORY PAPER 2
SQP

1: THE WARS OF INDEPENDENCE, 1286-1328

1. The candidate makes a judgement on how far **Source A** illustrates the problems caused by the death of Alexander III in terms of:

Points from the source which show the candidate has interpreted the significant views:
• Deaths of Alexander's children and grandchildren also
• Armed factions manoeuvred to gain the throne and many feared civil war and Edward feared instability on his northern border.
• As overlord it was up to Edward to put things right again/the issue was serious enough for Edward to travel from a distant country to deal with the matter
• Edward laid out his case for overlordship as part of the agreement for his intervention and he demanded that the Scottish nobility accept him as overlord, prior to helping.

Points from recall which support and develop those in the source:
• John Balliol, Robert Bruce and John Hastings all had strong legal claims to the throne of Scotland, by the time of the great cause the number had raised to 13, not including Edward himself. The Guardians decided to ask Edward to make a choice.
• Robert Bruce (the competitor) threatened a coup d'état; many believed that only Edward could prevent this
• Bishop Fraser of St Andrews was sufficiently worried that he personally wrote to Edward asking him to come to Scotland in order to maintain peace and help choose the rightful king.
• Edward pressured the Competitors to agree to his overlordship

Points from recall which offer a wider contextualisation such as:
• The Treaty of Birgham had established a secure future with England, through marriage. Yet there were signs of Edward's intent to establish his overlordship; he seized the Isle of Man and appointed the Bishop of Durham to help administer in Scotland.
• However the death of the Maid of Norway changed the situation dramatically
• Edward brought his army with him to Norham and organised his navy to prepare for a blockade of Scotland
• Edward raised new taxes to prepare for a possible war against Scotland, Edward's lawyers argued that it was up to the Guardians to prove that he was not overlord
• The Guardians were shocked by Edward's claims, though some historians believe that they should have seen it coming.
• Bishop Wishart admonished Edward, but Edward replied that he was ready to wage war on Scotland, diverting his troops from his planned crusade if need be
• Their reply demonstrated that they were anxious to secure their independence, but at the same time were afraid to cross Edward I
• Edward took possession of the main castles in Scotland, to maintain the peace he claimed, but it also gave him a secure hold on the kingdom
• The Guardians were persuaded to resign their position and they were replaced by a single English baron
• Any other relevant points.

2. The candidate makes a judgement on how far **Sources B** and **C** agree about the Scottish defeat at the Battle of Dunbar in terms of:

Overall **Sources B** and **C** agree that the battle was an easy victory the English. However **Source B** suggests that it was lack of courage amongst the Scottish knights that led to the

English victory, while **Source C** suggests it was due to the Scots' lack of military experience.

Points from **Source B**	Points from **Source C**
• The Scots army showed themselves boldly on the brow of a steep hill.	• The Scots were massed on the slopes of the Lammermuir Hills.
• Although the Scots columns were in close order and strong in numbers, before it was possible for the English to come close, they broke up and scattered more swiftly than smoke.	• The Scots broke ranks and charged, only to meet an ordered English battle line which overwhelmed them at the first onslaught.
• The fiercest of the Scots were the first to flee. Yet their foot soldiers would have stood firm had not the knights shown their heels and fled so readily.	• Although the Scottish knights had shown themselves to be brave in tournaments, they had no experience of the tactics of serious warfare
• No fewer than 10,000 rebels were killed.	• Thousands of Scottish foot soldiers were slain and the knights surrounded and made prisoner.

3. The candidate makes a judgement on how fully **Source D** shows the Scottish resistance to Edward I, 1296-1305 in terms of:

Points from the source which show the candidate has interpreted the significant views:
• Falkirk was a major blow to the Scots, but was not a crushing victory for the English
• The Scots nobility got away intact and they were able to re-organise later and continue the struggle against Edward, especially north of the Tay and in the south West
• The Scots infantry were destroyed at Falkirk
• The Scottish people had learned from the war, and were now tougher and more prepared to fight on after a defeat, than they were at Dunbar
• The defeat did mean the end of Wallace's leadership of the rebellion

Points from recall which support and develop those in the source:
• Wallace resigned his guardianship and dropped out of the limelight. He supposedly travelled to the court of Philip IV and later to Rome to petition the release of King John,
• Upon his return he joined forces with the Stewarts but was betrayed in 1305 and executed by Edward I
• John Comyn and Robert Bruce were named joint guardians and carried on the resistance to English rule
• Bruce carried on the struggle until 1302
• Comyn and his faction continued fighting until 1304

Points from recall which offer a wider contextualisation such as:
• Growth of resistance under Wallace, and Moray in the north
• Scottish victory at Stirling Bridge
• The Scots captured Stirling Castle shortly afterwards
• The war continued on despite the defeat at Falkirk
• Edward had to invade again in 1300, this time in Galloway; he captured Caerlaverock castle and defeated a small Scots army, before retreating back to Carlisle; the Scots resistance was still not crushed
• In 1301 he tried again, this time capturing Bothwell castle, before retreating for the winter
• In 1303 another great invasion was launched, this time he advanced as far as Kinloss, but had still not managed to force the Guardians into a decisive battle

• Edward over-wintered in Scotland, 1303-4, which broke the spirit of the Scottish resistance
• Stirling Castle held out, but surrendered to Edward's great war machines in 1304
• Most remaining Scottish nobles surrendered after Edward issued the "Ordinance for the order of the land of Scotland", in which he restored lands to nobles and allowed them more of a say in how the country was to be run
• Any other relevant points.

4. The candidate makes a judgement on how useful **Source E** is as evidence of showing the tactics used by Robert I to persuade the English to accept him as King of Scots in terms of:

Points from the source which show the candidate has interpreted the significant views:
• **Origin**: The Lanercost Chronicle is a primary source written around the time of the events of the wars, and probably written at Carlisle rather than Lanercost. Thus it draws upon contemporary sources for its information. Edward stayed at the Priory several times; it is safe to assume that the chronicler was recounting the typical English opinion of the time.
• It mainly relied upon second hand accounts, though the writer claimed to have witnessed some of the events, such as the siege of Berwick. This makes it reasonably useful account of the events.
• However, several times the Priory was attacked by Scottish marauders and by Wallace's forces in 1296 and again during Bruce's campaigns in Northern England. It is inevitable that the chronicle writer would have been biased against the Scots to some degree.
• **Possible purpose**: to demonstrate one aspect of the Scottish attempts to bring Edward II to the negotiating table.
• **Content**: the constant raids into northern England were designed to bring military pressure to bear and force a lasting truce. Examples of this which are useful:
  – Several large Scottish armies were advancing through northern England, led by Robert's chief lieutenants, Moray, Douglas and the Steward. These attacks were designed to put pressure on the English monarchy to reach a settlement
  – Douglas and Steward engaged in plundering while on the march, this was very common, Scots armies tended to profit during these raids
  – The people of Richmond decided to pay off the Scots, rather than fight, they had no defenders and in this case it was the lesser of two evils.

Points from recall which support and develop those in the source:
• The recapture of Berwick by Robert in 1319 pre-empted an invasion by Edward II. When Edward did eventually cross the border, Bruce refused to give battle, instead attacking Northallerton, Boroughbridge and Knaresborough.
• Douglas launched a daring attack on York late on in 1319, and threatened the home of the Earl of Lancaster.
• In 1322 Robert again attacked the North, this time Carlisle, again avoiding Edward II's foray north from Newcastle. The Scots deployed scorched earth tactics and again the English forces were forced to withdraw. Edward was surprised by a counter attack by Robert at Bylan Abby and only just managed to escape.
• These raids led to the truce of November 1319 – January 1322

Points from recall which offer a wider contextualisation such as:
• Edward Bruce was sent to Ireland in 1318, to open up a second front, this was part of an ambitious plan to create a Pan-Celtic alliance against Edward II

- Scottish bishops sent envoys to the Pope, in order to get him on side and to remove Robert's excommunication. The Pope agreed to a truce between the two warring kingdoms and demanded a settlement of the issue. However the truce negotiations broke down
- When the Pope renewed Robert's excommunication in 1320, Robert replied with several letters, one of which was the declaration of Arbroath, this was an impressive document that appealed the Scottish cause once again to the Pope.
- Any other relevant points.

2: THE AGE OF THE REFORMATION, 1542-1603

1. The candidate makes a judgment on how far **Source A** illustrates the weaknesses of the Catholic Church in terms of:

Points from the source which show the candidate has interpreted the significant views:
- Clergy were having children.
- They were using church revenues to gain status for their offspring.
- Only some priests were able to preach/ there was little preaching going on.
- Many clergy lacked knowledge of scripture and the Catholic faith.

Points from recall which support and develop those in the source:
- Clergy were supposed to be celibate but many kept a 'wife'.
- Illegitimate sons of clergy often inherited parishes from their father.
- To help improve teaching of the faith, Archbishop Hamilton introduced his catechism.

Points from recall which offer a wider contextualisation such as:
- Major problem facing Catholic Church was Pluralism – where one man took the income from several parishes.
- Income was often diverted from parishes to Bishops and Abbots.
- Monarchs placed their offspring in important positions in the Church.
- King James V had gained the right to appoint bishops and grant abbeys to laymen.
- Monastic life was in decline, with the exception of the Augustinian Canons who went out to the parishes.
- Nunneries were noted for spiritual and moral decay.
- The one part of the Catholic Church that did have some vigour was the Friaries.
- Any other relevant points.

2. The candidate makes a judgment on how far **Sources B** and **C** agree about the involvement of Mary, Queen of Scots, in the death of Darnley in terms of:

Overall, the sources disagree about Mary's involvement in the death of Darnley, with **Source B** suggesting that Mary was at the heart of the conspiracy to murder Darnley and that any tenderness towards Darnley was a disguise of her real intentions, while **Source C** says she was innocent and that Maitland was a major conspirator.

Points from **Source B**	Points from **Source C**
• Mary's journey to Glasgow took place at a time when she was openly expressing her distrust and hatred of Darnley.	• Mary went to Glasgow with nothing in her heart but the most loving devotion to her husband.
• She showed tenderness towards him and expressed hopes of being reconciled with him in order to persuade him to come with her to Edinburgh.	• She nursed him day and night during her visit and Darnley proposed that she should take him with her to Edinburgh.
• Kirk o' Field was selected as the most convenient place to commit the crime.	• Mary suggested Craigmillar as it was situated on higher ground and very healthy. Darnley refused to go there/Mary wrote to Maitland to provide a house and he recommended Kirk o' Field.
• Mary consented to reside at this house so that Darnley would not refuse to live there. On the evening before the murder she removed from the house all the furniture of any value that it contained.	• It is clear that Maitland was a member of the conspiracy who wanted to put Darnley into Kirk o' Field.

3. The candidate makes a judgement on how fully **Source D** explains the relationship between Monarch and Kirk during the reign of King James VI to 1603 in terms of:

Points from the source which show the candidate has interpreted the significant views:
- Problems came from a clash with the extreme Presbyterians led by Andrew Melville.
- Tension was not about belief as the King was also Calvinist.
- Those like Melville wanted a Theocracy – where the church would rule.
- Melville told James that he was just a member not the head of the church.

Points from recall which support and develop those in the source:
- Melville wanted a Presbyterian Church where there was no hierarchy.
- King James considered himself to be head of the church – this brought him into conflict with Melville.
- James was determined that the church be under the control of the crown.

Points from recall which offer a wider contextualisation such as:
- Tension had first developed under Morton's regency. He was determined to keep control over the Kirk.
- The second book of Discipline 1576 set forth the vision of a Presbyterian Church.
- The 'Black Acts' of 1584 had clearly stated the supremacy of the King in all matters. They had also tried to promote bishops in the Kirk.
- James was reluctant to enforce anti-Catholic laws.
- General Assemblies continually called for crown to take action against Catholic nobles and Jesuits.
- The 'Golden Act' 1592 allowed for Presbyteries to be set up but the King had the power to say where and when General Assemblies would meet.

- James would have the General Assembly meeting in Perth or Aberdeen where he could expect more ministers would support the King.
- 1597 Riot in Edinburgh, as a result of sermon preached against the King. James had the ministers of Edinburgh briefly imprisoned. No minister to be appointed without his consent. The town council was fined.
- James attended every General Assembly from 1597 to 1603.
- By the late 1590s Assemblies were becoming more agreeable to the King's aims.
- James believed in the Divine Right of Kings. He was answerable to God alone. This conflicted with Melville's views.
- In his book 'Basilicon Doron' James advised his son to allow no meetings of the Church without his approval.
- James' preferred form of Church government was by bishops.
- In 1600, James reintroduced bishops into parliament.
- Any other relevant points.

4. *Points from the source which show the candidate has interpreted the significant views:*
   - **Origin**: contemporary document from a Scottish burgh.
   - **Possible Purpose**: to record the proceedings of the Kirk Session.
   - **Content**:
     - Instructions as to how the poor are to be dealt with.
     - Only those that attend church or are prepared to do so will be given any assistance.
     - Poor should be imprisoned until their need is assessed.

   Points from recall which support and develop those in the source:
   - The Church distinguished between the deserving and the undeserving poor.
   - The Church controlled poor relief in the post reformation period

   Points from recall which offer a wider contextualisation such as:
   - The able bodied poor were not to be helped nor were vagrants and beggars; in fact they were often punished by whippings and branding.
   - Poor relief was to be provided in the parish where you were born or lived in for some time.
   - Beggars were only allowed to beg in their own parish being issued with a 'Beggars Badge'/gaberlunzie.
   - Church collections and payments for use of parish mort cloth as well as fines from those disciplined by the Church were used for poor relief.
   - Act of 1587 allowed magistrates to assess the inhabitants of the parish to provide for poor relief.
   - Income for poor relief was always short of ideal.
   - Any other relevant points.

3: THE TREATY OF UNION, 1689-1740

1. The candidate makes a judgement on far **Source A** illustrate the problems arising from a shared monarchy in terms of:

   Points from the source which show the candidate has interpreted the significant views:
   - Problems surrounding the succession due to Queen Anne being without an heir.
   - Religious obstacles to the restoration of the Stuarts.
   - English Act of Succession chose the House of Hanover without reference to the Scottish Parliament.
   - English Parliament assumed Scots would agree.

   Points from recall which support and develop those in the source:
   - Succession crisis: Scots afraid of losing legal and religious identity under Hanoverian rule
   - England concerned at possible threat from Scotland if the Stuarts were restored.

- The Scots were angered because they were not consulted but just expected to accept the Hanoverian succession

Points from recall which offer a wider contextualisation such as:
- Conflict of interest – monarch tended to sacrifice Scottish interests to those of England
- William's use of political management to control the Scottish Parliament.
- Collapse of the Darien Scheme and William's manipulation of this.
- Scots angered at being drawn into the war with France without consultation.
- English resentment at continued Scottish trade with France.
- Differences between Scottish and English interpretations of the Revolution of 1688-9 – Scots said James VII and II had forfeited the throne while English said he had abdicated.
- Articles of Grievances of 1689 by Scottish Parliament.
- Glencoe Massacre and William's role in this.
- Continued Jacobite support in some parts of Scotland.
- Additional tension arising from English Episcopalian opposition to Presbyterian church in Scotland.
- Any other relevant points.

2. The candidate makes a judgement on how far **Sources B** and **C** agree about the advantages of a union with England in terms of:

   Overall: the sources are diametrically opposed in their attitude to a union, with **Source B** giving only advantages and **Source C** only disadvantages.

Points from **Source B**	Points from **Source C**
England gains a considerable addition of brave and courageous men to their fleet, armies and plantations, and we are secured by their protection, and enriched by their labours.	The valiant and gallant soldiery will be sent to learn the plantation-trade abroad, while their old regiments are broken, the common soldiers left to beg.
We will send our commodities and useful manufactures to them and have money and other necessaries remitted to us.	The royal boroughs will be wormed out of all the branches of their old trade.
We will see our craftsmen improve.	The honest industrious craftsman will be loaded with new taxes, drinking water in place of ale.
Our land will be better cultivated and manured.	The laborious ploughman will have his corn spoiling upon his hands, for want of sale.

3. The candidate makes a judgement on the reasons for the passing of the Treaty of Union in terms of:

   Points from the source which show the candidate has interpreted the significant views:
   - No great opposition to Union in England.
   - 'Management' of English M.Ps.
   - English insistence made Union possible.
   - Fears for the security of England.

   Points from recall which support and develop those in the source:
   - War of Spanish Succession – possible French intervention in a war with Scotland.
   - Threat of invasion from Scotland, possibly with support from the French.
   - Threat of Jacobite resurgence in Scotland.

Points from recall which offer a wider contextualisation such as:
- Scotland's economic problems: impact of failure of Darien scheme.
- Incentive of share in trade with English colonies.
- Guarantee for the Presbyterian Church.
- Part played by bribery in Scotland to secure the passing of the Act of Union.
- The importance of the Equivalent.
- Concessions on salt, wool and liquor.
- Assurances that Scots peers would retain privileges even if they did not get one of the 16 Scottish seats in the House of Lords.
- Scottish laws and courts were to remain.
- Role of the Squadrone Volante who held balance of power.
- Role of the Duke of Hamilton in dividing opponents of union.
- Threat of invasion if Scotland did not accept the Union.
- Disunity of opposition to union in Scotland; all they had in common was opposition to the union – the Jacobites because it would prevent a restoration of the Stuarts and the extreme Presbyterians because of the dominant position of the Episcopal Church of England.
- Any other relevant points.

4. The candidate evaluates **Source E** as evidence of political problems following the Union in terms of:

Points from the source which show the candidate has interpreted the significant views:
- **Origin**: Written just after the Treaty was passed, by a Scottish member of the Queen's Council.
- **Possible Purpose**: to tell the Earl of Leven of the measures being taken by the Council to deal with the threat of invasion.
- **Content**:
  - Plan being drawn up to disarm possible opponents of the Union.
  - Government taking measures to secure finances.
  - Law being changed in order to arrest suspects.

Points from recall which support and develop those in the source:
- In 1708 there was an attempted Jacobite invasion – a fleet set out from France with Old Pretender on board.
- Mar was soon disappointed with his status in the government and raised the Jacobite standard in 1715

Points from recall which offer a wider contextualisation such as:
- Exiled Stewart dynasty saw the advantage of invasion when the Union was so unpopular.
- Jacobites said that they would end the Union if the Stewarts were restored.
- Jacobites had become the main focus for anti-union sentiment after the Union was passed.
- The Government introduced stricter English treason laws, an early example of infringement of the Treaty.
- Other measures passed by the Westminster parliament infringed the Treaty of Union, eg Patronage Act and no rotation of sittings between Edinburgh and London, and this led to disillusionment with England and the Union.
- Other examples of issues affecting Scotland (eg Malt Tax).
- Short-term economic dislocation resulting in unemployment and beggary led to unrest.
- Attempt to repeal the Treaty of Union only narrowly failed its passage in the Lords.
- Porteous Riot of 1736 in Edinburgh can be partly ascribed to disillusionment with the Union, as it was occasioned by the hanging of Andrew Wilson for smuggling, which became more widespread in Scotland after the Union.
- Any other relevant points.

4: MIGRATION AND EMPIRE, 1830-1939

1. The candidate makes a judgment on the issue of internal migration in terms of **Source A** and recalled knowledge, using evidence such as:

Points from the source which show the candidate has interpreted the significant views:
- Many crafts being undermined by urban competition post-1850
- Technology was destroying the textile industry in numerous villages
- Traditional markets in rural areas were threatened by spread of railway lines
- Changing attitudes of the farm labourers themselves a factor in migration

Points from recall which support and develop those in the source:
- Effects of Industrial and Agricultural Revolutions on Scotland's population
- Advancement in new technology on Scottish work-force
- Transport developments within Scotland

Points from recall which offer a wider contextualisation such as:
- The Highland Clearances and the effects on Scottish life
- The 'Highland Problem' – overpopulation, lack of economic opportunities, land
- Problems and decline in fishing
- Structure of service in Lowland Scotland resulted in high levels of internal mobility in rural areas
- Temptation there for workers to seek better wages, more experience, change of surroundings
- Towns exerted a strong appeal to many young rural workers-social attractions, for example
- Rural life had few attractions-long hours and habitual turnover of labour curtailed social life to a minimum
- Town occupations seemed less demanding than work in rural areas
- Any other relevant points.

2. The candidate makes a judgment on how far **Sources B** and **C** agree on the issue of Irish assimilation in terms of:

Overall: the sources are both in agreement that the Irish found it difficult to 'rise up the social ladder' and that the immigrants were isolated from mainstream Scottish society, though **Source C** says this was partly due to a conscious effort by the Catholic community to remain separate.

Points from **Source B**	Points from **Source C**
• Irish found comfort and strength in their religion	• Catholic religion was essential for the maintenance of their cultural identity
• Irish found work which was unskilled and low paid	• Irish dominated the unskilled labour market – labourers, coal hewers, sweated labour in textiles
• Catholic Church was crucial in their lives, giving immigrants opportunities to meet with each other and providing general help where possible	• Church activists created a wide variety of organisations for the immigrants' benefit eg. religious, charitable and social
• Irish immigrants were excluded from main areas of Scottish society	• Immigrants were excluded from Scottish society by the native Scots but also due to a conscious effort made by the priests to do so

3. The candidate makes a judgment on the impact made by Scots emigrants on the British Empire in terms of **Source D** and recalled knowledge, using evidence such as:

Points from the source which show the candidate has interpreted the significant views:
- In India Scots were responsible for development of tea plantations
- Contribution of individual Scots – state education, finance minister in India
- In Canada Scots dominated government, fur trade, education and banking
- In Australia Macarthur considered to be founder of Australia's sheep industry

Points from recall which support and develop those in the source:
- Development of jute industry in the Calcutta area
- Development of Scottish banking system in India
- Development of India's elite schools, universities
- Scottish investment into developing economies
- Development of Canada's business, professional and political life

Points from recall which offer a wider contextualisation such as:
- Scottish Churches and their role in the evangelisation of India
- Contribution of Scottish educational missions in India
- Spread of the English language
- Spread of the ideal of individual liberty
- Role of Scots in Army, Civil Service and press
- Creation of Canadian Pacific Railroad by George Stephen
- Founding of banks and support of enterprise through investment companies
- Role of Presbyterian ministers on Canadian society
- Andrew Fisher became Prime Minister of Australia in 1908
- Education/Presbyterian Church developed by John Dunmore Lang in Australia
- Scots removed native Australians from land and appropriated the land for themselves
- Traditional way of life of Aboriginal people placed under threat
- In New Zealand Scots founded banks and financial institutions to develop the country
- Presbyterian missionaries attempted to protect the Maori people
- James Busby responsible for concluding Treaty of Waitangi whereby Maori chiefs accepted British Crown as only authority able to buy their lands
- Peter Fraser became Prime Minister of New Zealand in 1940
- Brisbane became Governor of Australia and introduced tobacco, sugar cane and freedom of the press
- Any other relevant points.

4. The candidate evaluates **Source E** is as evidence of the contribution of immigrants to Scottish society in terms of:

Points from the source which show the candidate has interpreted the significant views:
- **Origin**: Description given by an eyewitness to Jewish settlement in the Gorbals as part of an interview.
- **Possible Purpose**: To inform public opinion regarding Jewish settlement in Glasgow area at a certain point of time.
- **Content**:
  - Mostly Jewish businesses in the Gorbals, eg bakery, jewellers, cabinet-makers and upholsterers.
  - People helped each other out.
  - People could get credit in hard times.

Points from recall which support and develop those in the source:
- Contribution of Jewish community to Scottish economy.
- Contribution of Jewish community to Glasgow culture and society.

Points from recall which offer a wider contextualisation such as:
- Invaluable contribution made by Irish immigrants to Scotland's industrialisation – role of the 'navvies'.
- Role of Irish immigrants in agriculture – seasonal as well as permanent.
- Contribution of Irish for Scottish society generally – religious, political and cultural.
- Contributions of Italians and Lithuanians to Scottish society.
- Economic contribution of immigrants in tailoring, food industry, coalmining.
- Examples of assimilation of immigrant groups into Scottish society – sports clubs, churches, marriage.
- Any other relevant points.

5: SCOTLAND AND THE IMPACT OF THE GREAT WAR, 1914-1928

1. The candidate makes a judgement on how far **Source A** illustrates the experience of Scots on the Western Front in terms of:

Points from the source which show the candidate has interpreted the significant views:
- trenches poorly constructed
- dug-outs were overcrowded and the atmosphere stifling.
- heavy, prolonged shelling caused casualties eg Donald McLean was killed by a rifle grenade as he settled down to lunch; John Miller, from Portobello, also died in the bombardment.
- dangers from sniping: Willie Brydie, from Merchiston, was sniped during 'stand to'.

Points from recall which support and develop those in the source:
- Development of detail regarding British trench construction.
- Development of detail regarding dangers of trench life.
- Detail of conditions such as rats.
- Such dangers were common to all combatant units.

Points from recall which offer a wider contextualisation such as:
- Scots units were heavily involved in the Somme offensive and suffered high casualties as a result
- 3 Scottish divisions 9th, 15th [Scottish] and 51st [Highland] took part in the battle of the Somme, as well as numerous Scottish battalions in other units: i.e. the Scots Guards in the Household Division. 51 Scottish infantry battalions took part in the Somme offensive at some time.
- Huge Scottish sacrifice: 16th [McCraes] Royal Scots lost 12 officers and 573 soldiers, 51st Highland division suffered 3,500 casualties following two attacks on High Wood.
- Scots units tended to be seen as impact attack formations
- Despite losses there was still a belief in victory: new tactics were learned, but some criticism of war and its slaughter began.
- Successes existed as well: the 51st [Highland] Division launched a successful attack at Beaumont Hamel with relatively few casualties in November 1918.
- Previous experience at Loos which saw the 'blooding' of Kitchener's New Army divisions, including the enthusiastic Scottish volunteers.
- Scottish losses were so dreadful and no part of Scotland was unaffected. Of the 20,598 names of the dead on the memorial at Loos: one third are Scottish.
- Bloody-minded attitude of the survivors: losses were replaced and the Scottish units got back to the job in hand.
- Any other relevant points.

2. The candidate makes a judgement on how far **Sources B** and **C** agree about conscientious objection to the war in Scotland in terms of:

Overall: **Source B** and **Source C** agree that varied groups were opposed to the war, but differ in emphasis and on the nature and organisation of that opposition.

Developed through detail:

Points from **Source B**	Points from **Source C**
• UDC represented a range of opinions and was not specifically anti-war, even representing some who fought in the war	• No-Conscription Fellowship specifically opposed introduction of Conscription
• Some opposed to the war on what would be called ideological grounds. They held it was a capitalist war in which the working class had no share and no business to take part.	• When the war broke out in 1914 I became convinced that socialists had no business getting involved in this struggle.
• Then there were those who objected on religious grounds. The Quakers opposed all war as being against Christianity and members of other churches took the same position.	• One of the miscellaneous band called conscientious objectors, of which the Quakers were the best known.
• Then there were those who objected on various other grounds: it was a very mixed lot.	• No-Conscription Fellowship membership consisted not only of men of military age, but of women and of men too old for military service.

3. The candidate makes a judgement on how fully **Source D** shows the impact of the war on the Scottish economy in terms of:

Points from the source which show the candidate has interpreted the significant views:
- The lost generation lay at the root of Scottish industrial problems in the 1920s and 1930s, not the weakness of management.
- Low unemployment in Scotland compared to London before the war was reversed by 1923: it was long-term, skilled affected more than the unskilled.
- The war brought about a major shift in the balance within Great Britain between the north and south with regard to rates of unemployment. Scottish rates rose relative to the rest of Britain.
- In engineering wage the gap in earnings between skilled and unskilled reduced

Points from recall which support and develop those in the source:
- Disproportionate affect of losses on middle-class officers during the war: one in seven graduates from Edinburgh and one in six of the graduates of Glasgow University died. These were the managers of the future.
- In general wages were high during the war, but the introduction of dilution affected some industries.

Points from recall which offer a wider contextualisation such as:
- War was good for the traditional industries of Scotland: steel output doubled during the war.
- 90% of armour plate produced came from Glasgow
- 24,000 men in full-time steel employment in the Clyde valley
- Immediate impact of war on Clydeside shipyards where most of Britain's ships were built. Between 1914 and 1918 a total of 481 warships were built on the Clyde, and profits were good.

- Diversification of industry owing to the war: Beardmore's produced aircraft and artillery pieces as well as ships. John Brown's produced tanks.
- Edinburgh industries such as the North British Rubber Company did well as did the railways.
- Dundee's jute industry boomed as demand for sack cloth rose to meet the demands of warfare.
- Both Dundee and Aberdeen benefited from shipbuilding work.
- War delayed long-standing problems for the Scottish economy
- Concentration on a narrow group of heavy industries meant Scotland was affected badly when the post-war boom turned into slump. Exemplification, such as decline in shipbuilding; between 1921 and 1923 the tonnage built on the Clyde went down from 510,000 to 170,000
- Fish production went into decline as a result of falling demand.
- Jute production was affected by declining orders and industrial action after the war.
- Decline in Highland population: 341,535 in 1911, 325,853 in 1921: emigration, loss of life and decline in agriculture were all responsible.
- Disillusionment over lack of land for returning soldiers in the Highlands and Islands: Land Raids.
- The 1919 Land Settlement (Scotland) Act released funds and allowed the Board of Agriculture to compulsory purchase of private land. However, the process was laborious. Land raids occurred, especially by ex-servicemen who expected land on their return from the trenches. Occurred in areas like Lewis, Uist, Skye and Sutherland.
- Any other relevant points.

4. The candidate makes a judgement on how useful **Source E** is as evidence of the growth of radicalism in politics in Scotland in terms of:

Points from the source which show the candidate has interpreted the significant views:
- **Origin**: Willie Gallacher: prominent militant trade unionist, member of Clyde Shop Stewards' movement, chairman of Clyde Workers' Committee and founding member of the Communist Party in 1920.
- **Possible purpose**: a memoir of the activities on Red Clydeside.
- **Content**:
  - The 'tuppence an hour' strike made a deep political change as any hope of spreading pro-war fever throughout the Clyde gone for ever/workers now knew their real enemies
  - Revolutionary agitators, under McLean's tuition, were increasing in number day by day and were warmly cheered at mass meetings wherever they went.
  - Difficult for the 'patriots' to get a hearing as Socialists of Glasgow took a firm stand against the war as seen through the example of pro-war Ben Tillett being booed.

Points from recall which support and develop those in the source:
- Gallacher was consistently anti-war, but socialists were split on the matter
- Social Democratic Party, the Independent Labour Party and Socialist Labour Party had been intensely anti-war and anti militarist before the war.
- Role of John McLean; seen as a great Scottish revolutionary by many, but although undoubtedly inspirational was a marginalised figure eventually paranoid and broken by many arrests.
- Origin of much radicalism from the Shop Stewards who were more militant than their national union leadership: evidence of the numerous strikes on the Clyde etc.

Points from recall which offer a wider contextualisation such as:

- Agitators may have been cheered, but their impact was more limited.
- Most workers supported the war and worked hard.
- Practical evidence of more radical opinions seen in the growth of the Labour Party.
- Radicalism after war: possible 'revolution': 1919 – George Square; but long term triumph of gradualist approach: Maxton, Kirkwood, Johnston, Wheatley compared to McLean.
- In the 1922 election Labour made the breakthrough as the second political party: 29 of their 142 seats were in Scotland: 10 of these were in Glasgow. Leaders like Maxton were elected as MPs.
- More radical nature of Glasgow's Labour MPs can be seen in the fact that they were members of the ILP which had a more socialist agenda than the Labour Party.
- In the 1922 general election in Scotland, 40 out of the total of 43 prospective Labour candidates were members of the ILP.
- In the 1924 election Labour won 34 seats in Scotland. Labour formed a minority government, led by a Scot, Ramsay MacDonald, with Liberal support. (John Wheatley was a Glasgow Labour MP and Minister for Health.) One of their more radical measures was the Wheatley Housing Act, which gave government funding for local council housing. In Glasgow 21,586 badly needed houses were built as a result.
- Any other relevant points.

HIGHER HISTORY PAPER 1 2011

1. Each question is marked out of 20.

2. In Paper 1 candidates will be rewarded according to:

    (a) **Knowledge and Understanding – 6 marks are allocated for** the relevant knowledge they use to address the question. Marks will be awarded for each accurate, full point they make; these points may be further developed, as in the following example, relating to the effectiveness of the Liberal Reforms:

    Old age pensions *(0 marks for stating this)* were given to all people over 70 *(1 mark)*; married couples received 7/6 and single people 5s *(a second mark for knowledge)*. This provision was not enough to live on, but old people were able to help pay their families if they lived with them *(no further mark for knowledge, but an argument which would receive credit under the category Argument and Evaluation).*

    (b) **Argument/Evaluation – 10 marks are allocated for** the quality of thought revealed in their answers by the arguments and evaluation demonstrated. This should be taken as including the extent to which the candidate:

    - gives an answer which is relevant to the question and relates explicitly to the question's terms;
    - argues a case;
    - makes the various distinctions required by the question;
    - responds to all the elements in the question, and to any isolated factor in particular;
    - explains, analyses, debates and assesses rather than simply describes or narrates;
    - answers with clarity and fluency and in language appropriate to historical writing at this level.

    (c) **Structure – 4 marks are allocated for** the appropriateness of the organisation of the answer, according to the degree to which the response

    - establishes the context of the question and the relevant factors to be considered in the introduction
    - demonstrates a development of the issue
    - responds to the question in the form of a balanced conclusion based on the evidence and arguments deployed.

3. The following descriptions provide additional guidance on the marks awarded to essays displaying various characteristics. Many essays will exhibit some, but not all, of the features listed; others will be stronger in one area than another.

KNOWLEDGE – Up to 6 marks can be awarded
These are for substantive points and points further developed which are relevant and accurate.

STRUCTURE – Up to 4 marks can be awarded if:
The introduction clearly sets the issue in its wider context, indicates relevant factors and demonstrates a solid line of argument.
There is a coherent development directly focused on the question.
The conclusion is balanced, summarising the arguments and coming to an overall judgement directly related to the question.

ARGUMENT –   Up to 10 marks can be awarded if:
The evidence is integrated into a sustained analysis.
The argument is sustained and balanced, with some awareness of alternative interpretations and/or historical debate.

Historical Study: British History

Church, State and Feudal Society

1. The candidate assesses whether or not nobles gained all of the benefits from the feudal structure, using evidence and arguments such as:

Arguments that the nobles received all the benefits and that the peasants received none:

Nobles (and Kings)

- Nobles (and Kings) received feudal dues from their tenants. Royal lands amounted to one fifth of the cultivated land in the kingdom. Nobles and the church had most of the rest. Feudalism made monarchs much more powerful; nobles had judicial rights in their lands, and the right to call upon tenants to fight for them. Feudalism allowed the king to control the nobles, and the nobles to control their tenants.

Peasants

- The feudal term of villein or serf indicated a peasant who was not free to leave his home farm or village. They were bought and sold along with the land. They were expected to work at least three days a week in the lord's lands without recompense and hand over the best of their produce in exchange for the rent of their farmland.
- Peasants or villeins tended to work hard, mostly in the agricultural sector. All the work had to be done by hand and this resulted in long hours of backbreaking work.
- Not all peasants received the same amount of good farm land, and often it was the case that land was rotated amongst the peasants. This dissuaded them from attempts to improve the land; many did not put in the extra effort when next year their neighbour would reap the benefit.
- Accommodation was often very poor, especially for the lower strata of peasant society. Many peasants lived in poorly constructed one-bedroom dwellings, which they shared with their animals. A single hearth provided all the heat, lighting and cooking facilities.
- Firewood was at a premium; peasants were forced to pay a penny to their lord for the right to pick up fallen wood for the fires.
- Food was basic and in times of famine starvation was a real threat.

Arguments that nobles had problems as well as benefits:

- The king and tenants in chief were supposed to offer protection, justice and guidance to their tenants. For example in England it was not uncommon for local lords to pay for several feasts throughout the year.
- The feudal structure did not just offer benefits for the nobility.
- Kings and Barons relied upon the loyalty of their followers, and needed to ensure that they did not lose that loyalty.
- Nobles still had duties to perform for the king, usually military service.

Arguments that the peasants received some benefits:

- Peasants played an important part in feudal society, beyond the need for a productive class working in agriculture. It was expected that peasants would run their own day-to-day lives without the need for the feudal lord's presence. Local reeves and bailiffs, appointed by the peasants or the lord himself would act in his stead.

- Villeins had to organise themselves through the local manor court. The court dealt with sharing the land, fined those that broke the rules, and even brought murderers to trial.
- While work was hard the manor court ensured that everyone had a fair share of the good land to grow their crops. During bad times there were systems in place to share out food so that no one in the village went hungry.
- As the 12th century progressed famine became rare in England, since the manor system pulled in isolated communities and helped create new more viable villages throughout the kingdom.
- Improvements in agricultural equipment and the use of ploughs drawn by horses instead of oxen sped up the work and reduced the hours required in the field.
- Archaeological evidence points to homes occupied by small nuclear families, some with upper rooms that indicate a level of privacy previously thought impossible.
- Evidence of leisure activities included cards, chess pieces, musical instruments and even a football. Peasants were no longer bound to their lord's land as they once were.

2. The candidate assesses the extent to which the Papacy maintained its authority in Scotland and England, using evidence and arguments such as:

Evidence of the Papacy maintaining is authority

- The simple fact that it was the church that crowned the kings led to the idea that the king was dependent on God for his role, and thus subservient to the church.
- Popes could apply religious sanctions against kings, through excommunication and interdicts. This was often used to bring political pressure against an opponent, as seen during the reign of King John in England and Robert Bruce in Scotland. The threat of such political powers was one way in which the church could enforce its will during the battle between itself and the state.
- The church's importance within the feudal structure remained. Kings needed the literacy and numeracy skills of the clergy in order to help administer their realms; therefore the clergy could hold high office in government.
- The wealth of the church came mostly from large grants of land by nobles and especially kings. Thus the church became an integral part of the feudal structure, holding lands in both Scotland and England and being subject to military duties. The regular church was also politically important.
- The development of canon law, along with papal lawyers, helped to focus the arguments for papal authority. Christ was 'Lord of the World', and the pope as his vicar was the dispenser of his power. Thus he passed that power to the kings when the Church crowned them. The improving education of the population of Europe helped the church to train their priests in canon law and develop a Christendom-wide structure.

Evidence of decline of the church

The Great Schism

- Europe was divided between two popes. Within a few months of Urban VI's election the majority of cardinals declared him deposed and elected a Frenchman, Clement VII, as pope in Avignon.
- Europe became divided between the two popes; allegiance divided along political lines, and local clergy followed the lead of their kings. Scotland and England supported different popes.
- The entire affair tarnished the reputation of the Papacy. People now condemned the political manoeuvring of the cardinals and the popes. Local bishops now looked to the secular kings of their area, rather than the Papacy, for guidance.

The Avignon Captivity

- While at Avignon the Papacy appeared to be more powerful than ever, but it was also seen as the tool of the French monarchy. The growing concern of the church in worldly matters, the increased taxation and pressure on kings meant that many questioned the autocratic nature of the Papacy and the church.

The Investiture Contest

- Henry I had many disputes with Archbishop Anselm of Canterbury over the choice of different bishops in his realm. Henry II argued with Becket over the trials of criminal clerics and the proper position of the church within England.
- William the Lion had the same issue when he tried to have his candidate for Bishop of St Andrews replace the Pope's choice. King David I used the monasteries to support his leadership and bring areas of the countryside under his law.
- In practice the king's hold over the English or Scottish churches tended to remain unbroken. Even after the murder of Becket, Henry retained the right to appoint bishops. The Scottish church remained free of control from the Archbishop of York thanks to the Papal Bull of 1192.
- Kings allowed the taxation of the church by the Papacy, but in England the royal government appointed most of the collectors and they kept the majority of the proceeds.
- The effects of excommunication and interdict were blunted through overuse. The Scottish church never carried out the excommunication of Robert Bruce, and the years of interdict in England seemed to have had little obvious impact.

Other Evidence

- Long term abuses by the clergy, heavy taxation and the lavish lifestyles of the higher clergy and the papal court increasingly brought the Papacy into disrepute. Monarchs could use this to challenge the Papacy.

3. The candidate assesses how far it can be argued that David I and Henry II successfully established centralised feudal monarchies using evidence and arguments such as:

Development of the economy

- David introduced numerous monasteries, which helped to develop the wool trade, eg Melrose Abbey, and cultivate barren land.
- David granted charters to over 15 towns.
- Trade was encouraged with Germany, Scandinavia and France. David introduced the first Scottish coins to help promote trade.
- Henry II established the exchequer under Nigel of Ely to rein in sheriffs who failed to pay taxes and ensure scutage and other forms of aid and direct taxes were paid on time.

Introduction of feudal landholding

- During his time in England, David became an admirer of the feudal landholding system. He introduced a form of military feudalism into areas of Scotland, notably the southwest, Lothian and the northeast. Noble families were given grants of land. In return they offered David their support, both politically and militarily.

Development of the royal government

- David created a small but loyal group that had specific roles to aid him in the running of his household and the kingdom. Sheriffs replaced thanes in the remote areas of the kingdom. They offered direct royal contact for those away from the traditional seat of power.
- Henry ordered an investigation into his sheriffs in 1170. Many were dismissed and replaced by Henry's loyal followers.

Development of the royal military forces

- The new feudal forces brought to David by his introduction of feudalism offered a significant advantage when dealing with the Celtic Mormaers. Traditionally it was the Mormaers who controlled the summoning of the common army of Scotland. Now David had an independent force loyal to him. However, this force often did not work well with the other elements of the Scottish forces, as seen at the disastrous Battle of the Standard.
- Henry's introduction of scutage allowed him to get around the problem of 40 days' knight service. He successfully restored order in England by dismantling illegally built castles and removing barons' armies of Flemish knights.

Development of the justice system

- New Scottish barons were given the rights to hold their own courts within their fiefs. This was an obvious extension of the king's law, rather than reliance on the traditional Celtic courts led by Brechons, experts in the law. Eventually these Celtic courts died out and were replaced with sheriff courts. The gradual acceptance of the king's law led the way to the decrease of importance of the Mormaers and the acceptance of central control.
- Henry successfully reformed criminal and civil law in England, through the Assizes of Clarendon (1166) and Northampton (1176) however, his attempt to reform ecclesiastical law was less successful.

Development of the Church

- Started by David's mother Margaret, the introduction of the Roman Church at the expense of the Celtic one offered a significant boon to the development of royal authority. As the Church preached the divine grace of the king, it was hard to justify any rebellions against him.
- Henry famously ran into trouble in his attempt to establish more authority over the church in his dispute with Thomas Beckett.

The Century of Revolutions 1603 – 1702

4. The candidate evaluates the importance of religion in causing the challenge to the authority of James I in England, using evidence and arguments such as:

Religion

- James I had lifelong hatred of Puritanism.
- Puritans existed in large numbers in House of Commons and were demanding church reform.
- King feared moves towards Presbyterianism; rejected the Millenary Petition at the Hampton Court Conference of 1604, saying "no bishops, no king".
- King vowed to maintain episcopalian Church of England.
- King relaxed Recusancy Laws against Roman Catholics.
- Gunpowder Plot of 1605.
- King allowed son to marry Roman Catholic French princess and allow her to celebrate mass privately at court.

Other factors

Finance

- James I wanted to exist financially independently of Parliament.
- King manipulated statute books to re-impose anachronistic laws designed merely to raise revenue.
- Fiscal devices such as monopolies and wardships were imposed
- King alienated natural allies in House of Lords by selling honours and titles.
- Increases in customs duties led to Bates Case in 1606 which James I won, though Parliament declared duties illegal in 1610.

Politics

- Since days of Henry VIII MPs felt they could criticise Crown freely.
- James I asserted Divine Right of Kings.
- House of Commons opposed him.
- King conceded defeat in Goodwin Case.
- James I attempted to curtail Parliamentary freedom of speech by imprisoning outspoken MPs in the Tower of London when Parliament was dissolved.
- Attitude of James I unfavourable to Parliament.
- Royal favourites resented by political rivals.

Law

- James I appointed judges who would favour Crown.
- Parliament objected to abuse of power.
- King imposed martial law in towns where troops were preparing to embark on foreign campaigns.
- Parliament opposed to martial law.
- King billeted troops in homes of civilians to enforce law.

5. The candidate evaluates the extent to which religious issues brought about the English Civil War, using evidence and arguments such as:

Religious issues

- 1628 Charles I made William Laud Archbishop of Canterbury.
- Laud wanted to stamp out Puritanism and believed in authority and discipline of the Church and sacred status of clergy.
- Anyone who offended the Church was brought to trial.
- Laud's High Church policies were detested by all Puritans, including many MPs.
- Charles I authorised Laud's punishment of Puritan preachers and clamp-down on conventicles.
- Tight censorship of printed word to prevent criticism of High Church.
- 20,000 Puritans fled England to America in 10 years.
- 1637 Laud imposed Prayer Book in Scotland.
- Prayer Book fiercely opposed by members of Scottish Kirk.
- Thousands of Scots signed National Covenant pledging to defend Presbyterianism.
- Charles I lost 1st and 2nd Bishops' Wars in 1639 and 1640 in attempt to enforce Prayer Book.
- Charles I allowed Queen Henrietta Maria to celebrate Mass publicly at court with representative of Pope in attendance, which infuriated Puritans in Parliament.
- King influenced by wife who encouraged him to relax laws against Roman Catholics, Laud who encouraged him to promote High Church policies, and Thomas Wentworth whose work made king more absolute.

Other factors

Economic issues

- Charles I wanted to be financially independent, but resorted to anachronistic methods of raising revenue, such as forced loans, forest laws and distraint of knighthood.
- Methods unpopular with MPs.
- Tonnage and poundage tax allowed kings a share in profits from farm-produce.
- Parliament only voted to grant this to Charles I for 1 year, but he continued to raise it without their consent.
- King used Court of Star Chamber to impose heavy fines on those committing crimes against royal policy.
- Charles used legal loopholes to sell monopolies to companies rather than individuals.
- 1634 he re-imposed Ship Money and in 1635 extended the tax inland.
- Parliament opposed this, as there was no guarantee that it would always be used for ship-building.

- Financial crisis between 1640 and 1642, Charles I asked for Parliamentary funding for Bishops Wars, MPs took advantage, demanding abolition of prerogative courts and ship money, introduction of Triennial Act, and impeachment of Wentworth who was condemned to death.

Political issues

- Charles I believed in Divine Right, treated promises to Parliament lightly, was poor judge of character and surrounded by advisors unsuited to their positions.
- Parliament tried to introduce bills and Charles I disapproved.
- He imprisoned MPs who criticised his stance against them and some remained in prison for up to 11 years.
- House of Commons antagonised the king by impeaching serving government ministers.
- Impeachments designed to show that ministers were responsible to Parliament as well as Crown.
- When Parliament was asked to support Charles I's foreign policy it drew up Petition of Right in 1628 and forced king to sign it.
- Although it reduced King's powers, in 1629 Charles I dissolved Parliament because it criticised his levying of tonnage and poundage.
- Between 1629 and 1640 – "Eleven Years Tyranny" – Charles I ruled without Parliament.
- Threats of Scottish invasion in 1640-2 led to drastic action by Parliament in forming its own army.
- Rebellion in Ireland, hostilities broke out in Ireland as people rose up against ruthless policies imposed by Wentworth during 1630s.
- Political crisis, January 1642, Charles entered Commons to try and arrest 5 Puritan MPs, but they escaped.
- Civil War, Charles I left London for the north, joined by two-thirds of Lords and one-third of Commons, by March 1642 Parliament formed an army and king responded by raising standard at Nottingham.

Legal issues

- Charles I's use of Court of Star Chamber caused resentment in Parliament.
- MPs believed Star Chamber was being used as instrument for enforcing royal policy.
- 1637: people were outraged by sentencing of 3 men to be pilloried, have ears cropped and be imprisoned for life merely for writing Puritanical pamphlets.
- King allowed Archbishop of Canterbury to use Court of High Commission to put on trial anyone who opposed his religious policy and to persecute Puritans.
- Thomas Wentworth, Earl of Stafford, was king's chief minister from 1628
- Wentworth used Council of the North to enforce ruthless "Thorough" policies in north of England, put down rebellions and influence justice system.
- 1633, Wentworth was made Lord Deputy of Ireland.
- There he revived Ireland's fishing, farming and linen industries but this was merely to generate more money for Crown and make Irish subservient to king.

6. The candidate evaluates the importance of the actions of James II within a wide context of factors in causing the Revolution of 1688-1689, using evidence and arguments such as:

James II

- Ascended throne in 1685 upon death of older brother.
- James II, who practised Roman Catholicism, attempted to rule absolutely.
- Dismissed Parliament in 1685.
- Replaced Anglican advisors with Roman Catholic ones; placed Roman Catholics in important posts at Oxford and Cambridge Universities.

- Stationed 13,000-strong army outside London.
- Re-established Prerogative Courts in 1686.
- 1687, used Suspending Powers to suspend laws against Roman Catholics.
- Used Dispensing Powers to dismiss these laws from statute books.

Other factors

Charles II
- Charles II, who had been exiled in France during Interregnum, had accepted limitations on his power when monarchy was restored in 1660.
- Prerogative law courts were abolished, non-parliamentary taxation was prohibited, and Triennial Act remained in place.
- Loopholes, however, meant king could still make policy.
- Puritans lost power in House of Commons.
- Charles II initially did not try to abuse power.
- In turn, Parliament realised that king could not live off own finances and granted him taxation on alcohol.
- Nevertheless, towards end of reign Charles II ruled without Parliament for 4 years.
- Divine Right preached from pulpits.
- It seemed old Stuart combative approach to rule was re-asserting itself over Parliament.

Religious issues
- Issue of church governance which arose before the Civil War had not been resolved.
- Many MPs fearful of continued Stuart dominance of Anglican Church policy.
- James II promotion of Roman Catholics to key posts antagonised Presbyterians.
- Heir to the throne to be raised as a Roman Catholic.
- Divide between Episcopalians and Presbyterians in Scotland created hostility from Scottish Parliament towards monarchy.

Political issues
- Divine Right and absolutism as practised by Stuart monarchs continued to provoke resentment from MPs.
- Status of monarchy questioned by Parliament.
- Charles II's dismissal of Parliament resembled Charles I's 11-Year Tyranny.
- James II's use of Suspending and Dispensing Powers seen as an abuse by Parliament.
- Questions raised over control of the army.

The role of Parliament
- Parliament resented James II's abuses of power but took comfort from thought that he would be succeeded by Protestant daughter Mary
- However, king married again and had son, to be raised as Roman Catholic.
- June 1688, Parliament wrote to Mary, by now married to Dutch Prince William of Orange, offering Crown.
- They arrived in November with army and on Christmas Day James II fled to France after younger daughter Anne as well as leading generals declared support for Mary.
- William and Mary became joint sovereigns on February 13th 1689.

Lines of authority Crown and Parliament
- There were no clear lines of authority.
- Questions existed over who held sway in religious matters; Parliament feared a monarch could try to impose Roman Catholicism on country.
- Still possible for monarch to be financially independent of Parliament and manipulate succession in favour of Roman Catholic line.

- Both Charles II and James II had proved it was possible for monarch to rule without Parliament, influence legislative and judicial procedure, control army for own means, and assert religious and political will on Scotland and Ireland.
- Parliament saw need to agree constitutional status for monarchy.
- With no Bill of Rights, any future monarchs, including William and Mary, could preach notions of Divine Right, absolutism and passive obedience.
- Future limitations on power of monarchy would have to be written into law.
- In 1689 Parliament drew up Bill of Rights, which legalised new relationship between Crown and Parliament.
- This would ensure no future king or queen could attempt absolutism.
- Bill of Rights would be part of wider set of legal provisions for new order in country.
- Settlement established that kings and queens should depend upon Parliament for finance, succession would be determined by Parliament and not sitting monarch, judicial system would be controlled by Parliament, and no future monarch could rule without Parliament.

The Atlantic Slave Trade

7. The candidate evaluates the extent to which British military victories in the eighteenth century were the main reasons for the development of the slave trade, using evidence and arguments such as:

Military victories
- The Treaty of Utrecht, at the end of the war of the Spanish Succession gave the British the asiento or right to be the sole supplier of slaves to Spain's colonies in South America for a period of 30 years. The contract for this was given to the newly formed South Sea Company. Queen Anne was given 22.5% of the Companies Stock.
- In 1714 George I inherited her shares and purchased more. Although in 1720 massive speculation in the company's shares produced the 'South Sea Bubble' where shares crashed ruining many of the investors. Nevertheless the company survived and between 1715 and 1731 transported approximately 64,000 African slaves.
- The Seven Years War was chiefly an imperial war fought between Britain, France and Spain and many of the most important battles of the Seven Years War were fought at sea to win control of valuable overseas colonies.
- Britain emerged from the war as the leading European imperial power, having made large territorial gains in North America and the Caribbean, as well as India. Slave labour was necessary to exploit these gains.

Other factors

The labour shortage
- Huge profits made from the trade in tropical crops created a demand for labour to work on plantations in the colonies. Crops such as sugar cane required a large labour force to plant, look after, harvest and process crop in harsh conditions.
- There was a high death rate among native populations due to lack of resistance to diseases brought by Europeans and ill-treatment at the hands of colonists created labour shortage in the West Indies.

The failure of alternative sources
- Few colonists were willing to work on plantations as manual labour. There was a limit to the number of British criminals who could be sent as forced labour.
- Some Britons, particularly Scots, sold themselves as indentured servants, but numbers were limited.

The legal position

- The legal status of slaves as property was long established. It took a series of court cases from the 1770s that dealt with the rights of former slaves within the British Isles to challenge the legality of slavery and the slave trade eg Granville Sharp's resolute campaign to prove the illegality of slavery in England that culminated in Lord Mansfield's decision in the Somerset case.

Racist attitudes

- The unequal relationship that was created as a consequence of the enslavement of Africans was justified by the ideology of racism – the mistaken belief that Africans were inferior to Europeans.
- Entrenched racism among members of the merchant and landowning classes meant that enslaving African captives was accepted by colonists.
- Many Europeans claimed that African captives would suffer if slave trade was abolished eg criminals and prisoners of war would be butchered and executed at home.
- Many colonists believed that slaves were fortunate to be provided with homes, protection and employment, in the care of enlightened Europeans rather than African despots.

Religious factors

- The Church of England had links to slavery through the United Society for the Propagation of the Gospel missionary organisations which had plantations and owned slaves. The Church of England supported the laws not to educate enslaved Africans.
- Some bible passages such as the Curse of Ham from Genesis were used to justify slavery. Other bible passages such as Exodus were banned in British colonies because they could be interpreted as being anti-slavery.

Importance of slave trade to British economy

- Financial, commercial, legal and insurance institutions emerged to support the activities of the slave traders. Slave traders became bankers and many new businesses were financed by profits made from slave trading.
- View that slavery provided the capital to finance the Industrial revolution in Britain.
- Immense individual fortunes could be made: slavery ports like Bristol, Liverpool and Glasgow benefited, recent counter-view that profits were more modest [5-10%] and that slavery involved considerable risk on the part of the traders.
- Recent work calculates that as a % of national income, slavery's return was modest: considerably less than 5% of national income by the time of Industrialisation, however agrees that it was important to Britain's long-term economic development as it contributed to the commercial dynamism of Britain.

8. The candidate assesses whether the fear of resistance and revolt determined how slaves were treated, using evidence and arguments such as:

Safety and the fear of revolt

- Both on slave ships and plantations there was a constant fear of a slave revolt. On ships, security was paramount, as crews were heavily outnumbered by their cargoes. This meant that slaves were kept under decks for long periods. It also meant that they were usually shackled for the whole passage.
- As the number of revolts in slave ships grew so did the cost as larger crews were required.
- On plantations, there was fear of slave resistance, both overt and otherwise. Draconian legal codes were enacted by island assemblies (dominated by planters) covering the treatment/ punishment of runaways as well as those who resisted openly.

- Escaped ex-slaves called Maroons raided plantations, killed militia and freed slaves. Due to the inability of the planters to crush them they entered into a Treaty with them which gave them some toleration in return for leaving the slave system alone.

Other Factors

Humanitarian concerns

- Humanitarian concerns had little impact on the treatment of slaves in Africa or on the Middle Passage. Participants were not in daily close contact with slaves and did not get to know them personally.
- The West Indian plantations, on the other hand, were small communities. Where members of the owner's family were present, bonds of affection did grow between slaves and free. Where such personal ties did not exist, there was less moderation of the brutalities of slavery.

Religious concerns

- Slave traders/owners were able to point to the existence of slavery in the Bible, and use this as a justification for the institution.
- Slave traders/owners claimed that slaves were being exposed to Christianity; enslavement was therefore good for them, as it gave them a chance of eternal salvation.
- Some participants were religious and moderated their treatment of slaves accordingly.

Financial considerations

- In essence, the slave trade and the institution of slavery were commercially based. Most participants entered the trade or owned or worked the plantations as a means of income. Financial considerations were usually paramount.
- The debate over 'loose' or 'tight' pack on board slave ships had little to do with humanitarianism. In loose pack, slaves were treated better and had better conditions, but the prime motivation was to transport as many slaves as possible to the auctions in the West Indies, alive.
- To extract as much work from slaves as possible on the plantations, slaves were often beaten or worse.
- As slaves were property, bought and paid for, they were valuable. On the other hand, they were cheap enough to work, or beat, to death. This was known as 'wastage'.

Racism and prejudice

- There was ignorance of African culture and achievements. Africans were regarded by some Europeans as almost another species. This was used as an excuse for extreme brutality.

9. The candidate evaluates the extent to which hostile propaganda was the major obstacle to the abolition of the slave trade, using evidence and arguments such as:

Propaganda against abolition

- The pro slavery lobby issued pamphlets to try to counter the arguments of the abolitionists.
- Supporters of slavery and the slave trade could try to claim that the enslaved on plantations were treated at least as well as the working classes in Britain.
- Abolitionists were accused of being radicals sympathetic towards the increasingly extreme revolutionaries in France.
- To be pro-abolition was seen as being unpatriotic as a result.
- Abolition, it was argued, would lead to the loss of the West Indian colonies to France or America.

Other factors

Events in France

- War with Revolutionary France from 1793, also took peoples attention away from the abolition campaign.

- It encouraged the belief among many MPs that the abolitionist cause was associated with revolutionary ideas eg Clarkson openly supported the French Revolution; radicals used the same tactics as abolitionists to win public support – associations, petitions, cheap publications, public lectures, public meetings, pressure on Parliament; some abolitionists were linked to radicals and therefore they had to be resisted because of fear that events in France might be repeated in Britain.
- In 1794, the radical (Jacobin) national Convention voted to end slavery in the French Colonies.
- British government became suspicious of radicals as represented by mass petitions.

Slave rebellion in Saint-Domingue
- Abolition was associated with this symbol of brutal violence and in turn led to an exaggerated, general fear of slave revolts. Toussaint I'Ouverture was denounced. This was linked to fears of Jacobinism.
- Slave violence played into the hands of the slave lobby, confirming their warnings of anarchy.
- Britain suffered humiliation when it attempted to take the rebel French Colony and was beaten by disease and the ex-slave army.

Attitude of successive British Governments
- These were influenced by powerful vested interests such as MPs and merchants from London, Liverpool and Bristol; abolitionists found it easier to win support from general public, most of whom could not vote, than persuade MPs to vote for abolition.
- Belief of slave owners and their supporters that millions of pounds worth of property would be threatened by the abolition of the slave trade.
- The slave trade was necessary to provide essential labour on the plantations; there was fear that abolition would ruin the colonies.

The importance of the slave trade to the British economy
- The trade generated finance; West Indian colonies were an important source of valuable exports to European neighbours; taxes would have to be raised to compensate for the loss of trade and revenue; abolition would help foreign rivals such as France as other nations would fill the gap left by Britain.
- British cotton mills relied on cheap, slave-produced cotton.
- British consumers benefited from cheap, slave-produced sugar.
- Ports like Liverpool, Bristol and Glasgow also benefited; names like Kingston Bridge and Jamaica Street show the importance of the trade in Glasgow.

Fears over national security
- Abolition could destroy an important source of experienced seamen it was argued thus there was a possibility that Britain would lose its advantage over its maritime rivals. On the other hand, the Triangular Trade was arguably a graveyard for British seamen.

Britain 1851 – 1951

10. The candidate evaluates the importance of the role of pressure groups in Britain becoming more democratic between 1851 and 1928 using evidence and arguments such as:

Role of Pressure Groups
- Impact of campaigns by Reform League and Reform Union in 1866-67 – large demonstrations.
- Dangers of withholding the franchise from working classes – alarm at Hyde Park riots of July 1866. Less evidence of popular pressure in 1884 Reform Act.

- Impact of campaigns by women's movements up to 1914 – role of NUWSS and WSPU in persuading people and keeping the issue in the news headlines, be it through outrages, or sympathy for their plight.

Other factors

Social and economic change
- The industrial revolution changed where people lived, how they worked, and how they felt about their position in society.
- Middle classes – wealth creators – argued they should have more of a say in running the country.
- Development of basic education and cheap popular newspapers raised working class political awareness.
- Spread of railways helped create national political identity. People were more aware of issues.
- Less fear of revolutionary "mob" – the skilled working class was more educated and respectable, as is shown in support for North in American Civil War by elements of artisan class; an argument for extending the vote in 1867.
- The skilled working class was vital to the economic success of Britain.
- Increasing urbanisation led to pressure for redistribution of parliamentary seats – 1867, 1885, 1918.
- Impact of the Great War on the key issue of votes for women; realisation of the economic role of women in wartime was a factor in passing the 1918 Act – fears of a revival of militant women's campaign.

Changing political attitudes
- Political reform was no longer seen as a threat of struggles for liberty in Europe and USA. Britain was usually supportive of this and therefore it was difficult to argue against democratic progress at home.
- American Civil War – influence of Lincoln's Gettysburg Address.
- Role of leaders like Gladstone of the Liberal Party in passing reforms, esp.1880-85 government.
- Development of political beliefs that argued for intervention such as Socialism: Labour argued for universal suffrage.
- Women accepted into local government and school board elections.
- Role of World War One in speeding up processes that were already occurring. Example of Asquith's change of opinion towards women and the vote.

Political advantage
- Politicians often believed they could gain political advantages from passing reforms eg the 1867 Reform Act was passed by the Conservatives after being in opposition for many years – arguably trying to win votes: 'dish the Whigs'.
- Liberal party also tried to gain political advantage. John Bright argued for secret ballot, to free working class electorate from fear of retaliation by bosses and landlords.
- Corrupt and Illegal Practices Act – it is possible to argue that it was a pragmatic move by the Liberals. By limiting amount spent on elections, they might reduce advantages held by the wealthier Conservatives.
- Reforms of 1880s – it could be argued that they served as a distraction from foreign policy problems facing the Liberal government; Redistribution of Seats Act – Liberals hoped for political advantage from urban voters now being more fairly represented.
- In contrast the opportunity of coalition government during World War One may be considered in light of the fact that no one political party was behind the reform and, theoretically, all could benefit from the extension of the franchise to men and women.

Example of other countries
- Britain considered herself to be the cradle of modern democracy. Other nations had extended the franchise and Britain could not be seen to be falling behind.
- Influence of the United States of America spreading Liberal ideas: anti-slavery sympathy in Britain where Radicals supported the North.

11. The candidate evaluates the statement that changing attitudes in British society towards women was a major reason why women received the vote in 1918, using evidence and arguments such as:

Changing attitudes towards women
- The campaigns for women's suffrage can be seen within the context of changing attitudes within society towards women in the late 19th and early 20th centuries. The historian Martin Pugh stated that 'their participation in local government made women's exclusion from national elections increasingly untenable'. Millicent Fawcett argued that wider social changes were vital factors in the winning of the franchise.
- Women became increasingly active in public affairs – town councils, Boards of Guardians, members of political organisations.
- Educational opportunities slowly opened up to women: University, medical school, etc.
- Professions opened up to women: Law, Medical profession.
- Legal developments giving women rights over property: 1882 Married Women's Property Act, etc.

Other factors

The importance of the Great War
- Britain declared war on Germany on 4 August 1914 and two days later the NUWSS suspended its political campaigning for the vote. Undoubtedly the sight of women 'doing their bit' for the war effort gained respect and balanced the negative publicity of the earlier Suffragette campaign. A WSPU pro-war propaganda campaign encouraged men to join the armed forces and women to demand 'the right to serve'.
- Women's war work was important to Britain's eventual victory. Over 700,000 women were employed making munitions.
- The creation of a wartime coalition also opened the door to change.
- The traditional explanation for the granting of the vote to some women in 1918 has been that women's valuable work for the war effort radically changed male ideas about their role in society and that the vote in 1918 was almost a 'thank you' for their efforts. But the women who were given the vote were 'respectable' ladies, 30 or over, not the younger women who worked long hours and risked their lives in munitions factories.
- Another argument about the 1918 act is that it only happened because politicians grew anxious to enfranchise more men who had fought in the war but lost their residency qualification to vote and women could be 'added on' to legislation that was happening anyway.
- The war acted more as a catalyst, but the tide was flowing towards female suffrage before it started.

The NUWSS
- The NUWSS believed in moderate, 'peaceful' tactics to win the vote such as meetings, pamphlets, petitions and parliamentary bills. Membership remained relatively low at about 6,000 until around 1909 but grew to 53,000 by 1914 as women angered by the Suffragettes' campaign found a new home.

The WSPU – the Suffragettes
- Emmeline Pankhurst formed the Women's Social and Political Union (WSPU) in 1903. WSPU adopted the motto 'Deeds Not Words'. The new strategy gained publicity with noisy heckling of politicians. Newspapers immediately took notice. The Suffragettes had achieved their first objective – publicity. Violent protest followed eg window smashing campaign and arson attacks aimed to provoke insurance company pressure on the Government. The prisons filled with Suffragettes.
- Women used starvation as a political weapon to embarrass the government. In response the government introduced the Prisoner's Temporary Discharge for Ill Health Act – the Cat and Mouse Act.
- The actions of the Suffragettes mobilised opinion for and against. It can be argued that were it not for the Suffragette campaign, the Liberal Government would not even have discussed women's suffrage before World War One. But for opponents the militant campaign provided an excellent example of why women could not be trusted with the vote.

Example of other countries
- By 1913 many states in the USA, in Scandinavia, Finland [1906] and countries in the British Empire, such as New Zealand [1893] had given the vote to women. This had not caused the disasters that had been predicted. In fact, most countries believed giving women the vote had helped them.

12. The candidate assesses the statement that the Liberals failed to deal with the real problems facing the British people using evidence and arguments such as:

Social problems
- The problems could be summarised as poverty, especially among the 'deserving poor' of the old, the young, the sick and the unemployed.

The young
- The Provision of School Meals Act allowed local authorities to raise money to pay for school meals but the law did not force local authorities to provide school meals.
- Medical inspections (1907) for children were made compulsory but no treatment of illnesses or infections found was provided until 1911.
- The Children's Charter (1908) Act banned children under 16 from smoking, drinking alcohol, or begging. New juvenile courts were set up for children accused of committing crimes. Remand homes were opened for children awaiting trial and borstals for children convicted of breaking the law. Probation officers were employed to help former offenders in an attempt to avoid re-offending. The time taken to enforce all legislation meant the Children's Charter only helped improve conditions for some children.

The old
- Pensions Act 1908: people over 70 were given between 1 shilling and 5 shillings a week depending on any income they might have. Once a person over 70 had an income above 12 shillings a week, their entitlement to a pension stopped. Married couples were given 7/6d.
- Levels of benefits were low. Few of the elderly poor lived till their 70th birthday. Many of the old were excluded from claiming pensions because they failed to meet qualification rules. Nevertheless there was a high uptake and many people were grateful for their pension – 'Thank God for that Lloyd George'.

The sick
- The National Insurance Scheme of 1911 applied to workers earning less than £160 a year. Each insured worker got 9 pence in benefits from an outlay of 4 pence – 'ninepence for

fourpence'. Only the insured worker got free medical treatment from a doctor. Other family members did not benefit from the scheme. The weekly contribution was in effect a wage cut which might simply have made poverty worse in many families. It helped some who had previously got no help.

The unemployed
• The National Insurance Act (part 2) only covered unemployment for some workers in some industries and like part 1 of the Act, required contributions from workers, employers and the government. For most workers, no unemployment insurance scheme existed.

Other reforms which could be argued helped meet 'problems' eg working conditions
• In 1906 the Workman's Compensation Act covered a further six million workers who could now claim compensation for injuries and diseases which were the result of working conditions.
• In 1908, miners secured an eight hour working day.
• In 1909, the Trade Boards Act tried to protect workers in the sweated trades like tailoring and lace making by setting up trade boards to fix minimum wages.
• In 1911, a Shops Act limited working hours and guaranteed a weekly half-day holiday.

Limitations
• Aspects of poverty such as housing were not dealt with, posing the argument that Liberal reforms were not entirely successful in dealing with poverty and need.

Britain and Ireland 1900 – 1985

13. The candidate evaluates whether the response of Unionists to the Home Rule Bill was the main reason for the growth of tension in Ireland up to 1914 using evidence and arguments such as:

Unionist responses to the Home Rule Bill
• Setting up of the UVF was example of the willingness to use violence to further the cause of those opposed to Home Rule and an indication of the extent in the breakdown in peace in Ireland.
• Signing of the Solemn League and Covenant in Belfast at Town Hall, to the world's press, 250 000 Ulstermen pledged themselves to use "all means necessary" to defeat Home Rule.
• The role of Carson and Craig. Sir Edward Carson's theatrical political performances caught the public imagination and brought the case of the Unionists to the nation.
• Orange and Ulster Unionist groups were revived.
• Curragh Mutiny.

Other Factors

Nationalist responses to the Home Rule Bill
• The Irish Volunteer Force (IVF) was set up. Members from the Gaelic League, the Gaelic Athletic Association, Sinn Fein and the IRB all joined hoping to use the IVF for their own purposes. By May 1914 it had 80 000 members, which also shows the extent in the breakdown in the willingness for peace in Ireland as a result of the Home Rule Bill.
• In 1913, a third private army was set up called Irish Citizen Army, under the leadership of James Connolly, a socialist. It had two clear aims. To gain independence for Ireland and set up a socialist republic, for working class of all religions to join up with to improve their lives.

• Minority opinions take different view: support for Irish Republic from groups like the Irish Republican Brotherhood – Connolly's views; supporters of a workers republic: Griffith; or Sinn Fein; Pearse and his supporters. Very much minority views at this time.

The British Position in Ireland
• In 1865 Gladstone wanted Home Rule and when the Liberals were re-elected in 1892 and Gladstone introduced the Second Home Rule Bill but the House of Lords, dominated by Conservatives were opposed to Home Rule and wanted to maintain the Union. Bill rejected.
• Support for the Unionists from British politicians like Bonar Law and the Conservative Party.
• In 1908 Bannerman was replaced as Prime Minister by Asquith, who by the end of 1909, declared that he was a supporter of Home Rule.
• After 1910 the Liberals needed the help of the Irish Nationalists to run the country as they would not have a majority otherwise so passed the third reform bill.
• With the support of John Redmond, the leader of the Nationalists, a Bill was passed to reduce the power of the House of Lords, which was dominated by Conservatives, from being able to block a Bill to only being able to hold up the passing of a Bill for two years. As a result the Home Rule Bill for Ireland, which was previously blocked by the House of Lords, could now be passed.

The Irish Cultural Revival and Re-emergence of Irish Republicanism
• In 1884 the Gaelic Athletic Association was set up "for the preservation and cultivation of our national pastimes." And games like Gaelic football and hurling became very popular.
• In 1883 the Gaelic League was also set up whose aim it was to revive, and preserve the Irish language and Gaelic literature.
• Setting up of Sinn Fein (Ourselves) by Arthur Griffith in 1904 to boycott all things British and for the Irish to set up their own parliament in Ireland, which Griffith thought would force the British Government to collapse.
• IRB was revived with Thomas Clarke recruiting young men in Dublin for the movement. These two groups both wanted an Ireland separate from Britain and both willing to use force.

Redmond and Home Rule
• Redmond believed that Home Rule Bill would lead to greater unity and strength in the Empire, which was supported by the majority in the south but vehemently opposed by those in Ulster.
• He also believed it would end ill-will, suspicion and disaffection in Ireland, and between Britain and Ireland.
• He believed Ireland would be happy, prosperous, united and loyal.
• Ireland would be peaceful at this time and could give up hostility towards Britain.
• Britain would be willing to treat Ireland equally, as part of the empire.
• Redmond's Party consistently strong throughout Southern Ireland, where there was strong support for Home Rule.

Distinctive economic and religious features of the Northern Counties
• Ulster was mainly Protestant and feared that a government lead by Dublin would see the imposition of laws on Northern Ireland based on Catholic faith, which they were opposed to.
• Ulster was worried they would lose the benefits they enjoyed economically from being part of the British Empire, such as the linen industry and the shipbuilding industry.

14. The candidate evaluates the importance of British conduct during the Anglo-Irish War in preventing a peace settlement in Ireland up to the Anglo Irish Treaty using evidence and arguments such as:

British conduct during the Anglo-Irish War
- Formation of the Black and Tans composed largely of World War I veterans, employed as auxiliaries by the Royal Irish Constabulary from 1920 to 1921 to suppress revolution in Ireland. Although it was established to target the Irish Republican Army, it became notorious for its numerous attacks on the Irish civilian population.
- Black and Tans used wholesale violence, theft, drunken rampages, attacks on villages such as the burning of Balbriggan, village creameries were burnt down and houses were destroyed.
- In March 1920 the Lord Mayor of Cork was shot dead by RIC men as well as murdering suspects, or "Shinners" as they were known, often on the merest of evidence, for being in the wrong place at the wrong time.
- Black and Tans fired in to the crowd killing 12 people and injuring 60 at Croke Park where there was a Gaelic football match taking place.
- The sacking of Cork City by the Black and Tans.
- RIC members were instructed to challenge Irish civilians from ambush and shoot them if they did not obey the RIC officers.
- RIC officers were encouraged to shoot suspicious looking people.
- If innocent people were killed then this could not be helped.
- No RIC officers were to get in to trouble for shooting people.
- Regular British Army also committed atrocities such as burning the towns of Mallow and Fermoy, but the Irish did not distinguish between them and the Black and Tans.
- The best houses in local areas to be taken and used, with the occupants evicted, if the local police station had been burned or destroyed, turning the Irish people against the British and increasing tension.

Other factors

Role of IRA
- IRA campaign also prevented peace in Ireland as their attacks on British troops and men working for Britain escalated the violence.
- Guerrilla tactics.
- Attacks on agencies of law and order: RIC, magistrates and police barracks.
- Ambush, assassination, the disappearance of opponents, the sabotage of enemy communications and the intimidation of local communities to not support the British forces.
- Attacks on British troops.
- Attacks on G-men (detectives concentrating on IRA atrocities).
- Attempted assassination of Lord French (Viceroy).
- Flying Columns: mobile IRA squads used in ambushes of RIC and army.
- Role of IRA leaders, particularly Michael Collins.

The General Election of 1918
- The success of Sinn Fein in this election, who opposed British rule, meant that Ireland would only want peace if Ireland gained independence from Britain.
- Sinn Fein won 73 seats, compared to winning none in 1910, showing increased resentment of British Rule.
- Sinn Fein membership had now reached 112 000.
- 34 were in prison, one had been deported, two were ill and 7 were absent on Sinn Fein business, so there was only 25 present when they held their first public meeting in January 1919. This meant control of the movement largely moved to the IRB and the IVF.

- Ballot boxes being stuffed and the "dead" voting. There were some complaints by soldiers that they did not get voting papers and these men were more likely to vote Nationalist rather than Sinn Fein. Moreover there were no Nationalist candidates in 26 of the constituencies, which helped the Sinn Fein party.
- Ulster Unionists won extra 10 seats and now had 26 seats in Westminster, making partition increasingly likely.

The Declaration of Independence and the Dail
- Republicans lead by Sinn Fein, did not attend Westminster, met at the Mansion House in Dublin and declared themselves "Dail Eireann" thus increasing division between Ireland and Britain.
- De Valera was made the President of Ireland, Arthur Griffith Vice President, Michael Collins was made the Minister of Finance which again caused division as these men were vehemently opposed to British Rule in Ireland.
- Most local councils in Ireland, except for those in Ulster, recognised the rule of this new assembly, as opposed to British Rule.
- By 1921 1000 Sinn Fein law courts had been set up and Collins raised £350,000 and many people paid their taxes to the Minister of Finance, Collins rather than the British Government.
- Dail failed to meet very regularly as many of its members were unable to meet but worked as couriers - carried communication between the different people in hiding but Irish were willing to even obey this rather than have British rule.
- Law and order maintained though as Dail relied on "alternative" courts, presided over by a priest or lawyer and backed up by the IRA. This system won the support of the Irish communities as well as the established Irish legal system but contravened British rule.
- Dail had won the support of masses, the Catholic Church and professional classes in Ireland thus increasing division between Ireland and GB as even the influential people of Ireland were moving away from British rule.
- Dail wrested power away from Britain to a reasonable extent due to military wing of the Dail.

15. The candidate evaluates the importance of political differences between the Protestant and Catholic communities in contributing to the developing crisis in Northern Ireland up to 1968 using evidence and arguments such as:

Political Differences
- Parliament in Northern Ireland opened June 1921, limited control and could be overruled by Westminster. James Craig the first Prime Minister refused to speak to Boundary Commission.
- Third of Ulster was Catholic and wanted unification the Protestant two thirds did not want it.
- Only on average 10 or 12 Nationalists in parliament whereas average 40 Unionists so Nationalists views were rarely listened to. In Westminster 10 or 12 Unionists to 2 Nationalists.
- Unionists support increased after De Valera in 1932 called for a Republic "in fact" and banned Governor General, right to appeal to Privy Council External Relations Act passed.
- 1959 Eire became a Republic, which heightened Unionist fears about pressure to end partition.
- In April 1951 Eire leader Browne forced to resign after party leaders insisted he respect the Catholic Church's stance on matters, Unionists worried about Catholic rule if Ireland unified.
- Unionists fears about giving Catholics fairer treatment so Orange Order and UVF revived.

Other Factors

Economic Issues

- De Valera's economic war with GB worried Unionists that GB might abandon them.
- Depression in 30's saw unemployment of over 25% for Catholics, but Protestants were mainly employed.
- South was poor, so North financially better off as part of the United Kingdom.
- North benefited greatly economically from helping GB during WWII eg factories, farms.
- Unemployment fell to 5% even some from the south employed, eg aircraft and ship building.
- Ulster shared mainland British suffering during war eg rationing.
- WWII underlined the economic and strategic importance of Ulster to Britain.
- Ulster benefited greatly from being part of British Welfare state, payments 50% – 67% higher than those in south for Unemployment benefit.
- GB gave extra money to Ulster to set up Welfare state 1961-63 £60m average, £160m by 1972.
- 1950's Eire had one of the poorest standards of living in Western Europe.

Cultural Differences

- 1923 Education Act amended, but Catholic Church retained control over Catholic schools.
- Protestants refused to acknowledge cultural identity of Catholics.
- In Eire, Irish language to be used in government and taught in schools.
- Gaelic League and other language groups sprung up. Irish music and dance thrived.
- Gaelic football, hurling, were more popular than soccer, rugby and cricket in Eire.

The Unionist Ascendancy in Northern Ireland

- Ulster was not willing to sever links with Britain, but ensure Unionist control.
- B Specials set up and RUC; both were issued with guns.
- Special Powers introduced – internment, prohibit meetings, special courts, death penalty.
- Votes in local Councils restricted to Householders and property owners so Catholics ruled out.
- Boundaries redrawn to secure Unionists councillors (gerrymandering).
- Proportional Representation abolished to reduce Catholic influence in politics.
- Unionist Councillors favoured Protestants for housing and job vacancies.
- Revival of Orange Orders in 60's, Protestants favoured in 70's.
- Role of Brookeborough: Ulster Unionist leader and Prime Minister of Northern Ireland, 1943-1963: kept Unionists largely unified.

Continuing Threat of IRA

- Catholics in North turned to IRA to defend them from Orange rioters.
- IRA shootings, Kevin Higgins assassinated, attacked Garda barracks led to Public Safety Act.
- During war attacked mainland Britain eg Coventry.
- Upsurge in violence in 50's but came to nothing and ended by 1962, a failure after which they were divided.

Issues of Civil Rights

- Catholics set up NICRA for equal rights, as young Catholics benefited from better education.
- Campaign for Social Justice set up, 1966 nationalists commemorate Easter Rising in Belfast.
- June 1966 Ian Paisley starts riot taking his supporters in to a Catholic area.
- Coalisland to Dungannon march, Peaceful Civil Rights march charged by police in 1968.
- October 1968 police in Londonderry attack NICRA march with violence, captured by media.
- Homeless Citizens League, Derry Citizens Action Committee (John Hume) set up.
- Devlin's People's Democracy Belfast – Londonderry march attacked by RUC and B Specials.
- Well known Nationalists and IRA members seen in Civil Rights marches.

HISTORICAL STUDY: EUROPEAN AND WORLD HISTORY

The Crusades, 1071 – 1204

16. The candidate evaluates the Pope's desire to channel the military power of the knightly class as the main reason for calling the First Crusade, using evidence and arguments such as:

Arguments for the importance of the Pope's desire to channel the military power of the knightly class:

- The introduction of Norman feudalism across Western Europe had created the knightly class. Their dedication to learning the arts of war had created a culture based around the skills of fighting. Even tournaments had come to be seen as integral part of the culture and as entertainment.
- However, for knights to use their skills in anger was a sin.
- Pope Urban had long considered how he could turn the nature of Western knighthood to a less aggressive, less damaging activity.
- Urban saw the Crusade as a way to channel this aggression in a way that would be of benefit to Christianity.
- Urban was well aware of the growing political instability of Italy. Northern Italy with its growing urban centres and rich Lombard provinces was a tempting target for both the Norman knights and the German Emperors. By calling a Crusade the Pope could channel this aggression away from Italy and the Church while at the same time exerting a moral control over the armed knights. This was a simple step from the already successful "Peace of God" and "Truce of God" attempts by the church in the 1020s.

Other factors

Papal authority and the Investiture Contest

- By 1075 the relationship between the Church and the Holy Roman Emperor, the church's supposed protector, had deteriorated badly. Pope Gregory VII had excommunicated Henry IV and Henry invaded Rome.
- Henry IV, the Holy Roman Emperor, had been locked in a power struggle with Urban over the Investiture contest, which had led to popes, including Urban, fleeing Rome. This was part of an ongoing struggle between the Church and State over the appointment of Bishops. The desire of the reforming popes (trained at Cluny) was to firmly establish the dominance of the papacy in this area.
- The papacy was anxious to re-join the two halves of the Christian church. Since the Great Schism of 1054, where the Pope of Rome and Patriarch of Constantinople excommunicated each other, it had been the goal of every pope to become head of the Greek Orthodox Church. The Crusade seemed to offer Pope Urban the opportunity to achieve this. A papacy that was able to accomplish this would be less vulnerable to the problems that had plagued the Papacy in the previous decades.

Fear over the expansion of Islam

- Pope Urban used the fear of Islamic expansion in his famous speech at Clermont in 1095. He pointed to the successful Reconquista in Spain. El Cid had captured Valencia in 1094 from the Moors.
- The Holy Lands had been annexed by the expanding Turks.
- There was a potential threat to the important pilgrimage routes; it was this threat that inspired the People's Crusade.
- However, Alexius was seen as a bulwark against this eventuality and his letter asking for help was taken very seriously.

Threat to Byzantium

- Urban pointed to the threat of the Turks to Byzantium, a topic that was already talked about across Europe. He claimed that the loss of Anatolia had 'devastated the Kingdom of God.' What Urban was referring to was the Disaster at Manzikert, where Emperor Romanus IV had been defeated by the Seljuk Turks. However, this battle happened in 1071, and had led to the Turkish conquest of Anatolia (modern Turkey). For centuries Byzantium had been the bulwark against the expansion of Islam, and in little over two decades half the empire had been swallowed up by the Turks. However, what Urban failed to mention is that the Empire was also under threat of attacks from Normans from Sicily.
- Urban used the fear of the fall of Byzantium as propaganda; he included details of Turkish actions such as torture, human sacrifice and desecration.
- The Seljuk Turks had been threatening the Empire for decades. There was fear in Europe that if it was allowed to fall then the expansion of this new aggressive Islamic group into central Europe would be hard to resist.
- The city of Constantinople was the largest Christian city in the world. Its fall to the forces of Islam would be highly damaging to the papacy and the Christian world.
- Byzantium was home to the Orthodox church, saving it would help reestablish cordial relations with the eastern Christians.

17. The candidate evaluates the success of the Crusaders with regard to the divisions amongst the Muslim states, using evidence and arguments such as:

Arguments for the importance of the division amongst Muslim states

- The Islamic response to the First Crusade was slow in getting under way. During the crusade Muslim leaders were more willing to fight among themselves than join forces against the common enemy. In fact many did not even realise that this was a common enemy. Kilij Arslan, for example, expected the 'Princes Crusade' to be no more of a concern than Peter the Hermit's followers. Thus he was off raiding his Muslim neighbours when Nicaea came under attack.
- Kerbogha's army abandoned him at the battle of Antioch in 1098. Many had feared that his victory would allow him to gain a semblance of authority over the other Seljuk Turkish leaders. There was tension in his army as the Turks mistrusted the Arab speaking Muslims and the different tribes of nomads. The lack of unity was clear among the divisions of Ridwan of Aleppo and Duquaq of Damascus.
- The fundamental division of Muslim between the Fatimids and the Seljuks is illustrated in the Egyptians seizure of Jerusalem. The Egyptian army used siege engines to reduce the walls of Jerusalem in a siege that lasted 6 weeks. This not only damaged the defences of the city but reduced the number of defenders available. The Fatimids even sent embassies to the crusaders offering them Jerusalem in exchange for an alliance against the Seljuks.
- For the Muslims this was not seen as a holy war, at least at the outset. To them, unifying to face the Christians was a more dangerous idea than the crusaders themselves.
- Religious divisions between Sunni and Shiite Islam.

Other factors

Military importance of the knight

- The First Crusade had been unexpected by local Muslim leaders. Those that had witnessed the ineptitude of the People's Crusade expected Christian knights to be as inept in combat. However Christian knights were often ferocious fighters, used to long campaigns in Europe, whereas the knights of the East were seen as gentlemen of culture and education.
- The mounted tactics of the knights were relatively unknown in the east and the sight of the largest concentration of knights in history assembled on the field was a truly awesome sight. This full frontal charge of the knights was in contrast to the tactics deployed by the Islamic forces. Their hit and run horse archers were not prepared for this aggressive style.
- Crusading knights used aggressive combat tactics, and utilised heavier armour and barding for their horses. The constant fighting of the 12th century had well prepared the organised and disciplined knightly classes for warfare. Many, such as Raymond of Toulouse, had combat experience against the Moors in Spain.

Misunderstanding of the Crusaders' intent

- Muslims misunderstood the threat of the Western knights. Many saw this as another expedition from Byzantium and thought them soldiers of Alexius. Such raids had occurred before; however this was different. Here the Christians had an ideological motivation not yet encountered by the Islamic leaders.

Help from Byzantium

- The First Crusade was the only Crusade to have significant support from Constantinople. Even though Alexius's army did not participate in the Crusade itself, they did cause problems, diverting a lot of Muslim resources.
- Alexius also provided much needed supplies at the sieges of Antioch and Jerusalem.

Religious Fervour

- The sheer determination of the Crusaders helped them through incredible hardships during their passage through the Taurus Mountains and at the sieges of Antioch and Jerusalem. Because they believed God would help them, they attempted the impossible, where most armies would have surrendered eg Battle of Antioch and the belief in the Holy Lance.
- The Muslims did not really understand this idea of a 'Holy War'; they assumed the crusaders were after land and territory and therefore they tended to underestimate what the crusaders could achieve.

18. The candidate assesses the extent to which it can be argued that Richard I was a greater military leader than Saladin, using evidence and arguments such as:

Arguments to suggest that Richard was a greater military leader than Saladin

Leadership

- Richard had established himself as an able leader prior to the Crusade.
- Richard was good at motivating troops, and his arrival at the siege of Acre galvanised the troops in a way that Philip had been unable to do. Even when confined to his bed due to illness he was still able to direct the operations.

Victories

- While journeying to the Holy Lands Richard captured Cyprus.

- Richard, despite being lured into a trap, won the Battle of Arsuf with an impressive charge of knights that routed Saladin's men. Saladin was defeated in battle and it helped raise morale; the great defeat of Hattin had been erased from the minds of the crusaders.
- Richard won the Battle of Jaffa against overwhelming odds. Saladin had failed to defeat Richard in battle, and he lost control of his men at Jaffa; they refused to obey his orders.

Use of Tactics

- Richard took his time to march to Jerusalem. He organised his men into well defended columns marching down the coastal route using his fleet to carry plenty of supplies.
- This way he was able to protect his vulnerable supply line from Turkish raids.
- Richard was enough of a military tactician to realise that he did not have the men to capture Jerusalem.
- Richard always lined up with the Templars in battle which was seen as the fiercest part of the fighting.

Arguments to suggest Richard was able to exploit Saladin's mistakes

- Saladin's decision to spare the crusaders at Tyre, in order to allow them a safe haven to board ships for the west was a grave military error. Conrad was able to successfully take over the defence of the city and use it as a base for the third crusade.
- Saladin was unable to keep his large army in the field for the whole year round. Many men were needed back on the farms, or were only expected to provide a certain numbers of days service.
- The fall of Acre to Richard's forces.
- The Battle of Arsuf, where Richard was outnumbered 3 – 1, and his men had fallen into Saladin's ambush. Richard held his men together and his all out cavalry charge smashed the Muslim forces.
- Saladin should have been able to capture or kill Richard at Jaffa; however, he failed to keep control of his men, whom were reluctant to fight Richard due to his growing reputation as an unbeatable opponent.

Arguments to suggest that Saladin was a greater military leader than Richard

Leadership

- Saladin brought effective military leadership and central authority to Egypt and Syria for the first time.

Victories

- In 1168 while Caliph of Egypt he destroyed the combined crusader/Byzantium invasion fleet/army at the port city of Damietta.
- In 1170 he followed this up with an attack on Gaza, massacring the Christian inhabitants of the city.
- Saladin's victory at the Battle of Hattin (1187) was all consuming. The military orders were devastated, King Guy had been captured, many of the nobles executed or taken into slavery. One by one the great forts and cities fell to Saladin's army.
- The capture of Jerusalem in 1187 made Saladin the hero of Islam. The eventual negotiated surrender saved much bloodshed.

Use of Tactics

- 1180 Saladin had successfully limited the attacks from Outremer by negotiating a peace treaty with Baldwin IV.
- Saladin's tactics leading up to Hattin were masterly. He provoked Guy of Lusignan into an unnecessary sally to aid a castle that was not seriously threatened. He avoided a pitched battle till the Crusaders were debilitated by heat and thirst, then further disabled them by lighting fires.

The American Revolution 1763 – 1787

19. The candidate evaluates the extent to which disagreement over the frontier was the key issue between Britain and the colonies by 1763, within a wide context of factors, using evidence and arguments such as:

Land claims/The Proclamation of 1763

- Quarrels arose after individual colonists and land companies unwittingly violated treaties agreed between Britain and Indian tribes.
- The Royal Proclamation of 1763 was issued October 7, 1763, by King George III following Great Britain's acquisition of French territory in North America after the end of the French and Indian War/Seven Years' War. The purpose of the proclamation was to organize Great Britain's new North American empire and to stabilise relations with Native North Americans through regulation of trade, settlement, and land purchases on the western frontier.
- The proclamation created a boundary line (often called the proclamation line) between the British colonies on the Atlantic coast and American Indian lands (called the Indian Reserve) west of the Appalachian Mountains. The proclamation line was not intended to be a permanent boundary between white and American Indian lands, but rather a temporary boundary which could be extended further west in an orderly, lawful manner. The proclamation outlawed private purchase of Native American land, which had often created problems in the past; instead, all future land purchases were to be made by Crown officials "at some public Meeting or Assembly of the said Indians". Furthermore, British colonists were forbidden to move beyond the line and settle on native lands, and colonial officials were forbidden to grant lands without royal approval. The proclamation gave the Crown a monopoly on all future land purchases from American Indians.
- Almost immediately, many British colonists and land speculators objected to the proclamation boundary, since there were already many settlements beyond the line (some of which had been temporarily evacuated during Pontiac's War), as well as many existing land claims yet to be settled. Indeed, the proclamation itself called for lands to be granted to British soldiers who had served in the Seven Years' War. Prominent American colonists joined with land speculators in Britain to lobby the government to move the line further west.

Other factors

The Seven Years War

- The war highlighted the status of the colonies as territories to be fought over by imperial powers. Britain, France and Spain all viewed America as a potential possession. The British fought the Seven Years War which prevented the colonies being ruled by France. Victory in 1763, and the acquisition of Canada, should have made British rule more secure, but the removal of the French threat meant that many colonists saw less need for British protection.

Old colonial system

- Britain treated colonies merely as a source of revenue, and plundered valuables from America. Those in New England and the Middle Colonies objected to being used as a dumping ground for British goods. Wealthy Southern plantation owners objected to members of the British government attempting to control them. Frontiersmen were frustrated at British attempts to prevent them from going beyond the Frontier. However, being part of the Empire meant protection from the British Army against the French and Indians.

Navigation Acts

- Passed in 1650s, these stated that colonists could only sell their goods to the British, could only buy goods from the British, and could only use British shipping. Royal Navy enforced the Acts by patrolling east coast of colonies for rogue Dutch, French or Spanish ships. However, the acts gave colonists a guaranteed market. During the Whig Ascendancy in mid-1700s many colonists were able to ignore the Acts as Royal Navy was unable to enforce them as strictly.

Political differences

- The colonies were more advanced politically than Britain, each having its own elected Assembly which passed local laws and raised local taxes, and so they resented the lack of representation in the British Parliament which sought to control their lives. However, the British Empire provided an order to the existence of the colonies. Britain acted out the role of Mother Country. Britain appointed a governor for each colony, whose payment by the colony ensured an element of control for the colonists over the governor.

George III

- When George III ascended the throne in 1760 he oversaw a re-imposition of British rule over the colonies. This was seen as tantamount to foreign invasion by many colonists who had acted in an independent spirit during the Whig Ascendancy. Colonies had their own militia and did not feel British Army was required in America. However, George III aimed to ensure the security of the colonies by maintaining a British military presence and together with Parliament planned an economic strategy to raise money from the colonists to pay for this.

Neglect by Britain

- During the Whig Ascendancy, colonist assemblies had assumed powers which should have been exercised by governors, and they resented Parliament's attempts to reverse this trend.

20. The candidate assesses how far the views of Edmund Burke were typical of British opinion towards the conflict with the American colonists in the period between 1763-1781, within a wide context of factors, using evidence and arguments such as:

Edmund Burke

- Burke studied American situation and took colonists' demands seriously.
- He made speeches in House of Commons, citing common bond of 'Englishness' which existed between Britain and America, and urging Parliament to 'loosen the reins' on colonists or lose America for good.
- However, Burke's views were dismissed as alarmist by many Parliamentarians.

George III

- George III, popular in Britain, sacked Grenville after Stamp Act and appointed Pitt (Earl of Chatham) as Prime Minister.
- He supported Parliament's right to tax colonies.
- He asserted his view that problems in America were 'localised' in New England, and declared colonies to be in 'rebellion' after 1775.
- However, king's actions led colonists to call him a tyrant, and critics in Britain, notably Burke, believed his actions to have accelerated move to war.

Parliament

- In House of Lords, Lord Sandwich and others disregarded warnings of impending crisis and seriously underestimated colonists' forces.
- However, as well as Burke and Chatham, others such as John Wilkes spoke in favour of radical change in policy towards America.

Earl of Chatham

- He had been Prime Minister during Seven Years War and again in mid-1760s when he repealed Stamp Act.
- He became more aware of colonists' plight in his final years, and repeatedly warned of impending situation in America.
- However, Chatham's warnings fell on deaf ears, as Parliament ignored his pleas for conciliation and his assertion that America could not be beaten if war broke out.

Thomas Paine

- Paine had been in America since November 1774, making republican speeches and meeting with colonists.
- He published 'Common Sense' in January 1776 and it sold 100,000 copies in America, and more than that in Britain and Europe.
- However, Paine was a radical, too radical for many colonists.
- Some in Britain read his work out of fascination rather than because they agreed with him.
- In America, many who may have been influenced by 'Common Sense' were already considering independence after rejection of Olive Branch Petition.

Also

- **British cotton industrialists** – Mill owners, including some MPs, wanted speedy resolution to crisis to ensure continued supply of raw materials from colonies.
- **Cotton workers** – Mill workers wanted trade to be maintained in order to preserve jobs.
- **Scotland and Ireland** – some Scots and Irish sympathised with colonists' resentment of "English" rule and understood their calls for greater autonomy.

21. The candidate evaluates the importance of French intervention to colonial victory in the American War of Independence, within a wide context of factors, using evidence and arguments such as:

French intervention

- Franco-American Treaty of Alliance in February 1778 was a turning point in the war. France contributed troops, ammunition, expertise and supplies to the colonists. The strength of the French navy meant Britain had to spread its forces worldwide, thus reducing its effort in the colonies. The entry of France into the war may have encouraged Spain and Holland to follow suit within the next two years. French intervention on the part of Admiral de Grasse preceded the final British surrender at Yorktown. However, the war had been taking place for over eighteen months by the time France entered. France's main contribution was at sea rather than on land.

Other factors

British military inefficiency

- On several occasions British generals did not act appropriately to orders received. Orders from London were misinterpreted. One example was Howe marching south to Brandywine instead of north into New England, thus isolating Burgoyne who subsequently surrendered his forces at Saratoga. Petty jealousies obstructed co-operation amongst British military leaders. Changes in personnel holding high office hindered progress. However, in many instances the British were forced into bad decisions by the tactics of Washington's army.

Distance between Britain and the colonies

- This caused a delay in communications between London and the generals, with orders from Britain often overtaken by events by the time they reached America.

George Washington

- Washington was an inspirational leader, a self-made Virginian whose choice as Commander of the Continental Army gave heart to many. He fought guerrilla warfare effectively. He taught his troops to fire accurately from distance in open battle. He had experience of the British Army during the Seven Years War. His speeches to troops offered them the incentive of independence if they won the war. However, Washington benefited from luck on several occasions, such as when inefficiency led the British into traps or when the French arrived at Yorktown.

Land war fought on American soil

- This gave the Continental Army an advantage, as the colonists' knowledge of the theatre of war meant they handled the terrain better than the British.
- Local people burned their crops rather than let them fall into British hands, reducing potential supplies for the British.

Role of other foreign powers

- Spanish and Dutch entry into the war – they stretched British resources even further and made the British less effective in the colonies.
- Armed League of Neutrality – Russian, Danish and Swedish willingness to fire on the Royal Navy placed extra pressure on Britain.

The French Revolution, to 1799

22. Candidates assess the extent to which the Third Estate had the greatest cause for complaint under the Ancien Regime by using evidence and arguments such as:

The role of the Third Estate

- The bourgeoisie – often individually wealthy, this social group nonetheless resented the privileges and exemptions enjoyed by the First and Second Estates. Although they had displayed their talents in business, the law and in education members of the bourgeoisie were denied access to political power and suffered higher tax burdens than their social 'superiors'. Businessmen were particularly bitter about trade barriers, different regional weights and measures and restrictive trade and working practices which inhibited the free inter-flow of trade and industrial expansion. Intellectually astute, they had taken on board the ideas of the Philosophes which had called for a more rational, fair and equal society where privileges, exemptions and restrictive practices would be ended. It is hardly surprising that the bourgeoisie were at the head of revolutionary political, social and economic change during 1788 and 1789.
- The Peasantry – as was said above, the peasants laboured under a hugely unfair burden of taxation. Their grievances were compounded by the failure of the grain harvest in 1789. This hit agricultural incomes and the economic crisis peaked at the point when the political future of France was being decided in the newly-formed National Assembly (June). The ending of feudalism (August 1789) also had much to do with peasant discontent reaching it peak during the 'Great Fear' in the countryside in July.
- The urban workers – the economic crisis in agriculture hit manufacturing in 1789 when rising bread prices cut the demand for manufactured goods. Lay-offs and falling incomes intensified revolutionary fervour in the great cities such as Paris. Overall, the greatest threat to the Ancien Regime came from the bourgeoisie but the influence of other social groups cannot be ignored.

Role of the Clergy

- The Clergy was split into the Upper and Lower Clergy. The Upper Clergy were almost wholly exempt from the payment of taxes and were tenacious in holding onto the privilege.

The Catholic Church owned 10% of land in France and extracted tax (the tithe) from the peasantry in order to fund the Church's operations.

- The Lower Clergy often sympathised with the peasants in their parishes who suffered under an enormous burden of taxation relative to income and this precipitated tensions within the hierarchy of the Church. It also explains why some of the clergy were prepared to lead protests against the Ancien Regime on behalf of their parishioners – eg in drawing up Cahiers des Doleances in preparation for the meeting of the Estates-General in 1789. The Cahiers revealed a catalogue of discontent and provided a platform from which an attack on the privilege, venality and exemption from taxation rife in the Ancien Regime – privileges and exemptions enjoyed by the Upper Clergy – could be launched.
- Moreover, attempts to increase government income through a Land tax levied on the Church and the Nobility were met by bitter opposition in the Assembly of Notables among whose number the Upper Clergy were prominent. This precipitated a financial crisis and the convocation in 1788 of the Estates-General. This decision led directly to the attack on privilege which culminated in the collapse of the Ancien Regime in 1789 with the establishment of the National Assembly in June, the end of feudalism in early August and the Declaration of the Rights of Man in late August.

Role of the Nobility

- Like the Clergy, the Nobility were almost wholly exempt from taxation. As a result they, too, have to accept a considerable degree of culpability for the Revolution. As with the Clergy, the Nobility was split – between the traditional Nobles of the Sword and the more recently ennobled Nobles of the Robe. The former gained access – often through birth rather than merit – to the highest and most lucrative offices of the State, Church and the Army. The 'old' nobility sought to protect these privileges against the 'new' nobility – and, indeed, the bourgeoisie. Clearly this precipitated tension and a desire for change.
- Many of the leaders of the movement which sought revolutionary change in 1788 and 1789 were drawn from the ranks of the lesser nobility. Their intellect, organisation and education made them formidable opponents of the Ancien Regime – often in alliance with the numerically larger bourgeoisie. It is also worth noting that the Assembly of Notables (bitter opponents of reform) counted many of the traditional nobility among their number.

23. The candidate evaluates how far Louis XVI was responsible for the failure of constitutional monarchy in 1792, using evidence and arguments such as:

The Role of Louis

- Even before the outbreak of revolution in July 1789, Louis had shown himself incapable of making the strong decisions necessary to save the monarchy by dismissing Finance Minister Calonne in the face of opposition from the nobility to the major tax reforms needed to save France from bankruptcy.
- After the Declaration of the Rights of Man in August 1789, Louis failed to openly endorse its principles and in the weeks ahead seemed to be preparing for a counter-revolution through the build-up of troops at Versailles. This aroused considerable suspicion and, even at this early stage, made the achievement of a constitutional monarchy unlikely.
- The so-called March of the Women which forced the Royal family back from Versailles into the Tuileries indicates how Louis' actions during July to September had robbed the monarchy of much support.

- In June 1791 the Royal Family attempted to escape the Revolution by slipping across the border. They were stopped at Varennes and returned to Paris. The mistrust generated by his persistent ambivalence towards the Revolution brought a significant upsurge of support – particularly in Paris – for a Republic. Although not the end of the monarchy, Louis' actions in June 1791 made its demise increasingly certain.
- Even before his veto on decrees against 'refractory' clergy and émigrés in December, Louis' actions during 1791 had done the monarchy immeasurable harm. His lukewarm support for the reforms of the Constituent Assembly had generated popular hostility in Paris from the spring of 1791 onwards.

Other factors

The émigrés promoted anti-revolutionary sentiment abroad which damaged the monarchy at home.
- The Declaration of Pillnitz (August 1791) in which Austria and Prussia threatened to intervene against the Revolution had been inspired by the king's émigré brothers. This intensified suspicion of the monarchy.

The National Assembly's decision to introduce the Civil Constitution of the Clergy
- This caused great controversy in a traditionally Catholic country and created deep divisions which polarised the Revolution. The monarchy – since it was historically associated with the Church – was irrevocably damaged in the eyes of the radicals who exploited the king's unease over the Civil Constitution for their own ends.
- Louis' failure to openly endorse this and his support for émigré nobles (many of whom had left France in the aftermath of the Civil Constitution of the Clergy) increased the hostility of large sections of the population towards the monarchy.

The Declaration of War (April 1792) and the Manifesto of the Duke of Brunswick (July 1792)
- These events radicalised the Revolution to the point where the position of the monarchy became impossible because of the king's identification with the enemy. Partly, as was said above, this was Louis' own fault but it should be remembered that France declared war on Austria in April 1792 and it suited the radical anti-monarchists who thought that a successful war would bring them increased support at home and prove a decisive blow to the monarchy. The final overthrow of the monarchy in August 1792 had become inevitable under the pressures exerted by the war.

24. The candidate evaluates the importance of the constitution of 1795 in bringing about Napoleon's coup of 1799, by using evidence and arguments such as:

The Constitution of 1795
- Policy-makers framed a new constitution which sought to reconcile the bitterness of the preceding years by imposing checks and balances against the emergence of one dominant individual, group or faction. In so doing, many historians argue that the new constitution was a recipe for instability in the years which followed.
  - A bi-cameral legislature was established wherein each chamber counter-balanced the power of the other. By so doing it inhibited strong and decisive government.
  - To ensure continuity, the new Convention was to include two-thirds of the outgoing deputies from the old. This enraged sections of the right who felt that the forces of left-wing radicalism still prevailed in government. The resulting mass protests in October 1795 were put down by the army under Bonaparte. The principle of using extra-

parliamentary forces to control the State had been established with Bonaparte right at the heart of it. It was to prove a dangerous precedent.
- Annual elections worked against consistent and continuous policy-making.
- So did the appointment of an Executive – the Directory – one of whose members rotated on an annual basis.
- Again, the counter-balance between the legislature and the executive may have been commendable but it was to prove inherently unstable in practice.

Other factors

The context of government in 1794/5
- In the late summer of 1794 France was emerging from two years of increasing radicalisation and resulting bitterness between opposing factions. The Jacobins under Robespierre had been overthrown and a 'White Terror' was soon to sweep the country in revenge for the excesses of the radical left during the Terror. France had been torn apart by civil war, threatened by foreign armies egged on by émigré nobles seeking to overthrow the Revolution and riven by religious conflict occasioned by the State's opposition to the primacy of the Catholic church.

Increasing intervention of the army in politics
- Even before the 1795 constitution was ratified the army had been used to quell sans-culottes insurgents who sought to invade the Convention and to repel an émigré invasion at Quiberon. Napoleon's use of a 'whiff of grapeshot' to put down the disturbances in October (see above) merely underlined the parlous nature of politics at the time.
- The deployment of the army in May 1796 to put down the left-wing Babeuf Conspiracy was followed by the Coup of Fructidor in September 1797 when the first 'free' Convention elections (where the two-thirds majority rule did not apply) returned a royalist majority.

Role of Sieyes
- Afraid that France would descend into anarchy as a result of the on-going political conflict and deeming the 1795 constitution unworkable, Sieyes enlisted the aid of Bonaparte in mounting a coup against it. The Convention, the Directory and the legislative councils had run their course and few, if any, mourned their passing.

Role of Napoleon Bonaparte
- Napoleon's swift rise through the military had not gone unnoticed by people like Sieyes. He was a popular war hero owing to successful campaigns in Italy against the Austrians and Egypt against the Mamlukes. He had shown himself willing to put down the mob in Paris as well: 'the whiff of grapeshot'. Yet he was unwilling to be a pawn and had political ambitions of his own.

Germany 1815 – 1939

25. The candidate evaluates the importance of cultural factors in the growth of national feeling in Germany between 1815 and 1850 using evidence and arguments such as:

Cultural factors – 'Romanticism'
- The main unifying force was language – 25 million Germans spoke the same language and shared through it the same culture and literature.
  - Writers and thinkers (eg Heine, Fichte, Goethe, Brothers Grimm, Schiller, Hegel) encouraged the growth of a German consciousness.
  - Post-1815 nationalist feelings first expressed in universities.
  - The Hambacherfest and student demonstrations – little accomplished by the students.

Other factors

Economic factors

- Urbanisation and industrialisation in the German states led to frustration at the political fragmentation of Germany which can be argued to be the most important obstacle to German economic development. Middle-class businessmen called for a more united market to enable them to compete with foreign countries.
- Prussian economic expansion proceeded steadily in the 19th Century. Prussia's gain of territory on the River Rhine after 1815 (leading to a drift in power away from Austria and towards Prussia as the latter began to build on the rich resources such as coal and iron deposits) meant it had good reason to reach an agreement with neighbours to ensure relatively free travel of goods and people between its lands in the east and the west. Businessmen complained that tax burdens were holding back economic development. Prussia created a large free-trade area within Prussia herself which aided the needs of businessmen.
- The Zollverein was the 'mighty lever' of German unification. By 1836, 25 of the 39 German states had joined this economic free-trade area (Austria was excluded).
- Railway/road development from the 1830s onwards ended the isolation of German states from each other. They enabled the transport and exploitation of German natural resources. Economic co-operation between German states encouraged those seeking a political solution to the issue of German unity.

Political factors

- Ideas of the French Revolution appealed to the middle classes in the German states.
- German princes had stirred national feeling to help raise armies to drive out the French, aiding the sense of a common German identity with common goals.
- Growth of Liberal political beliefs.
- The 1848 Revolutions in Germany raised consciousness greatly even though they failed.

Military factors

- The impact of Napoleonic wars meant many Germans saw that Napoleon/France had been able to conquer the separate, autonomous German states before 1815 due to their divisions.
- Growth of *Burschenschaften* pre-1815 dedicated to driving French from German soil – zealous but lacking a clear idea of how best to accomplish the task.

26. The candidate evaluates the extent to which resentment towards Prussia among the German states was the main obstacle to German unification by 1850, using evidence and arguments such as:

Background

- Nationalism was the idea that people with a common culture, language and history should have the right to rule themselves.
- Post-1815 nationalist feelings first expressed in universities of *Burschenschaften*.
- Pre-1815 dedicated to driving French from German soil – zealous but lacking a clear idea of how best to accomplish the task.

German states and Prussia

- Northern German states were mostly Protestant and southern states mainly Catholic.
- Generally, the northern states looked to Prussia for help and protection while the southern states looked to Austria.
- Many German states were suspicious of the motives of Prussia within 'Germany', believing it was striving to dominate the area.

- Jealousy existed among many German states towards Prussia – economic success of Prussia was envied.
- Prussian military strength was both admired and looked on with trepidation by many German states.

Other factors

Particularism

- The leaders of the German states also obstructed unification – protective of their individual power and position. They wanted to maintain the status quo which would safeguard this for them.

Austrian strength

- The states within 'Germany' had been part of the moribund Holy Roman Empire, traditionally ruled by the Emperor of Austria.
- Post-1815 the chairmanship of the *Bund* was given to Austria on a permanent basis, partly as she was considered to be the major German power.
- Metternich's work – to oppose liberalism and nationalism. His use of the weapons of diplomacy and threats of force. Use of the police state, repression and press censorship. Smaller German states were in awe of the power and position of the Austrian Empire. Austrian control over the administration and management of the empire, stamping authority on the *Bund*.
- Karlsbad Decrees and the Six Articles.
- Post-1815 Austrian military strength and bureaucracy continued to decline in effectiveness; shift in balance of power between Austria and Prussia.
- Treaty of Olmutz, 1850 – signalled the triumph of Austria and humiliation of Prussia. German nationalism was now a spent force apparently.

Weakness of nationalism

- Nationalists were divided over which territory should be included in any united Germany; *grossdeutsch* and *kleindeutsch* arguments.
- Failure of the Frankfurt Parliament – lack of clear aims and without an armed force to enforce its decisions. Lack of decisive leadership. Divisions among the 'revolutionaries' regarding aims and objectives. Self interest among German rulers led to opposition to the actions at Frankfurt.
- Popular apathy – most Germans had little desire to see a united Germany, nationalism affected mainly the educated/business classes.

Attitude of foreign states

- Foreign concerns over the idea of a united Germany.
- None of the Great Powers wanted to see the creation of a strong Germany which might upset the balance of power.
- Britain, Russia, Austria and France were all happy to see the German states weak and divided.

27. The candidate evaluates the importance of economic factors in the rise to power of the Nazi Party between 1919 and 1933, using evidence and arguments such as:

Economic factors

- 1922/23 (hyperinflation) – severe effects on the middle classes, the natural supporters of the Republic; outrage and despair at their ruination.
- Difficulties faced by farmers in Schleswig-Holstein gave the Nazis their first electoral breakthrough in 1928.
- The Great Depression of 1929 – arguably without this the Republic might have survived. Germany's dependence on American loans showed how fragile the recovery of the late 1920s was. The pauperisation of millions again reduced Germans to despair. Propaganda posters with legends such as "Hitler – unsere letzte hoffnung " struck a chord with many.

- The Depression also polarised politics in Germany – the drift to extremes led to a fear of Communism, which grew apace with the growth of support for the Nazis.

Other factors

Weakness of the Weimer

- The Constitution/Article 48 ('suicide clause') – arguably Germany was too democratic.
  'The world's most perfect democracy – on paper.'
- The Treaty of Versailles – acceptance by Republic of hated terms.
- 'A Republic without Republicans'/'a Republic nobody wanted' – lack of popular support for the new form of government after 1918.
- Lack of real, outstanding Weimar politicians who could strengthen the Republic, Stresemann excepted.
- 'Peasants in a palace' – commentary on Weimar politicians.
- Lukewarm support from the German Army and the Civil Service for Weimar.
- Inability (or unwillingness) to deal effectively with problems in German society by the Republic.
- Lack of authority.

Weaknesses and mistakes of opponents

- Alliance of the new government and the old imperial army against the Spartacists – lack of cooperation between socialist groups – petty squabbling rife.
- Divisions among those groups/individuals who purported to be supporters of the new form of government eg the socialists.
- Political intrigue – roles of von Schleicher and von Papen.

Role of Adolf Hitler and Appeal of the Nazis after 1928

- Hitler's oratory – ability to put into words the outrage and frustrations of millions of Germans over a variety of issues.
- The Storm Troopers (SA) – Hitler's contribution to the setting up of the private army of the Nazi Party. To a worried middle-class they looked like the only political party willing to take on the Communists.
- Post 1925 – Hitler's decision to improve the efficiency of the Nazi Party, develop the effectiveness of its organisation, especially its propaganda machine.
- Hitler's uncompromising stance against the Treaty of Versailles struck a chord with millions of Germans.
- Hitler's alliance with Hugenberg offered the Nazi Party widespread publicity – propaganda.
- Hitler's ruthlessness/pragmatic approach to matters – for example in his hard-headed negotiations with von Papen.
- Hitler's policies – something for everyone, despite often contradictory policies.
- Hitler gave people somebody to blame for their problems: November Criminals, Jews, etc.

Italy 1815 – 1939

28. The candidate evaluates the importance of Mazzini to the growth of Italian nationalism between 1815 and 1850, using evidence and arguments such as:

Role of Mazzini

- Radical nationalist Mazzini not only inspired dreams of a united, democratic Italian republic through his written works, but also formed an activist movement 'Young Italy' whose aim was to make these dreams a reality.
- Low literacy levels lessened the impact of his writing.
- Failure of Young Italy revolts in the 1830s damaged his credibility.
- Lack of popular support for the Roman Republic.

Other factors

Cultural factors

- The Risorgimento was inspired by Italy's past. Poets such as Leopardi glorified and exaggerated past achievements kindling nationalist desires. Poets and novelists like Pellico inspired anti-Austrian feelings amongst intellectuals as did operas such as Verdi's 'Nabucco' and Rossini's 'William Tell.'
- There was no national 'Italian' language – regional dialects were like separate languages. Alfieri inspired 'Italian' language based on Tuscan. The poet and novelist Manzoni wrote in 'Italian'. Philosophers spread ideas of nationalism in their books and periodicals.
- Moderate nationalists such as Gioberti and Balbo advocated the creation of a federal state with the individual rulers remaining but joining together under a president for foreign affairs and trade. Gioberti's 'On the moral and civil primacy of the Italians' advocated the Pope as president whilst Balbo, in his book 'On the hopes of Italy', saw the King of Piedmont/Sardinia in the role.

Effects of the French Revolution

- 'Italian' intellectuals had initially been inspired by the French Revolution with its national flag, national song, national language, national holiday and emphasis on citizenship.

Role of Bonaparte

- Napoleon Bonaparte's conquest inspired feelings of nationalism – he reduced the number of states to three; revived the name 'Italy'; brought in single system of weights and measures; improved communications; helped trade inspiring desire for at least a customs union. Napoleon's occupation was hated – conscription, taxes, looting of art – led to realisation that, individually, the Italian states were weak.

Resentment of Austrian Rule

- After the Vienna settlement in 1815, hatred of foreign control centred on Austria. The Hapsburg Emperor directly controlled Lombardy and Venetia; his relatives controlled Parma, Modena, Tuscany. Austria had strong ties to the Papacy and had alliances with other rulers. Conscription, censorship, the use of spies and the policy of promotion in the police, civil service and army only for German speakers was resented.
- Austrian army presence within towns like Milan and the heavily garrisoned Quadrilateral fortresses ensured that 'Italians' could never forget that they were under foreign control and this inspired growing desire for the creation of a national state.

Role of Nationalist Societies

- The growth of secret societies, particularly the Carbonari, led to revolts in 1820, 1821, 1831. Also 'Young Italy' and their revolts in the 1830s.
- By 1850s development of moderate nationalist groups like the National Society which rejected revolt and looked to Piedmont's liberal political system and growing economic power as the best way to achieve unity.

Economic factors

- Wealth lay in land (landowners were often reactionary) and trade (where the educated bourgeoisie were more receptive to ideas of liberalism and nationalism).
- Realisation that closer economic ties would benefit the Italian state.

Role of Pio Nono

- The election of a new, seemingly reformist Pope, Pius IX, in 1846 inspired feelings of nationalism particularly amongst businessmen and traders as he wished to form a customs union.

29. The candidate evaluates how important the influence of Austria was in preventing the unification of Italy between 1815 and 1850 using evidence and arguments such as:

Austrian strength
- Following Vienna Settlement Austrian Emperor Francis I had direct control of Lombardy and Venetia. Relatives of the Austrian Hapsburg Emperor controlled Parma, Modena and Tuscany (Central Duchies). Austria had agreements with the other states.
- Lombardy and Venetia were strictly controlled – censorship, spies, conscription (8 years), policy to employ German speakers (Austrian) in law, police, army civil service so controlled others (non Austrian).
- Austrian army was 'common sight' in major cities and in the Quadrilateral fortress towns on Lombard/Venetian border (Verona, Peschiera, Legnano, and Mantua). Austrian army sent in by Metternich to restore order following the Carbonari-inspired revolts in 1820, 1821 and 1831.
- Austria had first class commander, Radetsky. In 1848 Charles Albert's army won two skirmishes but Radetsky awaited reinforcements then defeated Albert at Custozza forcing an armistice. Radetsky re-took Milan in August.
- After Albert's renewal of war Radetsky took just three days to defeat him again (Novara). He then besieged Venetia until the Republic of St Mark surrendered on 22 August 1849. Austrians re-established control across north and central Italy.

Other factors

Popular indifference
- Patriotic literature inspired intellectuals and students but did not reach the vast majority of the population who were illiterate (90% in some areas). The mass of the population were indifferent to nationalist ideas.

Geography
- Geographical difficulties hindered the spread of nationalist ideas. It also led to problems of economic development: the industrial north and the rural south.

Attitudes of Italian rulers
- Individual rulers were opposed to nationalism. Pope Pius IX denounced nationalism in 1848.

Nationalist divisions/weakness
- Secret societies lacked clear aims, organisation, leadership, resources and operated in regional cells.
- Young Italy movement dead by 1850.
- Moderate nationalists feared extremists like Mazzini.
- The 1848/49 revolutions showed that nationalist leaders did not trust one another (Manin and Charles Albert) or would not work together (C. Albert and Mazzini).
- Failure to capitalise on Austrian weakness in 1848.
- There was division between those desiring liberal changes within existing states and those desiring the creation of a national state.

30. The candidate evaluates the extent to which Musolini achieved power by 1925 as a result of the weaknesses of Italian governments using evidence and arguments such as:

Weaknesses of Italian governments
- Parliamentary government was weak and ineffective. Liberals had no party structure. A narrow support base. Coalitions were corrupt. Bribery commonplace (trasformismo).
- New parties with wider support base threatened existing political system. Universal male suffrage and PR worsened situation resulting in unstable coalitions. Giolitti made electoral pact with Mussolini (1921). Fascists gained 35 seats then refused to support government. Liberals fragmented into at least four different factions grouped around former PMs.

- Once Mussolini was PM these groups felt they could control him and believed he could tame the extreme fascists. Majority of 'liberals' supported the Acerbo Law. Aventine Secession played into Mussolini's hands.
- Weak governments failed to deal with Italy's internal problems.
- Coalitions failed to deal with Italy's growing post WWI economic problems:
  - foreign loans and massive national debt
  - spiralling inflation
  - low wages
  - food shortages
  - escalating unemployment, strikes, demonstrations and occupation of factories
  - violence of both socialist and fascists.
- They did little to support the police as law and order broke down and fears of civil war/ revolution grew.
- The government did not stop D'Annunzio's seizure of Fiume Government ineffective over 'Biennio Rosso'.
- Weaknesses of the monarchy: King caved in over 'March on Rome'.

Other factors

Socialist weaknesses
- Revolutionary socialists dominated the leadership of PSI (socialists) and they refused involvement in 'liberal' coalitions. Biennio Rosso frightened middle/upper classes who feared communism. 1919 elections PSI did well but could not form government.
- Split into moderates, radicals and communists in 1921 – 1922 General Strike failed. Moderates failed to join an anti-fascist coalition. In 1925 Mussolini banned socialist parties.

PPI weaknesses
- Pope Pius XI constantly undermined Sturzo's PPI. PPI was divided over its attitude to fascism – the right preferred fascism over socialism. The left were anti-fascist. Mussolini exploited this by including two right wing PPI in his coalition.
- Pius directly negotiated with Mussolini over existing problems between church and state, and effectively sidelined Sturzo. PPI officially abstained over Acerbo Law. Pope rejected PPI involvement in the anti-fascist coalition of 1924. By 1926 Mussolini had banned all opposition parties.

Appeal of fascism
- Fascism promised strong government.
- Squadristi violence directed against socialism so gained support of elites and middle classes.
- Violence showed fascism was strong and ruthless.
- Appeal to nationalism, capitalising on the resentment towards the Paris Peace Settlement.

Mussolini's skills
- He seized his opportunities and changed political direction offering support to conservative elites: Pope; king; army.
- He kept fascist policies vague to attract support from different groups.
- He copied D'Annunzio's tactics – direct action; flags, banners, salutes, songs – fascism seemed dynamic.
- He used 'piazza politics' and his newspaper effectively.
- He outmanoeuvred fascist extremists.

Russia 1881 – 1921

31. The candidate assesses how secure the Tsar's hold on power was in the years before 1905, using evidence and arguments such as:

The Secret Police, 'Okhrana'

- The Secret police was set up to ensure loyalty to the Tsar and weed out opposition to the Tsar.
- The Secret police would do this by spying on all people of society irrespective of class. Would infiltrate opposition groups to find their key leaders, etc.
- Large numbers were exiled however they were unable to completely eradicate all of the ideas opposing the Tsar.

The Church

- The Church helped to ensure that the people remained loyal to the Tsar.
- The Church preached to the peasants that the Tsar had been appointed by God and that they should therefore obey the Tsar.
- The Church also ensured that the peasants were aware of the Fundamental Law.

Fundamental Law

- This was used to impose the authority of the Tsar over the peasants as it stated "To the emperor of all Russia belongs the Supreme and unlimited power. God himself commands that his supreme power be obeyed out of conscience as well as out of fear."

The Army

- The Army was controlled by officers who were mainly upper class and therefore conservative and loyal to the King.
- The army ensured that the population and the peasants in particular were loyal to the Tsar.
- Most of the soldiers had been peasants themselves, but had been taught to be loyal to the Tsar.
- The army was used to crush insurgence and to enforce order in the country and loyalty to the Tsar.

Civil Service

- The Civil Service was set up to ensure loyalty to the Tsar and weed out opposition to the Tsar.
- The Civil Service spied on all people of society irrespective of class with those showing any sign of opposition to the Tsar being imprisoned or sent in to exile.
- Large numbers of people were exiled however they were unable to completely eradicate all of the ideas opposing the Tsar.
- The Civil Service mainly employed middle class people, which therefore ensured the loyalty of the middle class people in general.
- The Civil Service was responsible for enforcing laws on censorship and corruption as well as about meetings, which made it very difficult for the revolutionaries to communicate.

Censorship

- Censorship controlled what people were able to read which therefore meant the Civil Service could control what University lecturers could say and also controlled access to schools as well as limiting books available in libraries. As a result the Civil Service were able to prevent reading anti-Tsarist literature.

Russification

- Russification was an effort to restrict the influence of the national minorities in the Russian Empire by insisting that Russian was the first language.
- The law and government of the country were conducted throughout the Russian Empire in the Russian language, which maintained the dominance of the Russian culture over that of the minority cultures.
- Due to Russification, discrimination of minority peoples became more widespread. There was State intervention in religion and education by the Tsarist government over the minority people to ensure Russification.
- The Tsarist state treated subjects from minority areas as potential enemies and inferior.

Zubatov Unions

- The Zubatov Unions were used to divert the attention of the workers away from political change by concentrating on wages and conditions in the factories
- The Zubatov Unions reduced the chances of the workers being influenced by the revolutionary groups.
- Unions in 1903 became involved in strikes and so were disbanded due to pressure from employers.

Revolutionary Groups Weak

- There were various revolutionary groups like the Social Revolutionaries (peasants unhappy at the mir system), Social Democrats (disillusioned and angry town workers) and Liberals (who wanted a British style parliament).
- The revolutionary groups alone were not powerful or popular enough to affect change.
- The revolutionary groups were further weakened by the fact they were not very organised and they did not cooperate.

32. The candidate assesses the extent to which the power of the Tsarist state was weakened in the years between 1905 and 1914 by using evidence and arguments such as:

October Manifesto

- The Duma received legislative powers, ie agree to new laws.
- The electorate was widened, and promised freedom of speech, to have meetings and liberty of conscience.
- This split the revolutionary forces with the moderate liberals accepting it.
- On the face of it there was change, but…

Duma (parliament) granted to buy off the middle classes

- Before Duma met the Tsar took back much of the power he had conceded. He announced the "Fundamental Laws" whereby the Supreme autocratic power belonged to the Tsar, in that no law could be passed without his approval.
- The Duma had two chambers. The first house was elected and the second house (state council) would be largely dominated by the Tsar and could veto lower chamber proposals.
- The Tsar could appoint and dismiss ministers who were not responsible to the Duma.
- The Tsar could dissolve the Duma, but had to call elections for a new one.
- Article 87 meant the Tsar could issue decrees "in exceptional circumstances" when the Duma was not sitting.

The Duma

- 1st Duma: Lasted from April to June 1906. Dismissed for demanding a full democratic parliament. "Vyborg Group" of liberals who resisted were arrested and banned from future elections.
- 2nd Duma: Lasted from Feb to June 1907. Few liberals in this Duma as most of them were part of the "Vyborg Group". Closed due to the Tsar's resentment to criticism of the administration of the army, thus showing power of Tsarist state.
- 3rd Duma: Lasted from 1907 to 1912. The rich dominated it and only 1 man in 6 could now vote. This Duma was very right wing and was accused of merely rubber-stamping Tsarist policies, however it helped Stolypin bring about Land Reform which was disliked by the nobles, questioned ministers, discussed state finances, and made proposals to modernise the army, showing that Tsarist policy could change, but was it weakened?

- 4th Duma: lasted from 1912 to 1914. It was of a similar make up to the 3rd Duma. It also criticised the government at times, such as it's handling of the Lena goldfield strike and the very heavy-handed style of the government in repressing working class protest, but although critical did it weaken the Tsarist State? Dissolved itself at the start of WWI.

Stolypin cracked down on Revolutionaries
- Government ministers in reality helped the Tsar in some ways: role of Stolypin.
- Many of the revolutionaries were stamped out.
- Stolypin set up tribunals, which sentenced to death every terrorist captured by the secret police.
- There was a reduction in opposition to the Tsar and his running of the country.
- The Soviets were crushed in 1905 as they were a focal point of opposition to the Tsar.

Agricultural Reforms
- Stolypin introduced these important reforms to win the support of the peasants. Redemption payments were ended.
- Peasants were given complete freedom to leave the Mir and they could turn their holdings in to their own property, this was to produce a rich class of peasants and help farming.
- These reforms reduced opposition to the Tsar as the peasants became loyal to the Tsar and allowed him to rule as he wished.

June 1907 Electoral Law Change
- Franchise restricted to favour the gentry and urban rich at the expense of the workers, peasants and nationalities, which tended to reinforce Tsarist power.

Army remained loyal to the Tsar.
- After 1905 this enabled the Tsar to repress opposition such as revolutionaries.

33. The candidate evaluates how important Bolshevik propaganda was in the success of the October revolution in 1917 using evidence and arguments such as:

Bolshevik Propaganda
- Lenin returned to Russia announcing the April Theses, with slogans such as "Peace, Land and Bread" and "All Power to the Soviets" which were persuasive and appealed to important groups such as the workers and peasants.
- Lenin talked of further revolution to overthrow the Provisional Government and his slogans identified the key weaknesses of the Provisional Government.

Other factors

The Provisional Government Lacked Authority
- The Provisional Government was an unelected government; it was a self-appointed body and had no right to exercise authority.

The Petrograd Soviet
- The old Petrograd Soviet re emerged and ran Petrograd.
- The Bolsheviks kept attending the Petrograd Soviet when most of the others stopped doing so and this gave them control of the Soviet, which they could then use against the Provisional Government.
- The Petrograd Soviet undermined the authority of Provisional Government especially when relations between the two worsened.
- Order No. 1 of the Petrograd Soviet weakened the authority of the Provisional Government as soldiers were not to obey orders of Provisional Government that contradicted those of the Petrograd Soviet.

The War
- The Provisional Government gave in to the pressure of the army and from the Allies to keep Russia in the War.
- Remaining in the war helped cause the October revolution and helped destroy the Provisional Government as the misery it caused continued for people in Russia.

Workers
- The workers were restless as they were starving due to food shortages caused by the war.
- The shortage of fuel caused lack of heating for the workers in their living conditions.
- The shortage of food and supplies made the workers unhappy and restless.

The Land Issue
- All over Russia peasants were seizing nobles land and wanted the Provisional Government to legitimise this.
- The failure of the Provisional Government to recognise the peasants' claims eroded the confidence in the Provisional Government.
- Food shortages caused discontent, and they were caught up by revolutionary slogans such as "Peace, Land and Bread".

The July Days
- The Bolsheviks staged an attempt to seize power, rising in support of the Kronstadt sailors who were in revolt.
- The revolt was easily crushed by the Provisional Government but showed increasing opposition to the PG, especially from the forces.
- The revolt also showed that the PG was still reasonably strong and able to crush opposition such as the Bolsheviks who now appeared to be weakened.

Kornilov Affair
- General Kornilov, a right wing general, proposed to replace the Provisional Government with a military dictatorship and sent troops to Petrograd.
- Kerensky appealed to the Petrograd Soviet for help and the Bolsheviks were amongst those who helped.
- Some Bolsheviks were armed and released from prison to help put down the attempted coup.
- The Bolsheviks did not return their weapons to the Provisional Government after they defeated Kornilov.
- Bolsheviks were able to act as protectors of Petrograd.

USA 1918 – 1968

34. The candidate evaluates the importance of racism in explaining changing attitudes towards immigration in the 1920s, using evidence and arguments such as:

Prejudice and racism
- Changing nature of immigrants. Old Immigrants – WASPs mainly from North and West of Europe. New Immigrants – mainly from Southern and Eastern Europe. New immigrants were Catholic or Jewish – worried WASP America.
- New immigrants unfamiliar with democracy – viewed as a threat to the American constitution.
- New immigrants continued to wear traditional dress and looked out of place.
- Huge numbers of new immigrants entering America after 1900.
- Prejudiced views saw new immigrants as inferior people and threats to 'traditional values'.
- Nativism – America for Americans.
- Rebirth of KKK appealing to 100% Americanism.
- Anti Immigration legislation of 1920s heavily stacked against 'new' immigrants from southern and eastern Europe.

Other factors

Anti immigration attitudes had already existed before 1920s

- Change in attitudes already apparent in the 19th century. 1884 Immigration Restriction League.
- 1882 Federal Immigration Act.
- Chinese Exclusion Act.
- 1913 Alien Land Law.

Isolationism, the First World War and anti immigration

- Wanted to keep out of foreign problems and concentrate solely on America.
- Many immigrants during the First World War had sympathies for their mother country. Many German immigrants had supported the German side in the war and society was split when the USA joined the war against Germany.
- Many citizens felt hostile to anything foreign.
- When the war ended, most Americans wanted a return to isolationism.

Social fears/fear of crime

- Immigrants congregated in ghettoes – blamed for high crime rates in cities.
- Fears of un-American values being promoted.
- Media promoted fears of immigrants bringing crime to USA and Sacco and Vanzetti case seemed to confirm the link between political extremism, foreign influence and crime.

Economic fears

- Trade unions believed that anything they did to improve conditions or wages was wrecked by Italian or Polish workers who were prepared to work longer hours for lower wages.
- 1919 strikes – new immigrants were used as 'strike breakers'. Caused huge resentment and an increase in the desire to stop immigrants coming into the country.

Fear of communism/revolution

- Russian revolution in 1917 had established the first Communist state committed to spreading revolution and destroying capitalism. Many immigrants came from Russia and eastern Europe.
- Activities of Wobblies (The Industrial Workers of the World) and anarchist groups raised suspicion.
- Bomb scares and widespread strikes in 1919 heightened tension.
- 'Red Scare' 1919 looked as if revolution was imminent. Palmer Raids – August 1919.

35. The candidate evaluates the accuracy of the statement that the weakness of the US banking system was the main reason in causing the depression of the 1930's, using evidence and arguments such as:

Weakness of the US banking system

- Major problem was lack of regulation.
- Banking system was made up of hundreds of small, state-based banks.
- When one bank collapsed it often led to a 'run' on other banks, resulting in a banking collapse and national financial crisis.

Other factors

Saturation of the US market

- New mass-production methods and mechanisation meant that production of consumer goods had expanded enormously.
- Cars, radios and other electrical goods had flooded the market and more was being made than people could buy.
- By 1929 those who could afford consumer goods had already bought them.

- Throughout the 1920's business had benefited from low tax policies. The result of this was that the bottom 40% of the population received only 12.5% of the nation's wealth.
- In contrast, the top 5% owned 33% of the nation's wealth. Therefore, domestic demand never kept up with production.

International debt issues

- Results of the First World War on European economies.
- All European states, except Britain, placed tariffs on imported goods.
- US economy could not expand its foreign markets.

Economic boom of the 1920s

- Republican administrations' policy of Laissez-Faire.
- Failure to help farmers who did not benefit from the 1920's boom.
- Low capital gains tax encouraged share speculation which resulted in the Wall Street Crash.
- The depression was also due to the actions – or inactions – of President Hoover.

Wall Street crash

- Atmosphere of uncertainty in October 1929 and shareholders began to sell their stocks.
  - 24 October 1929 Black Thursday.
  - 29 October 1929 Black Tuesday.
  - Share collapse caused panic.
- Stock market crash did play a role in the depression but its significance was as a trigger. Collapse of credit, and of confidence.

36. The candidate evaluates the importance of the emergence of effective organisations to the development of the Civil Rights after 1945 using evidence and arguments such as:

Effective black organizations formed

- 1957 Martin Luther King and other black clergy formed the Southern Christian Leadership Conference (SCLC) to coordinate the work of civil rights groups.
- King urged African Americans to use peaceful methods.
- 1960 a groups of black and white college students organised Non-violent Coordinating Committee (SNCC) to help the civil rights movement.
- They joined with young people from the SCLC, CORE and NAACP in staging sit-ins, boycotts, marches and freedom rides.
- Combined efforts of the civil rights groups ended discrimination in many public places including restaurants, hotels, and theatres.

The emergence of effective black leaders

- Martin Luther King.
- Malcolm X.
- Stokely Carmichael.

Other factors

Evidence of continuing racial discrimination

- The experience of war emphasized freedom, democracy and human rights yet in USA Jim Crow laws still existed and lynching went unpunished.
- The Emmet Till murder trial and its publicity.

Legal changes

- Education: 1954 Brown v Board of Education of Topeka; Little Rock Central High School.
- Transport: 1955 Rosa Parks and the Montgomery Bus Boycott.

Effects of the Second World War

- Black soldiers talked about the 'Double-V-Campaign': Victory in the war and victory for civil rights at home.
- Philip Randolf is credited with highlighting the problems faced by black Americans during World War Two.

- March on Washington.
- Roosevelt's response – Executive order 8802.
- Roosevelt also established the Fair Employment Practices Committee to investigate incidents of discrimination.
- Creation of the Congress of Racial Equality (CORE) 1942.
- Beginning of a mass movement for civil rights.

Appeasement and the Road to War, to 1939

37. The candidate evaluates the disappointment over the terms of the Peace Settlements of 1919 as an explanation for the aggressive nature of fascist foreign policies in the 1930s using evidence and arguments such as:

Terms of the Paris Peace Settlement
- German desire to get revenge for defeat in WW1.
- Determination to revise/overturn Paris Peace Settlement – German resentment of war guilt, reparations, disarmament, lost territory. Italian resentment of failure to gain control of Adriatic.

Other factors

Economic difficulties
- Germany and Italy's post-WW1 economic difficulties – eg labour unrest, unemployment, inflation.
- Fascist economic policies in Italy in the 1920s – relative recovery.
- The impact of the world economic crisis 1929-32 on the German and Italian economies, intensified international competition and protectionism.
- Continuing economic problems in the 1930s, eg needs of rearmament and domestic consumption.
- Economic imperatives, eg need for additional resources, leading to aggressive, expansionist foreign policies, eg Italy in Abyssinia, German drive to the east.

Imperialism
- Mussolini's 'Roman' ambitions in the Mediterranean and Africa; Hitler's ambitions in Eastern Europe and Russia.
- Militarism – fascist glorification of war; Prussian/German military traditions.

Ideology
- Pathological hatred of communism, anti-Soviet crusade; contempt for democracy.
- Irredentism, eg Hitler's commitment to incorporation of all Germans within Reich.

Leadership
- Extent to which foreign policies driven by Hitler's and Mussolini's own beliefs, personalities, charismatic leadership.

Weakness of the League of Nations
- Failure of the League. Divided response of other powers, eg British appeasement, French political divisions, US isolationism, mutual suspicion of Soviet Russia; relative weakness of successor states in East Europe.
- Example of success of Japan in Manchuria in defiance of League.
- No League enforcement powers.
- Not a League of all nations.
- Seen as victors club to enforce unfair terms of 1919 settlements.

38. The candidate evaluates the extent to which British public opinion explains the policy of appeasement between 1936 and 1938 using evidence and arguments such as:

British public opinion
- Versailles too harsh
- Early Nazi foreign policy justifiable – "only going in own front garden" – Rhineland 1936.
- Peace Pledge Union – 11 million signatures for anti war position.

- Peace Ballot 1935.
- Fulham by-election often used as evidence for appeasement support – questionable.
- Oxford Union debate – no strong support to fight for King and Country.
- Fear of bombing – as seen in newsreels (Guernica 1937) and also 'Things to Come' movie.
- Fear of return to horrors of Great War and also new technology fears – gas bombing of civilians.
- More important issues to spend money on.
- Many felt European problems were not our concern.
- Distractions of the Abdication crisis.

Other factors explaining the policy of appeasement between 1936 and 1938
- Military weakness.
- Run-down state of armed forces following WW1.
- Army: conscription ended post-WW1, scaled right down in size.
- Navy: not so run-down but not fully maintained; many obsolete ships.
- Air Force: lack of adequate air defences and fear of aerial bombing.
- Multiple threats – Japan in the East, Italy in the Mediterranean and North Africa, Germany in Central Europe.
- Warnings of Chiefs-of-Staff.
- Exaggerated assessments of German military strength.
- 1919 Peace Settlement was seen as too harsh on Germany and there was sympathy for what were seen by many as genuine grievances.
- Reluctance to enforce Treaty provisions and preference for policy of making concessions.
- Economic difficulties – impact of 1929-32 economic crisis and depression, reluctance to further damage international trade and commerce.
- Fear of communism – suspicion of Soviet Russia; Nazi Germany seen as a buffer and destabilising the Nazi regime might lead to questions over communist revolution in Germany.
- Perceived lack of reliable allies (but there are doubts as to how reliable Britain was as an ally herself).
- Failure of League of Nations, eg Manchuria, Abyssinia.
- French political divisions, military weakness and Maginot mentality.
- US isolationism.
- Mutual suspicions vis-à-vis Soviet Russia.
- Relative weakness of eastern European successor states.
- Doubts over commitment of Empire and the Dominions in event of war.
- Italy also appeased in vain attempt to prevent alliance with Germany.
- Belief that Hitler would moderate views in power and be reasonable.
- Chamberlain's personal convictions and control of foreign policy.

39. "The candidate assesses the extent to which the Munich Agreement could be described as a triumph for British policy using evidence and arguments such as:

Munich a victory?
- Hitler himself was dissatisfied by Munich – felt 'robbed' of a war with the hated Czechs.
- Czechoslovakian defences were effectively outflanked anyway following the Anschluss.
- Britain and France were not in a position to prevent German attack on Czechoslovakia in terms of:
  - geography – difficulties of getting assistance to Czechoslovakia
  - public opinion – reluctant to risk war over mainly German-speaking Sudetenland.

- Military unpreparedness for wider war – especially Britain's air defences.
- Lack of alternative, unified international response to Hitler's threats:
  - failure of League of Nations
  - French doubts over commitments to Czechoslovakia
  - US isolationism
  - mutual suspicion of Soviet Russia
  - strong reservations of rest of British Empire and Dominions concerning support in event of war.
- Attitudes of Poland and Hungary – willing to benefit from dismemberment of Czechoslovakia.
- Munich bought another year for rearmament which Britain put to good use.

Munich a defeat

- A humiliating surrender to Hitler's threats.
- Another breach in the post-WW1 settlement.
- A betrayal of Czechoslovakia and democracy.
- Czechoslovakia wide open to further German aggression – destruction of Czechoslovakia, March 1939.
- Further augmentation of German manpower and resources.
- Furtherance of Hitler's influence and ambitions in Eastern Europe.
- Further alienation of Soviet Union.
- Poland left further exposed.
- A British, French, Soviet agreement was a more effective alternative.

The Cold War 1945 – 1989

40. The candidate assesses the importance of ideological differences between east and west in the emergence of the Cold War up to 1955 using evidence and arguments such as:

Ideological differences

- Impact of 1917 Bolshevik revolution in Russia on relations with the western powers: Soviet withdrawal from WW1, involvement of West with anti-Bolshevik Whites: ideological differences between Communist and Capitalism. WW2: suspicion of USSR by allies because of Nazi-Soviet Pact of 1939.

Other factors

Experience of the Second World War

- Tensions within the wartime alliance as the defeat of Nazism became clear. Soviet Union felt they had done the bulk of the land fighting and wanted security for the USSR. Stalin determined to hang on to land gained and create a series of sympathetic regimes in Eastern Europe. The USA wanted to create a free trade area composed of democratic states. Exemplification through Yalta conference: Soviet actions in Poland, Romania, Bulgaria, etc and Allied actions in Western Europe, Greece.

Impact of the atom bomb and arms race

- Use of atom bombs on Hiroshima and Nagasaki had one aim of impressing the USSR and making them ready to make concessions in Eastern Europe. Stalin refused to be intimidated and in fact it made him even more suspicious of the USA and determined to make the Soviet Union a nuclear power as soon as possible; the development of the arms race.

The status of post-war Germany: Berlin crisis in 1949

- The Potsdam Conference and policy over Germany whereby the allied sectors remained free as compared to Soviet sector which was stripped of assets as reparations. The economic status of Germany: creation of Bizonia in West. Contrast between the developing capitalist west and centrally controlled east: introduction of Deutsche mark in West led to the Berlin Blockade in 1949.

Changing Soviet and Western diplomacy

- Truman and the policy of containment: British power had been destroyed; decline in their world commitments, specifically in Greece where civil war raged between Communists and Royalists. Fear of similar problems in Italy when allied troops left. Truman acknowledged world dividing into two hostile blocs in his speech to support free peoples and oppose totalitarian regimes.
- Marshall Plan exemplifies differences. Rejected by Soviets.
- Hardening of Western attitudes. Fulton speech by Churchill. Creation of competing military alliances.
- Creation of NATO and Warsaw Pact further polarised the world.

Cold War sealed with a Hot War: Korea

- Stalin encouraged Communist North Korea to invade Capitalist South. This led to American-led UN intervention on behalf of the South, and resultant Chinese intervention. Soviet and American pilots fought each other across Korea. Stalemate along 38th parallel.

41. The candidate assesses the accuracy of the view that the Cuban Crisis of 1962 was a direct consequence of the domestic pressures on Khrushchev using evidence and arguments such as:

Domestic pressures of Khrushchev

- Ongoing deadlock over Berlin and criticism of Khrushchev at home over cuts in the armed forces, economic failures and the issues surrounding de-Stalinisation, Hungary 1956, etc.
- Khrushchev believed a foreign policy coup would help improve matters for him at home.
- Khrushchev aware of need to raise the Soviet standard of living and to greatly expand his country's space program. He sought to increase international standing of USSR and his own authority.
- Khrushchev became premier after outmaneuvering rivals. He needed to maintain authority.
- Khrushchev wanted to avoid war with the Western nations and, at the same time, increase economic competition between Communist and non-Communist countries. The policy, known as peaceful co-existence, caused bitter quarrels between the Soviet Union and China. Khrushchev needed to maintain his status in Communist bloc.
- Khrushchev worried that if the Soviet Union lost the arms race it might invite a first strike from the United States. Soviet missiles placed in Cuba would solve that problem.

Other factors leading to the Cuban Crisis of 1962

Miscalculation by Khrushchev

- Khrushchev felt that Kennedy was a weak president after the Bay of Pigs, June 1961.
- Summit in Vienna to discuss Berlin. USA did little to oppose construction of Berlin Wall.
- Khrushchev felt that Kennedy lacked power and support to make concessions over the arms race. Events were to prove him wrong.
- Khrushchev had been advised that the installation could be done secretly and that the Americans would not discover the missiles until long after. The advice was wrong.

Ideological reasons

- Khrushchev was sympathetic to Castro. Some historians argue that he wanted to use Cuba as a launch pad for revolution in Central America. Missile deployment would provide protection for the revolution.

American policy over Cuba

- Domestic pressures for Kennedy as an explanation for the Cuban Crisis of 1962.

- In 1960 Kennedy became President. He promised tougher defense polices and progressive health, housing, and civil rights programs. But Kennedy won by just over 100,000 votes. He lacked a reliable majority in congress.
- Kennedy needed to show he had strength and determination to gain respect and support.
- Kennedy already embarrassed by Bay of Pigs fiasco where 1400 Cuban exiles landed and were crushed by Castro's army.
- Argument that this forced Castro to start preparing to defend himself against another attack and drew him closer to Khrushchev and the Soviet Union. Castro asked for significant conventional military aid.
- Kennedy under some pressure from CIA to continue to destabilize Castro's Cuba.
- America was very sensitive about the presence of a Communist state so close to Florida. American aggression seemed to be confirmed by the United States practising the invasion of a Caribbean island with a dictator named Ortsac: Operation Mongoose overseen by Robert Kennedy.

The nuclear arms race
- The Soviets wanted to place nuclear missiles in Cuba because they were trying to balance out the number of nuclear arms between themselves and the United States.
- The United States had placed their Jupiter missiles in Turkey and now the USSR felt very threatened. Kennedy had originally placed the Jupiter missiles in Turkey in 1961 because the United States had feared the possible nuclear capabilities of the Soviet Union. These missiles became a major threat to the Soviets because they were capable of striking anywhere in the USSR. Counter view that the missiles were obsolete.
- In order to defend themselves, and let the United States know what it was like to be surrounded by a deadly threat, the Soviets placed missiles in Cuba.

42. The candidate evaluates the importance of MAD in forcing the superpowers into attempts to manage the Cold War, using arguments and evidence such as:

Mutually Assured Destruction
- The development of vast arsenals of nuclear weapons from 1945 by both superpowers as a deterrent to the other side; a military attack would result in horrific retaliation.
- So many nuclear weapons were built to ensure that not all were destroyed even after a first-strike, and this led to a stalemate known as MAD. Arms race built on fear.
- In this it worked as the threat of nuclear war seemed very close on the discovery of Soviet nuclear missiles in Cuba in 1962. Before Khrushchev backed down nuclear war was threatened. It also illustrated the lack of formal contact between the superpowers to defuse potential conflicts.
- Introduction of a 'hot-line' between the Kremlin and White House in order to improve communication between the superpowers. Khrushchev and Kennedy also signed the Limited Nuclear Test Ban Treaty, the first international agreement on nuclear weapons.

Other factors

Technology: The importance of verification
- American development of surveillance technology (U2 and satellites) meant that nuclear weapons could be identified and agreements verified.
- Example of U2 flight over Cuba where Anderson photographed nuclear sites.
- Also U2 and satellite verification to make sure the Soviets were doing as promised at the negotiating table.
- Some historians think Arms Control would never have taken root, but for the ability of the sides to verify what the other was doing.

Economic reasons
- Developments in technology raised the costs of the Arms Race.
- The development of Anti-Ballistic Missile technology and costs of war led to SALT 1, and the ABM treaty.
- Limiting MIRV and intermediate missile technology led to SALT 2.
- The cost of 'Star Wars' technology also encouraged the Soviet Union to seek better relations.
- Khrushchev's desire for better relations between the superpowers in the 50s and 60s was, in part, about freeing up resources for economic development in the USSR. He hoped this would show the superiority of the Soviet system.
- Gorbachev wanted to improve the lives of ordinary Russians and part of this was by reducing the huge defence budget eg Intermediate Nuclear Forces Treaty, December 1987.

Co-existence and Détente
- Policies of co-existence and détente developed to defuse tensions and even encourage trade.
- Role of others like Brandt in West Germany in defusing tension through their policies of Ostpolitik, etc.

However there were also times of great tension between the superpowers.
- The Second Cold War – Soviet invasion of Afghanistan in 1979 and the advent of the Reagan presidency led to poor relations between the superpowers.
- Technology – also allowed both sides to continue to develop powerful armaments despite agreements. Intermediate and battlefield nuclear technology for example.

HIGHER HISTORY PAPER 2
2011

SPECIAL TOPIC 1: THE WARS OF INDEPENDENCE, 1286 – 1328

1. The candidate makes a judgement on how useful **Source A** is as evidence of why the Scots asked Edward to resolve the succession crisis in Scotland, in terms of:

Points from the source which show the candidate has interpreted the significant views:
- **Origin:** William Fraser, Bishop of St Andrews, the senior churchman in Scotland.
- **Possible purpose:** desire to avoid civil war by calling in independent, powerful neighbour; Fraser has also been accused of favouring Balliol's claim for the throne.
- **Content:**
  - A sad rumour reverberated among the people that our lady was dead, because of this the kingdom of Scotland is troubled and the community perplexed.
  - When the rumour was heard and published Sir Robert Bruce, who had not intended to come to the meeting came with a large retinue to confer with some who were there. Concern as his intentions are not known.
  - Fear of a general war and a large-scale slaughter unless the Most High, through your active involvement and good offices, administer a quick cure.

Points from recall which support and develop those in the source:
- Maid of Norway, only direct surviving blood relation to the dead Alexander III had died on reaching Orkney causing the succession crisis.
- Fraser believes that Edward should come to an understanding with Balliol, and this is the only way to avoid civil war.
- The Earls of Mar and Atholl were also collecting their army, which further led to fear of civil war.
- Scots were looking for Edward I to arbitrate between the two competitors.
- Fear that the guardianship would collapse.

Points from recall which offer a wider contextualisation such as:
- Alexander had had a good working relationship with Edward I of England.
- Edward I had a reputation as a statesman.
- Fraser's letter led to a reaction from the Bruce faction: letter of the seven earls.
- Balliol was also manoeuvring for the crown, he had established a close relationship with Bishop Bek, Edward's chief representative in Scotland.
- Desire of Edward to revive English claims of overlordship.
- The majority of Scots looked kindly on Edward's intervention, at least at the beginning.
- Any other relevant points.

2. The candidate makes a judgement on how fully Source B illustrates the relationship between John Balliol and Edward I:

Points from the source which show the candidate has interpreted the significant views:
- Balliol was aware that he needed to impress Edward if he wanted to secure the kingdom.
- John's inauguration as King of Scots was attended by English officials rather than the traditional Scottish nobles and churchmen.
- John was summoned, more than once, to Northern England by Edward and crumbled in face of demand he renew his homage to Edward as overlord.
- Edward insisted he hear appeals from Scottish courts at Westminster.

Points from recall which support and develop those in the source:
- Edward had decided that the Treaty of Birgham was no longer valid, since the marriage had not gone through; he demanded that John agree to this.
- It was only a week into his reign when the Burgesses of Berwick appealed to Edward over a court decision made by the Guardians, that John had upheld.
- Other appeals were quick in coming, such as the damaging Macduff case.
- Scottish kings were not used to being summoned to appear before an English court.
- Alexander III had refused to do homage for Scotland.
- John had to agree to some English members of his government.
- Edward forced John to release him of any promise he made about Scottish autonomy.
- John did try to resist but he backed down in the face of threats.

Points from recall which offer a wider contextualisation such as:
- In 1294 Edward ordered John to bring Scottish troops to fight for him in France.
- This angered the Scottish nobles who had good trading relations with France.
- Nobles elected a council of Guardians to help John stand up to Edward.
- John sent envoys to treat with the French king in 1295; this was formally ratified in 1296 after Edward's invasion.
- April 1296 John sent Edward a list of grievances with Edward's handling of the issue of overlordship, it has been suggested he was forced to do this by the guardians.
- John decided to submit to Edward hoping for leniency: he surrendered at Kincardine.
- From this John was brought before Edward at Brechin and ceremoniously stripped of his royal regalia, his surcoat stripped from his body.
- Here John earned his nickname from English soldiers, Toom Tabard.
- John was taken as a prisoner to London.
- Any other relevant points.

3. The candidate makes a judgement on the extent to which **Sources C** and **D** agree about career of William Wallace in terms of:

Overall **Sources C** and **D** both agree on Wallace about several events during his career. They agree that he started out as an outlaw, was defeated at Falkirk and was executed by Edward. However **Source C** paints Wallace in a very negative light demonstrating a lot of bias, whereas **Source D** offers a more balanced judgement of his career.

Source C	*Source D*
- Wallace was an outcast, robber and sacrilegious man. Wallace was a cruel robber who burnt churches and killed school boys.	- Wallace became an outlaw because his father did not sign the Ragman Roll, and the Sheriff of Lanark killed his mistress.
- Wallace could not resist the power of the English army at Falkirk, and fled leaving his people to be slain.	- Wallace's army were worn down by knights and archers, but he escaped after making sure that he rescued the survivors of his army.

Source C

- Wallace was taken prisoner by Edward's servants and taken to London.
- Wallace was executed, his head was placed on a stake on London Bridge and his body divided into four and sent to the 4 quarters of Scotland.

Source D

- Wallace was betrayed by Sir John Stewart of Mentieth.
- Wallace was put to death by being strangled and dismembered.

4. The candidate makes a judgement on how far **Source E** shows the opposition of many Scots to Robert Bruce in terms of:

Points from the source which show the candidate has interpreted the significant views:
- The letters, including the Declaration of Arbroath, were designed to show unity between the Scots in support of King Robert, but there were limits to this unity.
- Many lords did not like being associated with the letters because they had a deep distaste for Bruce's kingship which those letters championed.
- There was a rival claim by Edward Balliol, many Scottish nobles preferred his claim to the throne: Edward joined with Scots who had refused to enter Bruce's allegiance.
- Some nobles, including Agnes Comyn and William Soules conspired against Bruce.

Points from recall which support and develop those in the source:
- Barbour claimed that Soules was trying to assassinate Bruce, but in reality the conspirators hoped for a Balliol restoration and peace with England.
- Bruce learned about the conspiracy and struck first, arresting the ring leaders and sentencing many to death.
- This conspiracy was a reminder that some Scots believed Bruce was an usurper.

Points from recall which offer a wider contextualisation such as:
- Bruce alienated the powerful Comyn faction by murdering their chief, John "the Red" Comyn in 1306.
- Bruce forced to fight a civil war between 1306 and 1311 against the Comyns and their supporters.
- The Comyn family was defeated in the North East and Bruce brought fire and sword to the earldom of Buchan devastating the province for many years to come.
- Bruce's family had long been antagonists with other powerful West coast political powers, such as the MacDougalls.
- Bruce's bid for the throne saw the MacDougalls join his enemies.
- Bruce had held an armistice for many nobles at his Parliament in Cambuskenneth in 1314, but many had refused, they fled to England and forfeited their lands. These families became known as the Disinherited.
- Bruce forbade lords to have divided loyalties thus they could not swear an oath to Edward II for lands in England.
- Bruce was always willing to restore lands to the Disinherited, but they first had to swear loyalty to him.
- The issue that the lands of the Disinherited were given to favourites of Bruce. Perception that they were unfairly distributed.
- Any other relevant points.

SPECIAL TOPIC 2: THE AGE OF REFORMATION, 1542-1603

1. The candidate makes a judgement on how useful **Source A** is in showing evidence of the growth of Protestantism in Scotland before the Reformation in terms of:

Points from the source which show the candidate has interpreted the significant views:
- **Provenance:** Contemporary source written by a leading figure in the Reformation. Clearly biased and may have the benefit of hindsight.
- **Possible purpose:** To provide an account of the events surrounding the Reformation in Scotland and to encourage the new Protestant Church in Scotland.
- **Content:**
  - The death of Walter Myln increased fervour amongst the Protestants.
  - Perth was to become a Protestant town.
  - John Knox felt able to return to Scotland and openly preach in Perth.

Points from recall which support and develop those in the source:
- In the spring of 1559, Dundee and Perth declared themselves Protestant towns.
- Knox returned to Scotland and began preaching; causing a riot in Perth where religious houses were attacked.
- Knox had not been in Scotland at the time of Myln's death.

Points from recall which offer a wider contextualisation such as:
- There was a growing interest in Protestant ideas as bibles and other literature arrived from Europe.
- Acts of Parliament were passed to protect the Catholic Church in Scotland which indicates that Protestant ideas were becoming a threat.
- Impact of the preaching tour of George Wishart.
- Confidence had grown amongst the Scots Protestants after Elizabeth became Queen in England in 1558.
- By 1558 in some east coast burghs Protestant congregations were meeting and using the English Prayer book.
- The Beggars Summons – notices during winter of 1558-59 on Friary doors demanding that the Friars leave the friaries.
- Bonds had been entered into by some of the Scots nobility.
- Scottish Protestant Lords organised themselves as the Lords of the Congregation.
- Any other relevant points.

2. The candidate makes a judgement on how fully **Source B** explains why Mary, Queen of Scots lost her throne in terms of:

Points from the source which show the candidate has interpreted the significant views:
- Bothwell was regarded as the main suspect in the murder of Darnley.
- Mary failed to mourn for Darnley which did not look good.
- The trial of Bothwell was to prove to be a farce.
- Her marriage to Bothwell was Protestant which appeared hypocritical.

Points from recall which support and develop those in the source:
- Handbills went up in Edinburgh showing that popular opinion blamed Bothwell and implicated Mary.
- On the day of Bothwell's trial, Edinburgh was full of his armed supporters. This resulted in even Darnley's father, Lennox failing to give evidence.
- Catholics disappointed by Mary's actions; Mary did little to help the Catholic faith in Scotland.
- Marriage to Bothwell by Protestant rites alienated Catholics at home and abroad.

Points from recall which offer a wider contextualisation such as:
- Mary had the difficult situation of being a Catholic monarch in a land which had become Protestant.

- Marriage to Darnley lost Mary the support of her half brother James Stewart, Earl of Moray and other nobles. This led to the Chase-about-raid.
- Mary made a poor choice of husband in Darnley. His life style and his craving for power proved to be an embarrassment.
- Lack of attendance by Mary at Council Meetings was a likely cause of the Rizzio murder. Nobles feeling neglected.
- Mary's apparent closeness to Bothwell before the murder of Darnley heightened suspicion of her involvement.
- Murder of Darnley was a major blow to Mary's position but she may have survived if she had acted properly.
- The marriage to Bothwell was regarded as scandalous. Bothwell had just recently had his own marriage annulled.
- Bothwell was not a popular figure with many of the nobles.
- A sizeable number of the Nobles felt strongly enough to form the Confederate Lords and rise to overthrow Mary.
- In 1567, Mary was forced to abdicate by the Lords of the Congregation.
- She abdicated in favour of her infant son, with Moray returning as Regent.
- In 1568, she escaped and raised troops but was defeated by Moray. This resulted in her escape to England.
- Mary naively hoped that Elizabeth would provide her with troops; instead she was imprisoned until her execution in 1587.
- Any other relevant points.

3. The candidate makes a judgement on how far **Sources C** and **D** agree about James VI's attempts to control the Kirk in terms of:

Overall **Source C** agrees with **Source D** that King James used various methods to attempt to control the Kirk, although **Source C** also shows that the Kirk wished to control the doctrine of its ministers.

Source C	*Source D*
• General Assembly met at Perth as the king had requested.	• General Assembly met at Perth rather than St Andrews as ministers in the north more likely to support the King./The King could choose the place where the Assembly met.
• The King had the right to choose the date when the General Assembly would meet.	• No meeting to be held without the King's knowledge.
• In all the main towns ministers to be chosen by the congregation and the King.	• Ministers in the main towns should not be appointed without the consent of the King.
• No minister was to criticise the King and no man's name was to be rebuked from the pulpit.	• Restrictions were placed on ministers sermons in particular commenting on politics and censuring individuals.

4. The candidate makes a judgement on how far **Source E** explains the social impact of the Reformation on Scotland in terms of:

Points from the source which show the candidate has interpreted the significant views:
- The church sought to regulate the lives of everyone to an obsessive and unhealthy degree.
- Kirk Sessions aimed to regulate morals and manners to promote a godly society.

- People presumed guilty until proven innocent therefore a sizeable proportion of the population could expect to be before the session: example of St Andrews and number of cases of sexual misconduct.
- Elders policed their part of a parish and could even enter people's houses.

Points from recall which support and develop those in the source:
- From 1560 Kirk Sessions exercised the right of fining, imprisoning and excommunicating offenders against their authority in moral matters.
- 'Stool of repentance' used to chastise those who had broken the moral code. They would be rebuked in the presence of the congregation.

Points from recall which offer a wider contextualisation such as:
- Great emphasis was laid upon attendance at both daily and Sunday services and every effort was made by Kirk sessions to ensure that no possible diversions existed which might detain a congregation from their duties.
- Kirk Sessions enforced acts relating to the possession of Psalm Books and Bibles printed under the strict supervision of the General Assembly.
- Kirk Sessions were constantly occupied in their attempts to keep wedding and other celebrations within bounds.
- The observance of Festivals and Saint Days and the performance of plays were actively discouraged.
- From the 1570s increased Sabbatarianism.
- Increased interest in and persecution of witchcraft.
- Music and dancing were also at times actively discouraged.
- There were ambitious plans in the First Book of Discipline to provide for the poor from the revenues of the old church, but vested interests thwarted those ambitions and funds proved to be inadequate.
- Church distinguished between the deserving and the undeserving poor.
- The able-bodied poor were not to be helped nor were vagrants and unlicensed beggars; in fact they were often punished by whippings and branding.
- Poor relief was to be provided in the parish where you were born or lived in for some time.
- Those who were destitute were only allowed to beg in their own parish after being issued with a beggar's badge and becoming a licensed beggar or 'gaberlunzie'.
- Church collections and payments for use of parish mort cloth, as well as fines from those disciplined by the Church, were used for poor relief.
- Act of 1587 allowed magistrates to assess the inhabitants of the parish to provide for poor relief.
- Income for poor relief was always short of ideal.
- Kirk's efforts to extend Education had a major social impact as more Scots had a basic education. Although the aim to establish a school in every parish was slow to achieve.
- There was an increase in the numbers of universities in this period.
- Any other relevant points.

SPECIAL TOPIC 3: THE TREATY OF UNION, 1689-1740

1. The candidate makes a judgement on how useful **Source A** is as evidence of worsening relations between Scotland and England in terms of:

Points from the source which show the candidate has interpreted the significant views:
- **Origin:** Speech given by Stair in Parliament during the union debates.
- **Possible purpose:** remind Scots of treatment by England during Darien/support an incorporating union.

- **Content:**
  - Scotland suffered from a lack of co-operation from England.
  - England treated Scots as pirates and enemy aliens, not fellow British subjects.
  - England encouraged Spain to attack the Scots colony.

Points from recall which support and develop those in the source:
- King William objected to Darien as it threatened English trade.
- William influenced many English investors to withdraw from the Company, antagonised many Scots.
- William persuaded the Dutch to refuse to sell ships to the Scots.
- East India Company stopped foreign investment in Company of Scotland.
- William instructed English colonists in Jamaica not to offer help to the Scots.
- William was influenced by English foreign policy towards Spain and France.
- No security for Scotland from Union of the Crowns.

Points from recall which offer a wider contextualisation such as:
- King William firmly controlled Scotland to reduce threat of Jacobite rebellion.
- Glencoe Massacre (in which Stair himself had been complicit).
- England's war with France affected English dealings with Scotland.
- Jacobite plot to assassinate William further strained relations.
- Continued effects on trade of English Navigation Acts of the 1660's.
- Issues concerning the succession – Act of Settlement (England).
- Act of Security (Scotland) – threat to restore the Stuarts.
- Wool Act and Wine Act in Scotland.
- Alien Act in England threatening Scottish trade with England.
- Consequence of 1688-89 Revolution: Scottish Parliament – no longer willing to 'rubber stamp' decisions taken in England.
- Scotland's economic problems – seven ill years, no help from England.
- England's fear that France may use Scotland as 'back door' – threat of invasion.
- Influence of the English Court on Scottish government – Queen Anne would employ only those who would support the Hanoverian Succession.
- Distrust existing between Episcopalian Church and Presbyterian Church of Scotland.
- Captain Green executed in Leith.
- Covenanters still agitating for Covenant of 1638 to be observed.
- Any other relevant points.

2. The candidate makes a judgement on how fully **Source B** illustrates the arguments for and against the Treaty of Union in terms of:

Points from the source which show the candidate has interpreted the significant views:
- Scotland would become a province of England.
- Subjection of Scotland: Cornwall would send almost as many members to Parliament as whole of Scotland.
- Scots wanted to remain known as Scots and not British.
- Scotland had fought for honour as a nation and was recognised by foreign countries.

Points from recall which support and develop those in the source:
- The creation of 'Scotlandshire' was a genuine fear for opponents of union.
- 45 Scots MPs in the House of Commons was felt to be under-representation.

- Many cherished what Lord Belhaven called 'Mother Caledonia'.
- Opponents of union wanted Scotland to remain an independent nation.

Points from recall which offer a wider contextualisation such as:
Arguments against union
- British parliament would favour English trade over Scottish.
- Fear of loss of European trade.
- Royal burghs would be deprived of rights.
- Manufactures may be ruined.
- English currency, weights and measures might be introduced.
- Presbyterians feared a British parliament dominated by Anglican church with bishops' seats in the House of Lords.
- Fears of reduction in status of Scottish nobility in British parliament.
- Scots Episcopalians opposed union and Hanoverian succession – only Stuart dynasty might restore episcopacy to Scottish church.
- Fear of taxes
- Fear of taking on English debt
- Possible ruin of Scottish manufactures and economy

Arguments for union
- Advantages in commerce and trade.
- Economy would improve – national product would increase.
- Scotland's trade would catch up with other European nations'/Free trade with English colonies.
- Protection of being in Great Britain.
- Common interests already with England.
- Advantages of Scottish politicians being part of the court of the king in London.
- Hanoverian succession offered security to Protestantism thus reducing threat from Popery: compared with Edict of Nantes and persecution of Huguenots.
- Union reduced risk of war.
- Any other relevant points.

3. Overall **Source C** and **Source D** agree that the Squadrone and political management were reasons for the passing of the Treaty of Union, but they differ on the importance of the Equivalent.

Source C	*Source D*
Squadrone had key role in outcome of union vote.	Squadrone votes proved critical in securing approval for several articles.
The Equivalent was crucial in carrying the treaty.	The Equivalent did not bribe MPs – support for union depended on more than material gain.
The Equivalent was an inducement to the Squadrone Volante.	Eight of Squadrone did not benefit from government patronage.
Formidable political management machine of Court Party.	Court's success achieved by political management.

4. The candidate makes a judgement on how far **Source E** explains the economic effects of Union in terms of:

Points from the source which show the candidate has interpreted the significant views:
- Free trade only brought prosperity to a few.
- Most enterprising Scots after 1707 were smugglers or black marketers.
- Manufactures not swamped but only sluggish demand from England and colonies.
- Insignificant effects on agriculture.

Points from recall which support and develop those in the source:
- In the years immediately after 1707, the economic disadvantages severely outweighed the advantages; only by 1740 were the benefits becoming apparent.
- Only a small number of Scots engaged successfully with the colonies.
- Increased taxes and duties encouraged smuggling and black market.
- It was difficult for some industries to cope with English competition.

Points from recall which offer a wider contextualisation such as:
- Tobacco industry developed in Glasgow, but this was still in its infancy by 1740.
- Agricultural techniques improved.
- Increased investment in Scotland.
- 1727 – Royal Bank of Scotland founded.
- Board of Trustees for the Encouragement of Fisheries and Manufactures established.
- Paper industry failed.
- Scottish linen industry suffered in relation to English woollen industry.
- Merchant shipping benefited, particularly in trade with Baltic nations and the Caribbean.
- Trade with France was lost.
- Union forced many to emigrate.
- Increase in cattle trade in the Highlands.
- Malt Tax – resulted in increased cost of alcohol.
- Salt Tax – impact on fish curing industry.
- Any other relevant points.

SPECIAL TOPIC 4: MIGRATION AND EMPIRE, 1830–1939

1. The candidate makes a judgment on how useful **Source A** is as evidence of the reasons for Scottish migration and emigration in terms of:

Points from source which show the candidate has interpreted the significant views:
- **Origin:** Primary source; views of an emigration agent representing Canada.
- **Possible purpose:** to highlight a problem in attracting emigrants to Canada.
- **Content:**
  - Emigration Agencies actively working to attract emigrants.
  - New Zealand and Australian authorities work is widespread, offering free passages and other inducements and diverting potential recruits from Canada.
  - Newspapers also push their cause as they gain revenue from their advertisements.

Points from recall which support and develop those in the source:
- Domineering landlords and lack of real opportunities encouraged emigration from the Highlands of Scotland.
- Inducements offered by foreign lands eg free land in Canada.
- Use of free and assisted passages by many territories to encourage Scottish emigrants eg to both agricultural and urban workers.

Points from recall which offer a wider contextualisation such as:
- The Highland Problem.
- The Highland Clearances.
- Failure of the kelp and herring industries.
- Effects of the Agricultural Revolution on farming and employment.
- Effects of Industrial Revolution on craftsmen.
- Sub-division of land into crofts.
- Harsh employment conditions on the land.
- Government schemes to assist emigration eg Highland and Islands Emigration Society.
- Transport Revolution ie from sail to steam ships.

- Attractions of the 'big city' – employment, better wages, easier work.
- Discovery of gold in the USA.
- Any other relevant points.

2. The candidate makes a judgement on how far **Source B** illustrates the experience of immigrants in Scotland terms of:

Points from the source which show the candidate has interpreted the significant views:
- Members of Catholic Irish communities were involved – often in significant numbers – in strikes, trades unions and trades unions campaigns.
- This participation was both welcomed and sought by Scottish workers.
- Most of the (sectarian) incidents did not involve Scottish workers, but were instead 'Orange' and 'Green' disturbances involving Protestant Irish and Catholic Irish immigrants.
- Most Scottish workers remained aloof and let the immigrant groups continue their old battles.

Points from recall which support and develop those in the source:
- In the 1830s and 1840s many Scots were repelled by the poverty and disease of Irish immigrants, Catholic and Protestant alike.
- Riots by Scottish workers from the 1820s to 1850s were not sectarian in nature but directed against the activities of Irish strike-breakers (both Catholic and Protestant) and confined almost exclusively to Lanarkshire and Ayrshire.
- Mixed marriages between Catholics and Protestants became commoner as the century progressed, particularly in smaller communities where the choice of marriage partners was less.
- The Catholic church took steps to develop Catholic organisations and institutions (eg Celtic FC) to develop a distinct Catholic community.
- Pius X's 'Ne Temere' decree of 1908 on invalid marriages applied to every marriage of a Catholic, even when marrying someone who was not of his or her faith; this caused much heartache amongst non-Catholics who felt they were continually 'losing out'.
- The 1918 Education Act led to increasingly separate communities in religious terms.
- In the 1920s the Church of Scotland became overtly hostile to Roman Catholicism.
- As the Scottish economy collapsed in the 1920s and 1930s, workplace discrimination against Catholics grew.
- In the 1920s and 1930s a few anti-Catholic councillors were successful in local elections in Glasgow and Edinburgh (though many lost their seats at the first defence).
- Anti-Catholic (rather than anti-Irish) disturbances in Edinburgh in 1935 were condemned by the press and punished by the courts.
- The Protestant Irish assimilated more easily into Scottish society, but at the expense of their distinct identity.

Points from recall which offer a wider contextualisation such as:
- Lithuanian immigrants were largely employed in the coal industry; they changed their names to integrate more easily into Scottish society.
- Lithuanians were much fewer in numbers then Irish immigrants and not perceived as a threat to Scottish way of life by native Scots.
- Italians were accepted into Scottish society fairly readily, providing a service through cafes etc. Italians kept own identity through clubs and organisations.
- Italians suffered hostility in the years before World War II as concerns grew about Mussolini's actions.
- Jews settled in central Glasgow, typically setting up small businesses. As they prospered they moved to more affluent suburbs.

- Most immigrant groups suffered minor harassment at various times, both from native Scots and from other immigrant groups.
- Immigrants often settled initially in the poorest areas of towns and cities; in the nineteenth century this meant they suffered from deprivation in overcrowded slums.
- Immigrants in Glasgow particularly suffered alongside the poorer sections of native society from the epidemics of mid-century.
- By the 1890s, both Catholic and Protestant Irish were gaining apprenticeships and beginning to move up the social ladder.
- The First World War and the ensuing slumps led to the collapse of the Scottish economy; this prevented further upward social mobility to a large extent. It also meant there was little further immigration, so that those near the foot of the social structure tended to stay there.
- Any other relevant factors.

3. The candidate makes a judgement on how far **Sources C** and **D** agree about the contribution of Scots to the economic growth and development of the Empire in terms of:

Overall: **Source C** and **Source D** agree that emigrant Scots made a significant and positive contribution to the growth and economic development of the Empire, but while **Source C** is totally positive in the view, **Source D** adds a note of caution that some Scots made a less than positive contribution to their adopted land although the numbers are relatively few.

Developed through detail:

Source C
- Scots have played important roles in the economic development of New Zealand.
- Scots noted for their contribution to education, the first high school for girls in Otago opened in 1871 due to the efforts of a Scot.
- Scots were over-represented among those involved in health matters.
- Otago had strong links with the Edinburgh medical school and Scots-born people had a continuing impact in the scientific field.

Source D
- Enterprise of the Dunedin merchants has done much for the commerce and prosperity of Otago.
- The Scot has made his mark in the field of education, setting up schools in the area.
- Several of the Scots' descendants became doctors administering to the health of the local population.
- A Scot founded the Geological Survey Of New Zealand and managed New Zealand's premier scientific society.

4. The candidate makes a judgement on how **Source E** shows the importance of Empire to Scotland's development, in terms of:

Points from the source which show the candidate has interpreted the significant views:
- Empire enabled some firms and individuals to make great commercial fortunes.
- Empire offered opportunities of employment to the sons of the ascendant Scottish middle-class.
- Example of Jute trade: raw material came from the Indian province of Bengal. The textile manufactured from this imported good was subsequently exported all over the world.
- Heavy industries of Scotland exported a high proportion of their products. American grain might well be taken in sacks made in Dundee, by locomotives manufactured in Springfield near Glasgow, to be loaded onto ships built on the Clyde.

Points from recall which support and develop those in the source:
- Exemplification of firms and individuals who made fortunes, such as Clyde shipbuilders like Napier's, John Brown's and Beardmore's.
- Scotland exported to the Empire in great quantities: Springburn, produced one quarter of the world's locomotives in 1914.
- Scots exploited employment opportunities offered by Empire: Scottish middle-class boys had successful careers, especially in India, as civil servants, doctors and as soldiers.

Points from recall which offer a wider contextualisation such as:
- Scottish investors pioneer use of 'investment trusts' where professional managers enabled large numbers of modest investors to gain access to the rewards of large-scale investment. Cities like Edinburgh, Dundee and Aberdeen came to hold extensive investments abroad.
- Investment a double-edged sword as it also meant that capital left Scotland to finance projects abroad.
- Importance of commerce and Empire left Scotland vulnerable to international trade slumps.
- Low-wage economy encouraged in Scotland by export market led to considerable poverty for many with associated problems of poor housing, etc.
- Empire also allowed for the development of a skilled, literate working class in engineering, etc.
- Empire encouraged Scottish martial tradition: eg; Sir Charles Napier and Sir Colin Campbell in India.
- Any other relevant points.

SPECIAL TOPIC 5: THE IMPACT OF THE GREAT WAR, 1914 – 1928

1. The candidate makes a judgement as to how useful **Source A** is as evidence of the experience of Scots on the Western Front in terms of:

Points from the source which show the candidate has interpreted the significant views:
Origin:
- By Private Thomas McCall who fought in the assault at the Battle of Loos with the Cameron Highlanders. Useful as source is personal eyewitness account of the battle that became known as 'the Scottish battle'. The source also seems to be uncensored given the gory nature of content.

Possible Purpose:
- It was a record of what had occurred at the assault on Loos by a soldier of the Cameron Highlanders.

From source:
- Soldiers experienced fear of injury – "My God, I'm done for".
- Soldiers experienced camaraderie – "he lifted his wounded pal's kilt then gave a laugh."
- Soldiers experienced combat – "machine guns were raking the street and bayonet fighting was going on".

Distracter – details of hand-to-hand fighting or were the Jocks dealing with prisoners?

Points from recall which support and develop those in the source:
- Military tradition of Scots: kilted regiments considered to be good soldiers.
- Scots contribution to battle of Loos: deserves to be called a Scottish battle owing to the large number of Scottish troops in action. 30,000 took part in the attack.
- One third of British casualties were Scottish at Loos.
- Loos was first taste of action for Kitchener's New Army volunteers.
- The 9th and 15th Scottish Divisions were to be involved in the attack.

Points from recall which offer a wider contextualisation such as:
- Experience of Scots in Trenches: conditions such as trench foot, rats, etc.
- Experience of fighting and its effects: bombardment, shellshock, etc.
- Battle of the Somme: 3 Scottish divisions 9th, 15th [Scottish] and 51st [Highland] took part as well as numerous Scottish battalions in other units: ie the Scots Guards in the Household Division. 51 Scottish infantry battalions took part in the Somme offensive at some time.
- Battle of Arras: Saw concentration of 44 Scottish battalions and 7 Scottish named Canadian battalions, attacking on the first day, making it the largest concentration of Scots to have fought together.
- One third of British casualties were Scottish at Arras.
- Role in other battles, such as Cambrai and Third Ypres.
- Experience of Scottish women on Western Front: Scottish Ambulance Unit, etc as balance in question that asks only about "Scots on Western Front".
- Scots in leadership role: eg Douglas Haig.
- Any other relevant points.

2. The candidate makes a judgement on how fully **Source B** shows the impact of war on Scottish Society in terms of:

Points from the source which show the candidate has interpreted the significant views:
- Scottish recruitment was a "higher percentage than any other country in UK".
- "Scottish forces suffered disproportionately higher losses".
- "Wartime revolutionised the position of women in the economy".
- "The slaughter remained to haunt the nation".

Points from recall that support and develop those in the source:
Recruitment
- Recruitment and Conscription: By the end of the first week in September 1914, Glasgow was able to boast that it had recruited more than 22,000 men.
- By December 1914, 25% of the male labour force of western Scotland had already signed up.
- 13% of those who volunteered in 1914-15 were Scots.
- Young Scots urged to join the army through a mixture of peer pressure, feelings of guilt, appeals to patriotism, hopes for escapism and adventure, heroism, self sacrifice and honour. For the unemployed, the army offered a steady wage.
- Kitchener's campaign was a huge success: examples such as by the end of August 20,000 men from the Glasgow area had joined up.
- In Scotland there were no official 'Pals Battalions' but in reality – the Highland Light Infantry/Tramway battalion; the 16th battalion/the Boys Brigade.
- In Edinburgh, Cranston's battalion and McCrae's battalions became part the Royal Scots. McCrae's battalion was the most famous because of its connection with Hearts football club.

Casualty rates
- The official figure given at the end of the war calculated that Scotland had suffered 74,000 dead.
- Huge sacrifice of Scots during the war: of 557,000 Scots who enlisted in the services, 26.4% lost their lives. One in five British casualties were Scottish.
- Campaigners for a national war memorial claimed the figure was over one hundred thousand.

Women in Wartime economy
- Shift towards military and manufacturing employment and a temporary decline in some service industries.
- Number of women working increased from 593,210 in 1911 and 638,575 a decade later.

- Before the war less than 4,000 women worked in heavy industry in Scotland.
- Number of women employed in munitions in Scotland rose to 31,500 by October 1918.
- Many women workers were used for "dilution" of labour.
- Women worked as conductors on trams and buses, as typists and secretaries and nearly 200,000 women found work in government departments.

Remembrance
- Collective national grief in Scotland.
- Also great pride in the achievement of the Scottish units.
- Local memorials were erected around the country.
- Scots wanted their own memorial in tribute to their special sacrifice: Edinburgh castle houses the memorial and museum. It was officially opened in 1928. Over 148,000 Scottish names are carved on the national war memorial.
- The British Legion was set up and in 1921 the British Legion Scotland. Poppy day started at the same time. The act of silence at 11am on 11 November started in 1919.

Points from recall which offer a wider contextualisation such as:
- Pacifism and Conscientious Objectors: People objected for religious, ethical or political reasons.
- DORA took industries, communications and resources under direct Government control, censorship of the press, imprisonment of war protestors, civilians could be tried under court martial, reduced hours of public houses etc.
- Rent Strikes saw a prominent role played by women like Mary Barbour, Helen Crawfurd and Agnes Dollan.
- These women would even physically oppose evictions and won with the passing of the Rent Restriction Act freezing rent levels and introducing state intervention in the private housing rental market for the first time.
- Any other relevant points.

3. The candidate makes a judgement on how far **Sources C** and **D** agree about the economic effects of the war on Scotland in terms of:
Overall: **Sources C** and **D** broadly agree on the economic effects of the war on Scottish industries such as shipping, coal, jute and farming, although there are difference in the detail between the sources.

Developed through detail:

Source C	*Source D*
- The Clyde in 1913 launched 750,000 tons of shipping but by the end of the 1920s the Clyde was launching merely 56,000 tons of shipping.	- Between 1921 and 1923 shipbuilding on the Clyde dropped (and) the Clyde was already beginning to pay for the artificial boom which had rescued it during the war years.
- In 1913 Scotland employed 140,000 miners but 20 years later the coal industry was…producing a third less coal.	- Coal production suffered.
- The Dundee jute trade was deeply depressed.	- Jute production in Dundee was adversely affected by declining orders.
- In the late 1920s the value of Scottish farming was falling.	- According to the Board (of agriculture) the decline was not restricted to any particular part of the country but was widespread throughout Scotland.

4. The candidate makes a judgement on how far **Source E** explains reasons for the growth of radicalism in politics in Scotland in terms of:

Points from the source which show the candidate has interpreted the significant views:

- The most decisive feature was the collapse of Liberalism as an effective electoral force.... Among the working classes the Labour party was most likely to benefit from Liberal misfortunes.
- The rent strike had increased the prestige and influence of ILP.
- Labour also excelled in organisation. The focus was constantly on local issues.
- Labour gained the lion's share of the new post 1918 electorate.

Points from recall which support those in the source:

- Liberal Party split between Asquith's independent Liberals and Lloyd George's coalition Liberals.
- The Liberal government was blamed for being incompetent in its handling of the war.
- Liberal government blamed by working class for introducing dilution, passed legislation to regulate work practices, arresting strike leaders and initially supported landlords when they raised rents.
- Arguments within the party weakened its organisation and demoralised party workers. Party funds collapsed as members stopped paying subscriptions.
- Coupon Election.
- By 1924 the Liberals had only 8 MPs in Scotland.
- The Rent Strike did much to improve the credibility of the labour movement.
- Independent Labour Party instrumental in orchestrating and organising demonstrations.
- ILP supported workers grievances over prices and rents.
- Focus (of Labour party) was constantly on local issues of housing, rents and jobs. Both the ILP and the Labour party campaigned for reforms in housing and health after the war and their focus on local issues was a big reason for Labour's success in the 1920s.
- Effect of franchise reform of 1918 which almost trebled the size of the electorate from 779,000 in 1910 to 2,205,000 in 1918.
- By giving the vote to men on the basis of age then almost inevitably the new voters would come from the poorer sections of society and would be more likely to vote for the working class party representing their best interests – the Labour Party.

Points from Recall which offer a wider contextualisation such as:

- Catholic Irish vote deserted the Liberals and moved towards the Labour Party.
- Extension of the franchise to women. Many working class women had become politicised by their war work and the rent strikes. Women, such as Mary Barbour, Agnes Dollan and Helen Crawfurd became role models for women keen to make their voice heard politically for the first time.
- The effect of political developments such as the ILP and Red Clydeside.
- The Clyde Workers Committee (CWC) was formed to control and organise action for an extension of workers' control over industry.
- Papers like "Forward" and "Worker" suppressed.
- Influence of John MacLean, Willie Gallacher, Jimmy Maxton, John Muir, Tom Bell and Jock Smith. MacLean won the support of thousands of people with his socialist and anti war views.
- Forty Hours Strike and demonstration at George Square, waving of red flag, riot, troops and tanks appear on streets of Glasgow.

- In 1922 Labour won 29 seats in Scotland (10 in Glasgow) and then in 1924 they won 34 seats but saw this fall to 26 seats in second election in 1924 but in the same election the Liberals had fallen to 9 seats in Scotland.
- Any other relevant points.

HIGHER HISTORY PAPER 1
2012

1. Each question is marked out of 20.

2. In Paper 1 candidates will be rewarded according to:

(a) **Knowledge and Understanding – 6 marks are allocated for** the relevant knowledge they use to address the question. Marks will be awarded for each accurate, full point they make; these points may be further developed, as in the following example, relating to the effectiveness of the Liberal Reforms:

Old age pensions *(0 marks for stating this)* were given to all people over 70 *(1 mark)*; married couples received 7/6 and single people 5s *(a second mark for knowledge)*. This provision was not enough to live on, but old people were able to help pay their families if they lived with them *(no further mark for knowledge, but an argument which would receive credit under the category Argument and Evaluation)*.

(b) **Argument/Evaluation – 10 marks are allocated for** the quality of thought revealed in their answers by the arguments and evaluation demonstrated. This should be taken as including the extent to which the candidate:

- gives an answer which is relevant to the question and relates explicitly to the question's terms;
- argues a case;
- makes the various distinctions required by the question;
- responds to all the elements in the question, and to any isolated factor in particular;
- explains, analyses, debates and assesses rather than simply describes or narrates;
- answers with clarity and fluency and in language appropriate to historical writing at this level.

(c) **Structure – 4 marks are allocated for** the appropriateness of the introduction and conclusion, according to the degree to which the response

- establishes the context of the question, line of argument and the relevant factors to be considered in the introduction
- responds to the question in the form of a balanced conclusion based on the evidence and arguments deployed.

3. The following descriptions provide additional guidance on the marks awarded to essays displaying various characteristics. Many essays will exhibit some, but not all, of the features listed; others will be stronger in one area than another.

KNOWLEDGE – Up to 6 marks can be awarded
These are for substantive points and points further developed which are relevant and accurate.

STRUCTURE – Up to 4 marks can be awarded if:
The introduction clearly sets the issue in its wider context, indicates relevant factors and demonstrates a solid line of argument.
The conclusion is balanced, summarising the arguments and coming to an overall judgement directly related to the question.

ARGUMENT – Up to 10 marks can be awarded if:
The evidence is integrated into a sustained analysis.
The argument is sustained and balanced, with some awareness of alternative interpretations and/or historical debate.

Historical Study: British History

Church, State and Feudal Society

1. The candidate assesses the extent to which the contribution of the Church to society in medieval Scotland and England was confined to religion, using evidence and arguments such as:

Religious Role
- The medieval church offered the people the hope of salvation. The Church promised that in the afterlife things would improve, assuming that your soul was pure and free of sin This offered a certain amount of social control but offered comfort and stability, providing answers to difficult questions
- Church services such as christenings, marriages and burials were an important part of everyday life. The Church also celebrated holy days
- Religion offered a certain amount of understanding about the world. The existence of God helped to explain not only how the world worked but in a society without the benefit of science, the unexplained could often be frightening
- The importance of saints, relics and pilgrimages not only reinforced the power of God, but pilgrimage especially provided a way of opening new horizons and helping expand medieval Europe and trade
- Monasteries provided hope for a greater salvation through a life of prayer and devotion.

Social Role
- The Church often provided alms to the poor, offering the only real poor relief available
- The Church provided basic education for lay people, notably sons and daughters of nobility. The Church, particularly the monasteries, helped develop architecture, art and music. Universities provided degrees in theology, medicine and arts
- Church hospitals provided free medical care, especially for lepers
- The Church provided a social centre for rural and urban life; games and music were common after Sunday services.

Economic Role
- Monasteries made significant contributions to the economic development of the 12th century
- They helped to cultivate many barren areas of England and Scotland
- Some monasteries helped to fund and maintain important trades, such as the wool trade in Scotland.

Political Role
- The Church legitimised monarchs
- The papacy was a European power, able to influence other monarchs through the threat of excommunication and interdict
- Monarchs required the help of the clerics to run the government, count taxes and write laws
- In England the church was part of the feudal structure, able to raise armies to defend their lands, as the Bishop of Durham did at the Battle of the Standard in 1138.

2. The candidate assesses how successful David I of Scotland and Henry II of England's attempts to increase royal authority were, using evidence and arguments such as:

Development of royal authority

- Henry II faced a kingdom in turmoil after the civil war
- Bands of mercenaries roamed through the countryside, until Henry dismissed them
- English Barons had seized land, castles and taxes that they were not entitled to
- Henry successfully reformed criminal and civil law in England, through the Assizes of Clarendon (1166) and Northampton (1176). However, his attempt to reform ecclesiastical law was less successful
- David I was faced with several rebellions, the first in 1130, only six years after his inauguration
- New Scottish barons were given the rights to hold their own courts within their fiefs. This was an obvious extension of the king's law, rather than reliance on the traditional Celtic courts led by Brechons, experts in the law. Eventually these Celtic courts died out and were replaced with sheriff courts
- The gradual acceptance of the king's law led the way to the decrease of importance of the Mormaers and the acceptance of central control.

Development of the royal government

- David created a small but loyal group that had specific roles to aid him in the running of his household and the kingdom. Sheriffs replaced thanes in the remote areas of the kingdom. They offered direct royal contact for those away from the traditional seat of power
- Henry ordered an investigation into his sheriffs in 1170. Many were dismissed and replaced with Henry's loyal followers.

Development of the royal military forces

- The new feudal forces brought to David by his introduction of feudalism offered a significant advantage when dealing with the Celtic Mormaers. Traditionally it was the Mormaers who controlled the summoning of the Common army of Scotland. Now David had an independent force loyal to him. However, this force often did not work well with the other elements of the Scottish forces, as seen at the disastrous Battle of the Standard
- Henry's introduction of scutage allowed him to get around the problem of 40 days' knight service. He successfully restored order in England by dismantling illegally built castles and removing the barons' private armies of Flemish knights.

Development of the economy

- David introduced numerous monasteries, which helped to develop the wool trade, eg Melrose Abbey, and cultivate barren land. David granted charters to over 15 towns. Trade was encouraged with Germany, Scandinavia and France. David introduced the first Scottish coins to help promote trade
- Henry II established the exchequer under Nigel of Ely to rein in sheriffs who failed to pay taxes and ensure scutage (shield tax) and other forms of aid and direct taxes were paid on time.

Introduction of feudal landholding

- During his time in England, David became an admirer of the feudal landholding system. He introduced a form of military feudalism into areas of Scotland, notably the southwest, Lothian and the northeast. Noble families were given grants of land. In return they offered David their support, both politically and militarily.

Development of the Church

- Started by David's mother Margaret, the introduction of the Roman Church at the expense of the Celtic one offered a significant boon to the development of royal authority. As the Church preached the divine grace of the king, it was hard to justify any rebellions against him
- Henry famously ran into trouble in his attempts to establish more authority over the church in his dispute with Thomas Becket.

3. The candidate evaluates the extent to which the growth of towns led to the decline of feudal society, using evidence and arguments such as:

The growth of towns

- Townsmen had different rights than those living in the countryside
- Many had the rights to hold their own courts, and these were seen as free from feudal interference
- Towns could buy a charter, granting Burgh status, allowing them to freely trade with overseas merchants. Burgesses could buy and sell their holdings
- A villein who lived in the town for a year and a day would become a freeman
- The development led to creation of a sort of middle class gentry in the fifteenth century, the mediocre or middling sort.

Other factors

Gradual decline in the old feudal manor economy

- With markets for their goods fluctuating considerably, many nobles came to understand their weak economic position. For some it was better to let their peasants become tenants who rented their land than to continue as their feudal protector
- Without the need for a feudal lord and protector, there was little need for serfs or villeins. It was easier to hire laborers, and relying on fixed rates of income from rents or salaries became more common.

Changing social attitudes

- Peasants who could afford to purchase or rent extra land could propel themselves upwards on the social ladder
- The de la Poles family in Hull rose from traders to become royal bankers, and the Pastson family rose out of serfdom to become country gentry
- Social commentators like Peter Idley complained that it had become impossible to tell the difference from "knave and Knight", because they dressed alike.

Growth of trade/mercantilism

- It has been argued that the feudal structure and serfdom hampered entrepreneurial merchants in England and Scotland. Many found the freedom of burgh life allowed them to develop trade without the burden of labour services or restrictions in movement
- Others discovered that sheep were a far more profitable resource than peasants could ever be, leading to development of mercantile skills
- Development of an affluent merchant class.

Black Death

- The decline in the population meant that the survivors, particularly of the lower classes, could demand and often received better wages for their labour. Wage levels in England roughly doubled. Indeed, the shortage of laborers is often seen as causing the decline of serfdom in Western Europe
- Parliament in England attempted to halt this decline by passing the "Statute of Laborers" in 1351, but it wasn't very effective and was mostly ignored

- Landowners for the first time needed to negotiate for their serfs' services, leading to higher wages and better living conditions for those that survived
- The Black Death led to the old feudal relationship between lord and serf disappearing.

Peasants' Revolt

- In England, the attempts of the Statute of Laborers in 1351 to force peasants back into serfdom were widely and strongly resisted. The extent of the revolt and the impressive way in which it was organised shows that the old feudal consensus had broken down
- The Peasants' Revolt was a reaction to the attempts to force peasants to return to the old ideas of labour services.

The Century of Revolutions 1603 – 1702

4. The candidate assesses the effectiveness of Charles I's rule in Scotland between 1625 and 1642, using evidence and arguments such as:

Political policy

- Charles I's policies which took power and land from Scottish nobles
- King did not visit Scotland until 1633 when he was crowned there
- Appointed bishops rather than nobles to Scottish Privy Council
- John Spottiswoode appointed Chancellor, first non-secular official in this position since Reformation
- Charles I gave increasing power to bishops, undermining status of Scottish nobility
- Stuart notion of Divine Right of Kings was brought to an end by Scots opposition to Charles I's attempts to impose his will on Scottish people.

Religious policy

- Charles I introduced William Laud, the Archbishop of Canterbury, to Scotland in 1633
- Laud proceeded to oversee Anglican practice in Scottish churches
- Many resented influence of Laud
- King approved of unification of churches without consulting Privy Council
- 1635 Book of Canons declared that monarch had authority over Church of Scotland and introduced new Service Book, a Scottish bishops' variation of English Prayer Book
- 23 July 1637 English Prayer Book was read at St Giles Cathedral by Dean, John Hanna, who subsequently had a stool thrown at him by a serving woman, Jenny Geddes
- In chaos that ensued, Bishop of Edinburgh was shouted down by crowd in support of Geddes
- Across Scotland people declared opposition to Service Book, placing Charles I's Privy Council in difficult position, caught between king and his rivals.

The Covenanters

- Covenanting movement challenged Charles I over religious policies and was active politically
- Covenanters wanted to preserve Presbyterianism in Scotland
- National Covenant was signed in 1638
- Covenant designed to promote a church free from monarchical meddling
- Charles I failed to suppress Covenanters, contributing to outbreak of War of the 3 Kingdoms
- During war, English Parliament's treaty of alliance with Scottish Covenanters – the Solemn League and Covenant of 1643 – was key feature of positive change in fortunes of king's enemies.

1st Bishops' War

- 1st Bishops' War took place in 1639
- Charles I could not raise enough money to fight war effectively, was forced to agree to truce in June as part of Pacification of Berwick
- As well as conceding military failure, truce gave Scots religious freedoms
- Charles I's inability to put down Scots brought an end to his "Eleven Years' Tyranny" in England
- King recalled Parliament in 1640 to request revenue to continue war with Scotland
- Short Parliament lasted one month as king dissolved it rather than debate his role during Eleven Years as condition of Parliamentary granting of funds.

2nd Bishops' War

- 2nd Bishops' War was continuation of first but ended in equal humiliation for Charles I in Treaty of Ripon, October 1640
- Treaty cost England the price that Scottish Parliament had to pay for its forces
- Defeat by Scots forced king to recall Parliament, this time after being advised to do so by grouping of peers known as Magnum Concilium
- Long Parliament was to last longer than previous one, but still represented downturn in king's fortunes, as English Civil War shortly followed.

5. The candidate evaluates the importance of religious issues in causing the Revolution of 1688 to 1689, using evidence and arguments such as:

Religious issues

- Issue of church governance which arose before Civil War had not been resolved
- Many MPs fearful of continued Stuart dominance of Anglican Church policy
- James II promotion of Roman Catholics to key posts antagonised Presbyterians
- Heir to the throne to be raised as a Roman Catholic
- Divide between Episcopalians and Presbyterians in Scotland created hostility from Scottish Parliament towards monarchy.

Other factors

Political issues

- Divine Right and absolutism as practised by Stuart monarchs
- Status of monarchy questioned by Parliament
- Charles II's dismissal of Parliament resembled Charles I's 11-Year Tyranny
- James II's use of Suspending and Dispensing Powers seen as an abuse by Parliament
- Questions raised over control of the army.

Lines of authority Crown and Parliament

- There were no clear lines of authority
- Questions existed over who held sway in religious matters; Parliament feared a monarch could try to impose Roman Catholicism on country
- Still possible for monarch to be financially independent of Parliament and manipulate succession in favour of Roman Catholic line
- Both Charles II and James II had proved it was possible for monarch to rule without Parliament, influence legislative and judicial procedure, control army for own means, and assert religious and political will on Scotland and Ireland
- Parliament saw need to agree constitutional status for monarchy.

The role of Parliament

- Parliament resented James II's abuses of power but took comfort from thought that he would be succeeded by Protestant daughter Mary
- However, king married again and had son, to be raised as Roman Catholic
- June 1688, Parliament wrote to Mary, by now married to Dutch Prince William of Orange, offering Crown
- They arrived in November with army and on Christmas Day James II fled to France after younger daughter Anne as well as leading generals declared support for Mary
- William and Mary became joint sovereigns on February 13th 1689
- With no Bill of Rights, any future monarchs, including William and Mary, could preach notions of Divine Right, absolutism and passive obedience
- Future limitations on power of monarchy would have to be written into law
- In 1689 Parliament drew up Bill of Rights, which legalised new relationship between Crown and Parliament
- This would ensure no future king or queen could attempt absolutism
- Bill of Rights would be part of wider set of legal provisions for new order in country
- Settlement established that kings and queens should depend upon Parliament for finance, succession would be determined by Parliament and not sitting monarch, judicial system would be controlled by Parliament, and no future monarch could rule without Parliament.

James II

- Ascended throne in 1685 upon death of older brother
- James II, who practised Roman Catholicism, attempted to rule absolutely
- Dismissed Parliament in 1685
- Replaced Anglican advisors with Roman Catholic ones; placed Roman Catholics in important posts at Oxford and Cambridge Universities
- Stationed 13,000-strong army outside London
- Re-established Prerogative Courts in 1686
- 1687, used Suspending Powers to suspend laws against Roman Catholics
- Used Dispensing Powers to dismiss these laws from statute books.

Legacy of Charles II

- Charles II, who had been exiled in France during Interregnum, had accepted limitations on his power when monarchy was restored in 1660
- Prerogative law courts were abolished, non-parliamentary taxation was prohibited, and Triennial Act remained in place
- Loopholes, however, meant king could still make policy
- Puritans lost power in House of Commons
- Towards end of reign Charles II ruled without Parliament for 4 years
- Divine Right preached from pulpits.

6. The candidate assesses the validity of the view that financial reform was the most significant change brought about by the Revolution Settlement, using evidence and arguments such as:

Finance

- In time of James I and Charles I, monarchy could exist financially independently of Parliament. This now impossible
- King and Queen were granted £700,000 for court expenses in 1689
- From then on Parliament voted to give Crown money annually as part of Civil List system
- Procedure of audit established for MPs to check expenditure of monarch

- Fiscal power now in hands of House of Commons
- However monarch would not have to make unpopular moves of raising taxes himself from now on.

Religion

- Before 1688, Crown dictated religious development of country
- After Settlement, hundreds of High Anglicans were expelled from their posts because they refused to recognise authority of William III
- Toleration Act of 1689 passed which provided for free public worship for all except Roman Catholics and Unitarians
- Roman Catholics still ineligible for elected posts in towns or Parliament
- Parliament now held more sway in religious matters
- However monarch still enjoyed political advantages of being head of church.

Legal

- Stuart monarchs had abused legal system and courts
- Legal settlement established Parliamentary control over these areas
- Later, Act of Settlement of 1701 stated judges could only be removed from their positions if Parliament demanded this
- From now on ministers impeached by House of Commons could not be pardoned by Crown
- 1695, Law of Treason altered to give defendants right to be given copy of indictment against them, right to be defended by Counsel and call witnesses in their defence
- An act of treason needed two witnesses against defendant instead of previous one
- Parliament now enforcing own control over judicial procedure
- However monarchs could still appoint judges who might be favourable to them.

Political

- In days before Civil War, Stuart monarchs had been able to rule without Parliament and curtail Parliamentary freedom of speech
- Revolution Settlement provided for another Triennial Act in 1694, which was intended to keep MPs more closely in touch with public opinion
- Licensing Act repealed in 1695, removing restrictions on freedom of press to report Parliamentary criticism of Crown
- William and Mary had to agree to Bill of Rights before they were given throne, legalising new relationship between Crown and Parliament
- This ensured no future king or queen could attempt absolutism
- Members of Parliament could now speak freely when voicing their opinion of monarch
- However, monarch could still dismiss Parliament at will.

The succession

- Before Settlement, monarchs approved own successors
- Bill of Rights declared no Roman Catholic could become king or queen
- Later, Act of Settlement of 1701 stated if William and Mary had no heirs the throne would pass to Sophia of Hanover, Protestant daughter of Elizabeth of Bohemia, sister of Charles I
- Act said all future monarchs should be members of Church of England
- Parliament now governed question of who ascended throne.

Differences between England and Scotland

- Settlement now allowed Scotland to have own church, Presbyterian Kirk
- Scottish Parliament had greater share in government of Scotland.

The status of the army
- Charles I had been able to raise army in 1642
- Revolution Settlement meant Parliament gained partial control of army
- Monarch not given enough money to maintain standing army
- Mutiny Act of 1689 legalised army, this act had to be passed annually by Parliament, which forced king to summon Parliament in order to do so
- Implications for implementation of foreign policy
- Royal authority over military matters now passed to the House of Commons.

Loopholes
- Although Revolution Settlement handed a lot of power from Crown to Parliament, loopholes in agreement meant monarch still held executive power and controlled foreign policy, declaring war and signing treaties
- Monarch still the source of patronage in army and navy
- Monarch still created peers, and could therefore control House of Lords
- Revolution Settlement, therefore, did not completely hand over power to Parliament
- It was a compromise which acted as a halfway-house between Crown and Parliament, and government business was negotiated and conducted between the two.

The Atlantic Slave Trade

7. The candidate assesses the extent to which the slave trade was the major factor in the development of the British economy in the eighteenth century, using evidence and arguments such as:

Evidence that the slave trade was important
- Importance of the slave trade to the development of the economy: profits accruing from tropical crops: financial, commercial, legal and insurance institutions emerged to support the activities of the slave traders. Slave traders became bankers and many new businesses were financed by profits made from slave trading
- The slave trade played an important role in providing British industry with access to raw materials and this contributed to the increased production of manufactured goods
- Ports such as London, Bristol and Liverpool prospered as a direct result of involvement in the slave trade; other ports such as Glasgow profited from trade with the colonies. Thousands of jobs were created in Britain supplying goods and services to slave traders
- Liverpool became a major centre for shipbuilding largely as a result of the trade
- Manchester exported large percentage of cotton goods to Africa
- The slave trade was important to the economic prosperity and well-being of the colonies
- Investment from the slave trade went into the Welsh Slate Industry
- The slave trade was an important training ground for British seamen, providing experienced crews for the merchant marine and the Royal Navy
- Wealth generated by the slave trade meant that domestic taxes could be kept low
- Argument that the slave trade was the vital factor in Britain's industrialisation was put forward in Williams' Capitalism and Slavery thesis.

Evidence that other factors were important
- Changes in agriculture: these created an agricultural surplus which:
  – fed an expanding population
  – produced a labour force in the towns for use in factories

  – created a financial surplus for investment in industry and infrastructure.
- Technological innovation: development of water and steam power; new machinery; transport changes
- Mineral and energy resources, particularly iron and coal
- Political stability
- Much of the profits of slavery were dissipated in conspicuous consumption eg landed estates.

8. The candidate evaluates the validity of the view whether the slave trade was too important to the British economy to allow it to be abolished, using evidence and arguments such as:

The importance of the slave trade to the British economy
- It generated finance – West Indian colonies were an important source of valuable exports to European neighbours. Taxes would have to be raised to compensate for the loss of trade and revenue. Abolition would help foreign rivals such as France as other nations would fill the gap left by Britain
- British cotton mills depended on cheap slave produced cotton
- Africa provided an additional market for British manufactured goods
- Individuals, businesses and ports in Britain prospered on the back of the slave trade
- Shipbuilding benefited as did maritime employment.

Other factors

Pressure exerted by vested interests
- Successive British Governments were influenced by powerful vested interests such as MPs and merchants from London, Liverpool and Bristol
- Slave owners and their supporters argued that millions of pounds worth of property would be threatened by the abolition of the slave trade. The slave trade was necessary to provide essential labour on the plantations. Abolition of the slave trade would ruin the colonies.

The events of the French Revolution
- These encouraged the belief among many MPs that the abolitionist cause was associated with revolutionary ideas eg Clarkson openly supported the French Revolution. Radicals used the same tactics as abolitionists to win public support – associations, petitions, cheap publications, public lectures, public meetings, pressure on Parliament. Some abolitionists were linked to radicals and therefore they had to be resisted because of fear that events in France may be repeated in Britain.

Slave rebellion in Saint-Domingue
- Abolition was associated with this symbol of brutal violence and in turn led to an exaggerated, general fear of slave revolts. Toussaint l'Ouverture was denounced. This was linked to fears of Jacobinism
- Slave violence played into the hands of the slave lobby, confirming their warnings of anarchy.
- Britain suffered humiliation when it attempted to take the rebel French Colony, beaten by disease and the ex-slave army.

Propaganda against abolition
- Supporters of slavery and the slave trade could try to claim that the enslaved on plantations were treated at least as well as the working classes in Britain.

Fears over national security
- Abolition could destroy an important source of experienced seamen it was argued thus there was a possibility that Britain would lose its advantage over its maritime rivals. On the other hand, the Triangular Trade was arguably a graveyard for British seamen.

9. The candidate evaluates the significance of the campaign organised by the Anti-Slavery Society in bringing about the abolition of the slave trade, using evidence and arguments such as:

The campaign of the abolitionist movement
- Thomas Clarkson obtained witnesses for the Parliamentary investigations of the slave trade which provided Wilberforce with convincing evidence for his speeches
- Books and pamphlets published eg eyewitness accounts from former slaves such as Olaudah Equiano
- Campaigns to boycott goods produced by slaves in the West Indies such as sugar and rum
- Petitions and subscription lists, public meetings and lecture tours involving those with experience of slave trade eg Olaudah Equiano, churches and theatres used for abolitionist propaganda, artifacts and illustrations eg Wedgwood pottery
- Lobbying of Parliament by abolitionists to extract promises from MPs that they would oppose the slave trade. Effective moderate political and religious leadership among the abolitionists influenced major figures such as Pitt and Fox; abolitionists gave evidence to Parliamentary Commissions.

Other factors

The role of Wilberforce
- Wilberforce put forward the arguments of the Society for the Abolition of the Slave Trade in Parliament for eighteen years
- Wilberforce's speeches in Parliament were graphic and appealing
- Wilberforce's Christian faith had led him to become interested in social reform and link the issues of factory reform in Britain and the need to abolish slavery and the slave trade within the British Empire
- Wilberforce was prepared to work with other abolitionists to achieve his aims, eg Thomas Clarkson.

Effects of slave resistance
- Successful slave rebellion in Saint-Domingue led to an exaggerated, general fear of slave revolts.

Economic factors
- Effects of wars with France – slave trade declined by two-thirds as it was seen as harming the national interest in time of war. The slave trade had become less important in economic terms – there was no longer a need for large numbers of slaves to be imported to the British colonies. There was a world over-supply of sugar and British merchants had difficulties re-exporting it.

Military factors
- Napoleon's efforts to restore slavery in the French islands meant that the abolitionist campaign would help to undermine Napoleon's plans for the Caribbean. The Act banning any slave trade between British merchants and foreign colonies in 1806 was intended to attack French interests.

The Religious Revival
- Role of the Quakers and other non-conformists
- Role of people like John Newton: ex slave ship captain and now clergyman
- Religious arguments against slavery.

Britain 1851 – 1951

10. The candidate assesses the validity of the view that Britain was still far from being a democratic country by 1928, using evidence and arguments such as:

The vote
- In 1867 most skilled working class men in towns got the vote
- In 1884 many more men in the countryside were given the vote
- In 1918 most men over 21 and some women over 30 gained the vote
- Finally in 1928 all men and women over 21 were given the vote.

Fairness
- Secret Ballot 1872 freed voters from intimidation
- Corrupt and Illegal Practices Act 1883 limited the amount spent campaigning
- Re-distribution of seats in 1867, 1885 and 1918 all helped created a fairer system of voting
- The effectiveness of these varied; they were less effective in areas where the electorate was small, or where a landowner or employer was dominant in an area, eg Norwich.

Choice
- Although the working class electorate increased by 1880s there was no national party to express their interests. The Liberals and Conservatives promoted middle, even upper class capitalist values. The spread of socialist ideas and trade unionism led to the creation of the prototype Labour Party – the LRC – by 1900 thereby offering a wider choice to the electorate.

Access to information
- Education – in the later 19th Century there was a great increase in literacy and hence access to information on which to base choice. Also railways spread information nationally and were important to the growth of democracy.

National Party Organisation
- As the size of the electorate grew individual political parties had to make sure their 'message' got across to electorate eg development of National Liberal Federation, Conservative Central Office, Primrose League.

Power of Lords
- From 1911 Lords could only delay bills from the House of Commons for two years rather than veto them. They had no control over money bills.

Widening opportunity to become MP
- The property qualification to be MP was abolished 1858. Payment for MPs began in 1911 enabling working class men to sit
- By 1928 Parliament was much more fully representative of the British people.

Points still to be resolved included
- Undemocratic anomalies – plural votes and the university constituencies – were not abolished until 1948
- In 1949 the two year delaying power of the House of Lords was reduced to only one year, but the power of House of Lords in law making still continues
- Voting system still first past the post in UK.

11. The candidate assesses the extent to which the Liberal reforms of 1906 to 1914 made a significant improvement to the lives of the British people, using evidence and arguments such as:

The young
- Children were thought to be the victims of poverty and unable to escape through their own efforts. In this way they were seen as 'the deserving poor'. Child neglect and abuse were seen as problems associated with poverty
- The Provision of School Meals Act allowed local authorities to raise money to pay for school meals but the law did not force local authorities to provide school meals
- Medical inspections after 1907 for children were made compulsory but no treatment of illnesses or infections found was provided until 1911

- The Children's Charter of 1908 banned children under 16 from smoking, drinking alcohol, or begging. New juvenile courts were set up for children accused of committing crimes, as were borstals for children convicted of breaking the law. Probation officers were employed to help former offenders in an attempt to avoid re-offending
- The time taken to enforce all the legislation meant the Children's Charter only helped improve conditions for some children during the period.

The old
- Rowntree had identified old age as the time when most people dropped below his poverty line. Old age was inescapable so was clearly associated with the problem of poverty
- Old Age Pensions Act (1908) gave people over 70 up to 5 shillings a week. Once a person over 70 had income above 12 shillings a week, their entitlement to a pension stopped. Married couples were given 7 shillings and 6 pence
- The level of benefits was low. Few of the elderly poor would live till their 70th birthday. Many of the old were excluded from claiming pensions because they failed to meet the qualification rules.

The sick
- Illness can be seen as both a cause and consequence of poverty
- The National Insurance Scheme of 1911 applied to workers earning less than £160 a year. Each insured worker got 9 pence in benefits from an outlay of 4 pence – 'ninepence for fourpence'
- Only the insured worker got free medical treatment from a doctor. Other family members did not benefit from the scheme. The weekly contribution was in effect a wage cut which might simply have made poverty worse in many families.

The unemployed
- Unemployment was certainly a cause of poverty
- The National Insurance Act (Part 2) only covered unemployment for some workers in some industries and like (Part 1) of the Act, required contributions from workers, employers and the government. For most workers, no unemployment insurance scheme existed.

Other reforms which could be argued helped address problems associated with poverty
- In 1906 a Workman's Compensation Act covered a further six million workers who could now claim compensation for injuries and diseases which were the result of working conditions
- In 1909, the Trade Boards Act tried to protect workers in the sweated trades like tailoring and lace making by setting up trade boards to fix minimum wages
- The Mines Act and the Shop Act improved conditions.

12. The candidate assesses the validity of the statement that the Labour Government of 1945 to 1951 met the needs of the people 'from the cradle to the grave', using evidence and arguments such as:

Beveridge Report in 1942 identified 5 giants of poverty: Want, Disease, Ignorance, Squalor and Idleness.

Want
- 1946 the first step was made: the National Insurance Act: consisted of comprehensive insurance sickness and unemployment benefits and cover for most eventualities
- It was said to support people from the 'cradle to the grave' which was significant as it meant people had protection against falling into poverty throughout their lives.
- This was very effective as it meant that if the breadwinner of the family was injured then the family was less likely to fall further into the poverty trap, as was common before. However, this act can be criticised for its failure to go far enough
- Benefits were only granted to those who made 156 weekly contributions

- In 1948 the National Assistance Board was set up in order to cover those for whom insurance did not do enough
- This was important as it acted as a safety net to protect these people
- This was vital as the problem of people not being aided by the insurance benefits was becoming a severe issue as time passed. Yet, some criticised this as many citizens still remained below subsistence level showing the problem of want had not completely been addressed
- Family Allowance Act.

Disease:
- Est. of the NHS in 1948 dealt effectively with the spread of disease
- The NHS was the first comprehensive universal system of healthcare in Britain
- Offered vaccination and immunisation against disease, almost totally eradicating some of Britain's most deadly illnesses
- It also offered helpful services to Britain's public, such as childcare, the introduction of prescriptions, health visiting and provision for the elderly, providing a safety net across the whole country: the fact that the public did not have to pay for their healthcare meant that everyone, regardless of their financial situation, was entitled to equal opportunities of health care they had previously not experienced
- NHS could be regarded as almost too successful. The demand from the public was overwhelming, as the estimated amount of patients treated by them almost doubled
- Introduction of charges for prescriptions, etc.

Ignorance
- Reform started by the wartime government: The 1944 Education Act raised the age at which people could leave school to 15 as part of a drive to create more skilled workers which Britain lacked at the time. Introduction of school milk, etc
- Labour introduced a two-tiered secondary schooling whereby pupils were split at the age of 11 (12 in Scotland) depending on their ability. The smarter pupils who passed the "11+ exam" went to grammar and the rest to secondary moderns
- Those who went to grammar schools were expected to stay on past the age of 15 and this created a group of people who would take senior jobs in the country thus solving the skills shortages. Whilst this separation of ability in theory meant that children of even poor background could get equal opportunities in life, in practice the system actually created a bigger division between the poor and the rich
- Labour expanded university education: introduction of grants so all could attend in theory.

Squalor
- After the war there was a great shortage of housing as the war had destroyed and damaged thousands of homes; and the slum cleaning programmes of the 1930s had done little to rectify the situation which was leading to a number of other problems for the government
- Labour's target for housing was to build 200,000 new homes a year. 157,000 pre-fabricated homes were built to a good standard, however this number would not suffice and the target was never met
- Bevan encouraged the building of council houses rather than privately funded construction
- The New Towns Act of 1946, aimed to target overcrowding in the increasingly built up older cities. By 1950, the government had designed 12 new communities
- In an attempt to eradicate slums the Town and Country Planning Act provided local communities more power in regards to building developments and new housing
- By the time Labour left government office in 1951 there was still a huge shortfall in British housing.

Idleness
- Unemployment was basically non-existent so the government had little to do to tackle idleness
- The few changes they did make were effective in increasing the likelihood of being able to find work, because they increased direct government funding for the universities which led to a 60% increase in student numbers between 1945-46 and 1950-51 which helped to meet the manpower requirements of post-war society. This provided more skilled workers and allowed people from less advantaged backgrounds to pursue a higher education, aiming to keep unemployment rates down
- Labour government also nationalised 20 percent of industry – the railways, mines, gas and electricity. This therefore meant that the government were directly involved with people employed in these huge industries which were increasing in size dramatically
- This tackled idleness by the government having control which meant that employees were less likely to lose their job through industries going bankrupt and people were working directly to benefit society
- Marshall Plan: financial aid from U.S.A.

Britain and Ireland 1900 – 1985

13. The candidate assesses how far World War One changed political attitudes towards British rule in Ireland, using evidence and arguments such as:

Irish attitudes to World War I
- Initially war brought prosperity to Ireland - manufacturing and farming, low unemployment thus improving relations between GB and Ireland
- Propaganda – powerful Germany invading helpless and small Catholic Belgium so Ireland supported GB
- Ulster very supportive of Britain to ensure favourable treatment at the end of the war
- Nationalists and Redmond backed war to get Home Rule, urging Irish men to enlist
- Press gave support to the war effort
- Irish Volunteers gave support to help Home Rule be passed after the war
- Recruitment was successful in the south as almost ¼ million men join up.

The Nationalist Movement
- Opposition to war very much a minority in 1914 but supported by Sinn Fein and Arthur Griffith (not powerful at this time), as well as Pearse, Connolly and their supporters and also a section of the Irish Volunteers. This damaged relations with Britain.

Easter Rising
- Rebels saw war as chance to rid Ireland of British by force
- Felt it was opportunity to gain independence by force as Britain had their troops away fighting the Germans in World War I. This greatly strained relations between Britain and Ireland
- Britain had to use force to suppress rebellion, such as using the Gunboat, 'Helga' to sail up the River Liffey and fire on the rebels in the GPO, thus distracting GB's attention and resources away from War effort, thus straining relations
- Strong criticism of Rising initially from the public, politicians, churchmen, as well as press for unnecessary death and destruction. 450 dead, 2500 wounded, cost £2½ million, showing that majority still sided with GB therefore indicating that there was not too much damage to relations between the two countries
- Initial hostility by majority of Irish people to Rising by small group of rebels, majority of people supported Redmond and the Nationalist Party
- Strong hostility and criticism by Dubliners to rebels for destruction of city centre.

Changing attitudes towards British rule after 1916
- The secret court martial, execution of leaders over 10 days as well as imprisonment without trial and at least one execution without a trial saw the rebels gain a lot of sympathy from the Irish public, turning them against British rule
- These political developments meant a growth of sympathy and compassion for rebels who were seen as martyrs and replaced the initial condemnation of the Rising
- Sinn Fein, initially blamed for the Rising, saw a subsequent rise in support for them
- Catholic Church and business community became more sympathetic to the cause of independence.

Anti Conscription Campaign
- Irish opposed conscription and pushed people to Sinn Fein who openly opposed it
- Caused the Nationalists to withdraw from Westminster
- Sinn Fein and Nationalists organised campaign eg general strike April 23rd
- Catholic Church, Mayor of Dublin drew up the National Pledge opposing conscription
- Conscription was not extended to Ireland which Sinn Fein was given credit for
- Conscription campaign drove Sinn Fein underground which improved their organisation.

Decline of Nationalist Party
- Irish Convention failed to reach agreement, which weakened position of Nationalists
- Led to feeling British could not be trusted and Nationalists could not deliver
- Three by-election wins for Sinn Fein gave impression they spoke for people not Nationalists which increased tension between Ireland and Britain politically
- March 1918 Redmond died which accelerated the decline of the Nationalists. Sinn Fein gained influence and popularity as a result
- Many moved from the Nationalist Party as they felt Sinn Fein was doing more for Ireland.

Rise of Sinn Fein
- Release of rebel prisoners from Frongoch meant Sinn Fein's struggle against British Rule in Ireland gained momentum
- Michael Collins was building up IRB and Irish Volunteers when in prison
- Collins ready to encourage anti-British activity in Ireland on release
- Collins and De Valera improved Sinn Fein's leadership
- Opposition to Britain due to martial law, house searches, raids, control of press, arrest of "suspects" without trial, and vigorous implementation of the Defence of the Realm Act
- Hunger striker Thomas Ashe died in 1917. His funeral became a propaganda tool for Sinn Fein.

14. The candidate evaluates the contribution of economic issues to the developing crisis in Northern Ireland up to 1968, using evidence and arguments such as:

Economic issues
- Northern Ireland was left relatively prosperous by World War Two, with the boom continuing into the 1950s. But by the 1960s, as elsewhere in Britain, 'many' industries were in decline, eg Harland and Wolff profitable 'til early' 60s, but government help in 1966. Largely Protestant workforce protected as a result
- Catholic areas received less government investment than their Protestant neighbours. Catholics were more likely to be unemployed or in low-paid jobs than Protestants in Northern Ireland. Catholic applicants also routinely excluded from public service appointments

- The incomes of mainly Protestant landowners were supported by the British system of 'deficiency payments' which gave Northern Ireland farmers an advantage over farmers from the Irish Republic
- Brookeborough's failure to address the worsening economic situation saw him forced to resign as Prime Minister. His successor, Terence O'Neill set out to reform the economy. His social and economic policies saw growing discontent and divisions within his unionist party.

Other factors

The Unionist Ascendancy in Northern Ireland and challenges to it

- Population of Northern Ireland divided: two-thirds Protestant and one-third Catholic: it was the minority who were discriminated against in employment and housing
- In 1963, the Prime Minister of Northern Ireland, Viscount Brookeborough, stepped down after 20 years in office. His long tenure was a product of the Ulster Unionist domination of politics in Northern Ireland since partition in 1921
- Unionist ascendancy: Before 1969 elections not held on a "one person, one vote" basis: gerrymandering used to secure Unionist majorities on local councils. Local govt electoral boundaries favoured Unionist candidates, even in mainly Catholic areas like Derry/Londonderry. Also, right to vote in local elections restricted to ratepayers, favouring Protestants, with those holding or renting properties in more than one ward receiving more than one vote, up to a maximum of six. This bias preserved by unequal allocation of council houses to Protestant families
- Challenges as Prime Minister O'Neill expressed desire to improve community relations in Northern Ireland and create a better relationship with the government in Dublin, hoping that this would address the sense of alienation felt by Catholics towards the political system in Northern Ireland
- Post-war Britain's Labour government introduced the welfare state to Northern Ireland, and it was implemented with few concessions to traditional sectarian divisions. Catholic children in the 1950s and 1960s shared in the benefits of further and higher education for the first time. This exposed them to a world of new ideas and created a generation unwilling to tolerate the status quo
- Many Catholics impatient with pace of reform and remained unconvinced of Prime Minister O'Neill's sincerity. Founding of the Northern Ireland Civil Rights Association (NICRA) in 1967. NICRA did not challenge partition, though membership mainly Catholic. Instead, it called for the end to seven 'injustices', ranging from council house allocations to the 'weighted' voting system.

Role of the IRA

- Rioting and disorder in 1966 was followed by the murders of two Catholics and a Protestant by a 'loyalist' terror group called the Ulster Volunteer Force, who were immediately banned by O'Neill
- Peaceful civil rights marches descended into violence in October 1968 when marchers in Derry defied the Royal Ulster Constabulary and were dispersed with heavy-handed tactics. The RUC response only served to inflame further the Catholic community and foster the establishment of the Provisional IRA by 1970 as the IRA split into Official and Provisional factions
- The Provisional IRA's strategy was to use force to cause the collapse of the Northern Ireland administration and to inflict casualties on the British forces such that the British government would be forced by public opinion to withdraw from Ireland
- PIRA were seen to defend Catholic areas from Loyalist attacks in the summer of 1970.

Cultural and political differences

- The Catholic minority politically marginalised since the 1920s, but retained its distinct identity through its own institutions such as the Catholic Church, separate Catholic schools, and various cultural associations, as well as the hostility of the Protestant majority
- Catholic political representatives in parliament refused to recognise partition and this only increased the community's sense of alienation and difference from the Unionist majority in Northern Ireland
- Nationalists on average 10-12 in NI Parliament compared to average 40 Unionists. In Westminster 10-12 Unionists to 2 Nationalists
- As the Republic's constitution laid claim to the whole island of Ireland, O'Neill's meeting with his Dublin counterpart, Seán Lemass, in 1965, provoked attacks from within Unionism, eg the Rev. Ian Paisley
- Violence erupted between the two communities, in 1966 following the twin 50th anniversaries of the Battle of the Somme and the Easter Rising. Both events were key cultural touchstones for the Protestant and Catholic communities.

The issue of Civil Rights

- From the autumn of 1968 onwards, a wide range of activists marched behind the civil rights banner, adopting civil disobedience in an attempt to secure their goals. Housing activists, socialists, Nationalists, Unionists, Republicans, students, trade unionists and political representatives came together across Northern Ireland to demand civil rights for Catholics in Northern Ireland
- The demand for basic civil rights from the Northern Ireland govt was an effort to move the traditional fault-lines away from the familiar Catholic-Protestant, Nationalist-Unionist divides by demanding basic rights for all citizens of Britain
- Civil rights encouraged by television coverage of civil rights protest in USA and student protests in Europe. Also by widening TV ownership: 1954, 10,000 licences, by 1962 there were 200,000 leading to increased Catholic awareness of the issues that affected them
- As the civil rights campaign gained momentum, so too did unionist opposition. Sectarian tension rose: was difficult to control, and civil disobedience descended into occasions of civil disorder.

15. The candidate evaluates the importance of religious and communal differences between both communities in preventing peace in Ireland between 1968 and 1985, using evidence and arguments such as:

Religious and communal differences

- The Protestant majority in Northern Ireland belonged to churches that represented the full range of reformed Christianity, while the Catholic minority was united in its membership of a Church that dominated life in the Republic and much of Europe. These religious divisions made it very difficult for both communities to come together
- These divisions further enhanced by traditions embraced by both communities, such as the 'marching season', which became a flashpoint for sectarian violence. Also differences in sport, language
- Many Catholic political representatives refused to recognise partition and their views only heightened the Nationalist community's sense of alienation and fostered Unionist hostility towards the Catholic minority
- The speeches and actions of Unionist and Nationalist leaders such as Reverend Ian Paisley and Gerry Adams polarised views in the province, and emphasised the divisions between both communities.

Other factors

Economic differences

- From 1973, the Common Agricultural Policy changed the decision making environment for food prices and farm economics, and employment in the farming sector continued to decline. Traditionally this sector had been dominated by the Unionist community
- Discrimination against Catholic applicants for employment declined steadily during this period as Catholics in the province began to enjoy the same civil rights enjoyed by the population of the rest of the UK.

Hardening attitudes – the role of terrorism

- Paramilitary groups began to operate on both sides of the sectarian divide, while civil rights marches became increasingly prone to confrontation
- In late 1969, the more militant 'Provisional' IRA (PIRA) broke away from the so-called 'Official' IRA. PIRA was prepared to pursue unification in defiance of Britain and would use violence to achieve its aims
- Unionist paramilitaries also organised. The UVF was joined by the Ulster Defence Association, created in 1971
- Examples of terrorist activity: by the end of 1972 sectarian violence had escalated to such an extent that nearly 500 lives were lost in a single year
- PIRA prisoners protest at loss of special status prisoners leading to hunger strikes Second hunger strike in 1981, led by Bobby Sands. Sands was put forward for a vacant Westminster seat and won. Sands and nine other hunger strikers died before the hunger strikes called off in October 1981
- Sinn Fein won the by-election following Sands' death in June 1983, these electoral successes raised the possibility that Sinn Fein could replace the more moderate SDLP as the political voice of the Catholic minority in Northern Ireland
- Indiscriminate terrorism meant Eire public opinion turned against PIRA
- In 1985 the violence of Northern Ireland's paramilitary groups still had more than a decade to run and the sectarian divide remained as wide as it had ever been.

British government policies – Internment

- New Prime Minister Brian Faulkner reintroduced internment ie detention of suspects without trial, in 1971 in response to unrest. Policy a disaster, both in its failure to capture any significant members of the PIRA and in its sectarian focus on Nationalist rather than Loyalist suspects. The reaction was predictable, even if the ferocity of the violence wasn't. Deaths in the final months of 1971 over 150.

Direct Rule

- A number of reforms had followed on from the Downing Street Declaration, ie on allocation of council housing, investigate the recent cycle of violence and review policing, such as the disbanding of the hated 'B Specials' auxiliaries
- The British government, now led by Prime Minister Edward Heath, decided to remove control of security from the government of Northern Ireland and appointing a secretary of state for the province leading to resignation of Stormont government. Direct rule imposed
- Despite attempts to introduce some sort of self-rule, such as the Sunningdale agreement of 1973, which failed in the face of implacable Unionist opposition and led to the reintroduction of direct rule. It would last for another 25 years.

The role of the British Army

- The so-called 'Battle of Bogside' in 1969 only ended with the arrival of a small force of British troops at the request of Chichester Clark. An acknowledgement that the govt. of Northern Ireland had lost its grip on the province's security

- By 1971 policing the province was fast becoming an impossible task, and the British Army adopted increasingly aggressive policies on the ground
- On 30 January 1972, the army deployed the Parachute Regiment to suppress rioting at a civil rights march in Derry. Thirteen demonstrators were shot and killed by troops, with another victim dying later of wounds. Appalling images of 'Bloody Sunday; led to increased recruitment by Provisional IRA
- The British Army's various attempts to control the PIRA, such as house-to-house searches and the imposition of a limited curfew, only served to drive more recruits into the ranks of the paramilitaries.

The role of the Irish government

- Irish government's role in The Anglo-Irish Agreement, signed in November 1985, confirmed that Northern Ireland would remain independent of the Republic as long as that was the will of the majority in the north. Also gave the Republic a say in the running of the province for the first time
- The agreement also stated that power could not be devolved back to Northern Ireland unless it enshrined the principle of power sharing.

HISTORICAL STUDY: EUROPEAN AND WORLD HISTORY

The Crusades, 1071 – 1204

16. The candidate evaluates the importance of religious factors in the decision of Europeans to go on crusade, using evidence and arguments such as:

Religious motives

- It was generally believed that the Remission of Sins offered by Pope Urban was an attractive solution to the dilemma of knights. Salvation was a constant worry for those trained to kill. Urban successfully resolved the need to protect Christianity from the Muslim threat and the general desire to re-establish the pilgrimage routes to the Holy Lands
- The promise of remission of current sins was also a great relief to those knights worried about their eternal soul. Tancred's biographer wrote about both his worry over this dilemma and his relief at Urban's suggestion
- The appeal of the People's Crusade shows the power of the belief that they were doing good and helping God
- Of the leaders of the Princes' Crusade, Raymond of Toulouse, is often held up as an example of a knight riding to the defence of the Holy Lands. His decision to take Tripoli in 1100 casts a shadow over this interpretation of his motives
- In later Crusades many of the religious aspects of the Crusade are adopted and modified by the growing idea of chivalric codes.

Other factors

The desire to acquire territory in the Holy Land

- Many of the great magnates on this expedition had intentions to acquire new estates for themselves. The motives of many of the leaders of the Princes' Crusade have been put down to this
- Bohemend and Baldwin in particular showed little zeal in carrying on with the Crusade once they had acquired Antioch and Edessa respectively.

Peer pressure

- The pressure put on knights by their families to take the cross was at times severe. Noblemen's wives tended to be keenly aware of the politics at court and had a role in influencing the decisions of some

- Stephen of Blois had married Adela, daughter of William I of England. It would have been unthinkable for such a notable knight not to go on the Crusade.

Seeking of fame and riches
- Some knights did go seeking glory. The Crusade had provided the solution to the problem of knights and their need for salvation. Killing was only wrong if you killed Christians. Urban indicated that the killing of a Muslim was a just act, and the equivalent to prayer or penance
- Seeking of riches per se was uncommon; land was the real source of wealth and power.

The sense of adventure
- Going on crusade was exciting and engendered a sense of adventure
- Pilgrimages had always been seen as important, and the idea of this as an armed pilgrimage was very appealing. It offered a way out for many serfs from their lives in bondage, or perhaps a chance to see the Holy Land.

Overpopulation and famine
- Many were forced to leave because of the lack of available farmland in an already overcrowded Europe.
- Several famines have also been suggested as a possible motive. It was popularly believed that the Holy Land was a land of plenty.

17. The candidate assesses the validity of the view that while Richard was a greater military leader and Saladin was a better diplomat, using evidence and arguments such as:

Diplomatic strengths and weaknesses

Saladin's strengths as a diplomat
- Despite being a Sunni Muslim in Shi'ite-dominated Egypt, he was successful in bringing much needed stability to the troubled court. His religious tolerance and fair judiciary earned him the respect of the Shi'ite citizens
- While ruler of Egypt Saladin was able to keep Nur-ed-Din at bay by evading the main contentious issue of religious conformity. When Nur-ed-din died in 1174, Saladin was able to step in and take over from his 10 year old son
- Saladin brought effective military leadership and central authority to Egypt and Syria for the first time
- In 1180 Saladin had successfully limited the attacks from Outremer by negotiating a peace treaty with Baldwin IV
- The capture of Jerusalem in 1187 made Saladin the hero of Islam. The eventual negotiated surrender saved much bloodshed.

Richard's weaknesses as a diplomat
- Many historians have pointed out that Richard, like his father Henry II, had something of a fiery temper. However it is questionable as to what extent this lost him the prize, Jerusalem. There is evidence that Richard was a poor diplomat; certainly at times he failed to understand the nature of his allies but he was perhaps better at understanding the nature of his enemy. His temper did result in the loss of potential allies. His treatment of Leopold of Austria, the leader of the much-reduced German contingent, resulted in an injury to the pride of Leopold and the loss of his German knights to the cause
- Richard's inability to share the spoils taken during this attack on Cyprus with Philip Augustus helped persuade the ill king of France that he was needed at home. The one thing Richard had wished to do was keep Philip with him on the Crusade; now he had to worry about French incursions into his Angevin Empire
- Against advice Richard backed Guy de Lusignan to become King of Jerusalem, against the popular Conrad of Montferrat, perhaps because he was the favourite of Philip.

This continued support of Guy resulted in a compromise that no one liked. The assassination of Conrad was even whispered by some to be Richard's fault. The end result was the withdrawal of the support of Conrad's forces and those of the Duke of Burgundy's remaining French knights.

Richard's strengths as a diplomat
- Richard proved himself in the art of diplomacy during the Crusade, when he successfully negotiated with Al-Adill, Saladin's brother. The two instantly got on, and a bond was forged between them. Saladin was increasingly concerned when Richard knighted one of Al-Adill's sons and even offered his sister in marriage. Al-Adill's connection to Richard was enough of an incentive for Saladin to agree to a truce with Richard.

Saladin's diplomatic weaknesses
- Not all of his supporters were happy with the peace treaty of 1180. Many felt that this contradicted the jihad and gave support to the Christian claim to Jerusalem
- Saladin was panicked into peace with Richard. Saladin was worried over the close relationship between Al-Adil and Richard. If he had held out it was probable that Richard would have had to return to England anyway without the peace treaty.

Military strengths and weaknesses

Richard's leadership
- Richard had established himself as an able leader prior to the Crusade
- Richard was good at motivating troops, and his arrival at the siege of Acre galvanised the troops in a way that Philip had been unable to do. Even when confined to his bed due to illness he was still able to direct the operations.

Richard's victories
- While journeying to the Holy Lands Richard captured Cyprus
- Richard, despite being lured into a trap, won the Battle of Arsuf with an impressive charge of knights that routed Saladin's men. Saladin was defeated in battle and it helped raise morale; the great defeat of Hattin had been erased from the minds of the Crusaders
- Richard won the Battle of Jaffa against overwhelming odds. Saladin had failed to defeat Richard in battle, and he lost control of his men at Jaffa; they refused to obey his orders.

Saladin's leadership
- Saladin brought effective military leadership and central authority to Egypt and Syria for the first time.

Saladin's victories
- In 1168 while Caliph of Egypt he destroyed the combined Crusader/Byzantium invasion fleet/army at the port city of Damietta
- In 1170 he followed this up with an attack on Gaza, massacring the Christian inhabitants of the city
- Saladin's victory at the Battle of Hattin (1187) was all consuming. The military orders were devastated, King Guy had been captured, many of the nobles executed or taken into slavery. One by one the great forts and cities fell to Saladin's army
- The capture of Jerusalem in 1187 made Saladin the hero of Islam. The eventual negotiated surrender saved much bloodshed.

Use of tactics
- 1180 Saladin had successfully limited the attacks from Outremer by negotiating a peace treaty with Baldwin IV
- Saladin's tactics leading up to Hattin were masterly. He provoked Guy of Lusignan into an unnecessary sally to aid a castle that was not seriously threatened. He avoided a pitched battle till the Crusaders were debilitated by heat and thirst, then further disabled them by lighting fires.

18. The candidate assesses how far the crusading ideal had declined by the Fourth Crusade in 1204, using evidence and arguments such as:

The Fourth Crusade
- The initial inspiration of the Forth Crusade had a strong crusading ideology behind it. Pope Innocent III was a highly effective pope. He had managed to settle the problem of the investiture contest with Germany, and hoped to sort out the issue of the Holy Lands as well. Innocent believed that the inclusion of medieval monarchs had caused the previous two Crusades to fail, unlike the First Crusade that was nominally under the command of Bishop Adhemar. This Crusade would fall under the command of six papal legates. These men would hold true to the ideal of the Crusade and not be bound by earthy greed of politics
- However, the Fourth Crusade has also been described as the low point of the crusading ideal. Hijacked by the Venetians, the Crusade instead became a tool for their growing political and economic ambitions
- While attacking Zara, Alexius, son of the deposed emperor of Byzantium, arrived with a new proposal for the Crusaders. He asked them to reinstate his father, who had been imprisoned by his brother, and if they agreed they would be handsomely rewarded. He also promised to return control of the Byzantine Church to Rome. The church was against such an attack on another Christian city, but the prospect of wealth and fame led the Crusade to Constantinople
- When the Crusaders discovered that Alexius and his father could not, or would not, meet the payment as agreed, the Crusaders stormed the city. The murder, looting and rape continued for three days, after which the crusading army had a great thanksgiving ceremony
- The amount of booty taken from Constantinople was huge: gold, silver, works of art and holy relics were taken back to Europe, mostly to Venice. Most Crusaders returned home with their newly acquired wealth. Those that stayed dividing up the land amongst themselves, effectively creating several Latin Crusader States where Byzantium had once stood.

Role of Venice
- By 1123 the city of Venice had come to dominate maritime trade in the Middle East. They made several secret trade agreements with Egypt and North African emirs, as well as enjoying concessions and trade agreements within the Kingdom of Jerusalem. Byzantium however, remained a constant rival for this dominance of trade and in 1183 Venice was cut off from the lucrative trading centres of the empire
- Venice's participation in the Crusade was only secured when the Pope agreed to pay huge sums of money to Venice for the use of its ships, and supplies as well as half of everything captured during the Crusade on land and sea
- Venice's leader, the Doge Enrico Dandolo, had sold the Crusaders three times as much supplies and equipment as required for the Crusade. The crusading leader, Boniface of Montferrat, found that he was unable to raise enough money to pay, and the Crusaders were all but imprisoned on an island near Venice. Dandolo's proposal to pay off the Crusaders' debt involved attacking Zara, a Christian city that had once belonged to Venice but was now under the control of the King of Hungary, a Christian monarch. Thus the Crusade had become a tool of the Venetians
- The Fourth Crusade's intended target, Egypt, was totally unsuitable from a Venetian perspective. Thus when the Pope's representative approached the Venetians in 1201 they agreed to help transport the Crusaders, hoping to divert the Crusade to a less friendly target. The final target for the Fourth Crusade was therefore determined by politics and economics.

Coexistence of Muslim and Crusading states
- Attempts at peace between Muslim and the Crusading states during the reign of Baldwin IV, before his death and the fall of Jerusalem
- Also other examples, such as the treaty of mutual protection signed between King Alric of Jerusalem and the Emir of Damascus prior to the Second Crusade.

The corruption of the crusading movement by the Church and nobles
- Popes were willing to use crusades against Christians, such as the Albegensian Crusade against the Cathar heretics of Languedoc (Toulouse and southern France) in 1209-1229. The Cathars did not believe in the hierarchy of Rome, all you needed was to be able to read the Bible. This is only the first of many such Crusades in Europe, seen as diluting the crusading ideal, ie killing Muslims
- Examples of nobles using the Crusade for their own ends are all over the place, from Bohemond and Baldwin in the First Crusade, to arguably Richard in the Third. The Fourth Crusade is littered with examples.

Effects of trade
- Trade links directly into the Fourth Crusade and the influence of Venice
- Pisa and Genoa both had a lot of influence in events during the Third Crusade, they both had favoured candidates for the vacant throne of Jerusalem for example and used trade rights as a bargaining chip to get what they wanted.

The American Revolution 1763 – 1787

19. The candidate evaluates the importance of the rejection of the Olive Branch petition in the colonists' declaration of independence in 1776, within a wide context of factors, using evidence and arguments such as:

Rejection of Olive Branch Petition
- George III rejected the colonists' last attempt at compromise
- 2nd Continental Congress had written appeal to king pledging its allegiance to crown and bitterness towards Parliament, yet appeal fell on deaf ears as George III declared colonists to be in rebellion
- Many colonists started to consider independence as only means of changing relationship with Britain
- However, petition was expression of loyalty to George III which masked many colonists' intentions to declare greater autonomy for themselves, regardless of king's reaction
- George III rejected the Olive Branch Petition, possibly as a consequence of increased colonist military activity, eg Lexington and Bunker Hill.

Other factors

Disputes over taxation
Stamp Act
- This first form of taxation on colonies, in 1765, was objected to by colonists because they were not represented in British Parliament which imposed these taxes
- "No taxation without representation" became familiar protest during this time
- Act stated that official stamp had to be bought to go on any printed matter, and colonists subsequently refused to pay for this
- Colonists stated that they already paid financial dues to British through Navigation Acts and other restrictions, and that they had their own militia and did not need to pay for the British Army to protect them
- However, British said taxation would contribute to costs of Seven Years War and also pay for continued presence of British Army in America to protect colonies.

Townshend Duties

- After Stamp Act was repealed in 1766, these Duties, which were on glass, tea, paper and lead, were imposed in 1767
- Colonists challenged right of Parliament to impose duties that seemed designed purely to raise revenue
- However, British insisted that duties be paid in order to maintain costs of acting as Mother Country to protect colonies.

Boston Massacre

- Massacre occurred in 1770
- Although 5 working-class men died, including one black man, reports of 5 middle-class white men dying caused outrage amongst politically-minded colonists
- Committees of Correspondence meant that news of Massacre spread quickly around 13 colonies
- Acquittal of British soldiers led many colonists to fear for their personal liberty and believe that they would one day be enslaved by British
- However Massacre was an incident which animated people mainly in New England area, something which later caused George III to voice his belief that problems in America were "localised".

Punishment of Massachusetts

- Tax remained on tea from 1770 in order to maintain British right to tax colonists
- Boston Tea Party in December 1773 was expression of some colonists' frustrations at British policy towards them
- The British response to the Boston Tea Party, in a series of acts starting in March 1774, known to colonists as Intolerable Acts – closing port of Boston, altering constitution of legislature of Massachusetts, billeting British troops in colonial homes, and suspending trial by jury in colony
- Other colonists acted in sympathy with Massachusetts and showed unity at First Continental Congress in September 1774
- However, British spoke of punishments as Coercive Acts, which were an attempt to get colonists to see that acts of hostility towards Britain would not be tolerated.

British intransigence

- Britain retained an uncompromising attitude in face of continued colonist protest and pleas for compromise.

Influence of Thomas Paine

- Republican pamphlet 'Common Sense' was published in January 1776 and sold 100,000 copies.

20. The candidate evaluates the extent to which the colonists' advantage of fighting on home ground led to their eventual victory in the American Revolution, using evidence and arguments such as:

Colonists' advantage of fighting on home ground

- Land war fought on American soil: this gave the Continental Army an advantage, as the colonists' knowledge of the theatre of war meant they handled the terrain better than the British
- Local people burned their crops rather than let them fall into British hands, reducing potential supplies for the British.

Other factors

George Washington

- Washington was an inspirational leader, a self-made Virginian whose choice as Commander of the Continental Army gave heart to many
- Washington fought guerrilla warfare effectively. He taught his troops to fire accurately from distance in open battle. He had experience of the British Army during the Seven Years War
- Washington's speeches to troops offered them the incentive of independence if they won the war

- Washington benefited from luck on several occasions, such as when inefficiency led the British into traps or when the French arrived at Yorktown.

French entry into the war

- Franco-American Treaty of Alliance in February 1778 was a turning point in the war
- France contributed troops, ammunition, expertise and supplies to the colonists
- Strength of the French navy meant Britain had to spread its forces worldwide, thus reducing its effort in the colonies
- French intervention on the part of Admiral de Grasse preceded the final British surrender at Yorktown
- Entry of France into the war may have encouraged Spain and Holland to follow suit within the next two years
- However, the war had been taking place for over eighteen months by the time France entered. France's main contribution was at sea rather than on land.

British military inefficiency

- On several occasions British generals did not act appropriately to orders received. Orders from London were misinterpreted; eg Howe marching south to Brandywine instead of north into New England, thus isolating Burgoyne who subsequently surrendered his forces at Saratoga
- Petty jealousies obstructed co-operation amongst British military leaders
- Changes in personnel holding high office hindered progress
- However, in many instances the British were forced into bad decisions by the tactics of Washington's army
- Distance between Britain and the colonies caused a delay in communications between London and the generals, with orders from Britain often overtaken by events by the time they reached America.

British political mistakes

- The government ignored pleas by those such as Chatham (Pitt the Elder) to reconcile with America
- Burke's attempts in the House of Commons to persuade the government to make peace were also dismissed
- George III and British ministers treated Americans as rebels and therefore ignored arguments for the colonies' rights to autonomy, self-legislation and self-taxation.
- George III and British ministers' dismissal of Olive Branch Petition in 1775 led colonists to believe the war must be won
- Inefficiences at the Admiralty under Lord Sandwich's tenure as First Lord meant Royal Navy was ill-prepared for attacks on Britain by French and Spanish which diverted British efforts in America
- Lord North's attempts to conciliate the colonists later in the war were too little too late; the colonists were motivated by independence.

Control of the seas

- Spanish and Dutch entry into the war – they stretched British resources even further and made the British less effective in the colonies.
- Armed League of Neutrality – Russian, Danish and Swedish willingness to fire on the Royal Navy placed extra pressure on Britain.

21. The candidate assesses the accuracy of the statement that the American Constitution of 1787 was an answer to the problems highlighted by the experience of British rule, using evidence and arguments such as:

The experience of rule by Britain

- As part of the British Empire, colonists had been ruled by the King and the British Parliament, who together made key policy decisions, set laws and taxes, and enforced the law; there were no checks and balances

- Colonists feared the potentially tyrannical power of a monarch, and designed the Constitution to prevent any such future threat
- Branches of government were to be predominantly elective, to ensure the participation of the people.

Significance of the Constitution
- When the colonists drew up their Constitution, they built in a separation of powers providing checks and balances within the political system. The Bill of Rights established liberty for individuals in states within a federal union of all states, and set out clear lines of authority between federal government and individual states. This would avoid central government exerting a controlling power over people's lives
- The hierarchy which existed under rule by Britain was altered by the Constitution, which stated that 'all men are created equal' and that everyone was entitled to 'life, liberty and the pursuit of happiness'. Now people would be asked to ratify many of the stages within the democratic processes at state and national level. However, women and blacks were excluded from the franchise, and in reality only one-fifth of eligible voters turned out for national elections.

Executive: role of President
- Executive power was vested in the elected President, and his Vice-President and Cabinet. The President acted as head of state and Commander-in-Chief but would have no vote in the law-making process, although he could veto legislation. The President would make all key decisions and establish policy. Members of the Executive could be removed from office by the electorate or the other branches of government if it was felt they were not doing their job properly.

Legislature: Congress
- Legislative power lay in the hands of an elected Congress which was divided into two Houses, the Senate and Representatives. Congress passed laws and raised taxes, as well as having responsibility for international trade, war and foreign relations. No one in the legislature could serve in the judiciary or executive without first resigning from the legislature. Congressional elections were held regularly to ensure that Congressmen remained in touch with the people they served.

Judiciary: Supreme Court
- Judicial power was granted to the Supreme Court of the United States. The Supreme Court acted as the highest court of appeal in the country. It also debated the legality of new laws passed by Congress. Supreme Court judges were nominated by the President and their appointment was ratified by Congress after a rigorous checking process. Appointees to the Supreme Court could be removed from their position if they acted improperly.

The French Revolution, to 1799

22. The candidate evaluates the extent to which revolution broke out in France in 1789 as a result of the economic crisis of 1788 to 1789, using evidence and arguments such as:

The economic crisis of 1788/9
- Bad harvests and grain shortages inspired unrest among the peasantry and the urban workers in Paris and in provincial cities throughout France, exerting critical pressures on the Ancien Régime
- There was less demand for manufactured goods, which led to unemployment increasing amongst the urban workers
- The nobility were increasingly blamed as peasants started to take political action
- The economic crisis clearly created an environment in which the Ancien Régime was struggling to survive.

Other Factors

Financial problems of the Ancien Régime
- Because of exemptions the crown was denied adequate income. The privileged orders were an untapped source of revenue but it would require reforms to access it
- This created resentment amongst the 3rd Estate
- Exacerbated divisions that already existed between the estates
- Tax-farming meant not all revenues were reaching the government
- By the 1780s France faced bankruptcy due to heavy expenditure and borrowing to pay for wars
- Government failed to gain agreement on tax reform
- This was arguably the biggest threat facing the Ancien Régime. The opposition which this generated not only led to Calonne's dismissal in 1787 but more importantly to the convocation of the Estates General in 1788. When it met in May 1789 the long-standing divisions between the three Estates unleashed forces which culminated in the overthrow of the Ancien Régime.

Influence of the Enlightenment
- The Enlightenment encouraged criticism, and freedom of thought, speech and religion, and was seen as the end of man's self-imposed irrationality at the hands of the Church in particular
- Ideas of philosophes like Voltaire who attacked god, Montesquieu who favoured a British system of government and Rousseau who put forward the idea of direct democracy
- Very much appealed to the middle-classes, who led the revolution.

The American Revolution
- This war contributed to the financial crisis which came to a head in France post–1786 but for many in France at the time they also represented the practical expression of the enlightened views of the Philosophes in terms of the rights of the individual, no taxation without representation and freedom from tyrannical government. The wars inspired many of the lesser nobility and the bourgeoisie to seek the same freedoms.

The political crisis of 1788/9
- The convocation of the Estates General in August 1788 sharpened divisions between the three Estates which came to a head between May and August 1789. The Cahiers des Doleances revealed the depth of dissatisfaction with the existing order, especially among the bourgeoisie and the peasantry. The creation of the National Assembly, the abolition of feudalism and the Declaration of the Rights of Man and the Citizen all contributed to a revolutionary change in French government, society and economy.

Actions of Louis XVI
- Louis was largely under the influence of his wife, Marie Antoinette who, although strong minded, failed to grasp the serious nature of situation and was also unpopular as she was Austrian
- Louis XVI's handling of the Estates-General contributed towards the start of the Revolution. He wanted to make reform difficult by making the three Estates meet separately, in the hope that the First and Second Estates would vote the third down
- This backfired: opposition to the King grew, the Third Estate refused to act separately, and many of the clergy changed sides, changing the balance of power
- Louis allegedly closed the meeting halls, which led to the Tennis Court Oath from members of the Third Estate. He later agreed to a constitution when the Third Estate representatives occupied the royal tennis courts

- The King had lost more political ground than if he had just listened to the grievances of the middle classes and the Third Estate from the start.

Role of Bourgeoisie

- As part of the Third Estate resented paying the taxation
- Dominated the Third Estate representatives in the Estates-General
- Were outside the political process unless they bought a noble title: wanted access to power
- Very attracted to ideas of a constitutional monarchy as advocated by people like Montesquieu
- Provided the leadership for the revolution.

23. The candidate evaluates the extent to which army intervention in politics brought about Napoleon's coup of 1799, by using evidence and arguments such as:

Increasing intervention of the army in politics

- Even before the 1795 constitution was ratified the army had been used to quell sans-culottes insurgents who sought to invade the Convention and to repel an émigré invasion at Quiberon
- Napoleon's use of a 'whiff of grapeshot' to put down the disturbances in October merely underlined the parlous nature of politics at the time
- The deployment of the army in May 1796 to put down the left-wing Babeuf Conspiracy was followed by the Coup of Fructidor in September 1797 when the first 'free' Convention elections returned a royalist majority.

Other factors

Role of Sieyes

- Afraid that France would descend into anarchy as a result of the on-going political conflict and deeming the 1795 constitution unworkable, Sieyes enlisted the aid of Bonaparte in mounting a coup against it
- The Convention, the Directory and the legislative councils had run their course and few, if any, mourned their passing.

Political instability

- In the late summer of 1794 France was emerging from two years of increasing radicalisation and resulting bitterness between opposing factions
- The Jacobins under Robespierre had been overthrown and a 'White Terror' was soon to sweep the country in revenge for the excesses of the radical left during the Terror
- France had been torn apart by civil war, threatened by foreign armies egged on by émigré nobles seeking to overthrow the Revolution and riven by religious conflict occasioned by the State's opposition to the primacy of the Catholic Church.

The Constitution of 1795

- Policy-makers framed a new constitution which sought to reconcile the bitterness of the preceding years by imposing checks and balances against the emergence of one dominant individual, group or faction. In so doing, many historians argue that the new constitution was a recipe for instability in the years which followed
- A bi-cameral legislature was established wherein each chamber counter-balanced the power of the other. By so doing it inhibited strong and decisive government
- To ensure continuity, the new Convention was to include two-thirds of the outgoing deputies from the old. This enraged sections of the right who felt that the forces of left-wing radicalism still prevailed in government
- The resulting mass protests in October 1795 were put down by the army under Bonaparte. The principle of using extra-parliamentary forces to control the State had been established with Bonaparte right at the heart of it. It was to prove a dangerous precedent

- Annual elections worked against consistent and continuous policy-making
- So did the appointment of an Executive – the Directory – one of whose members rotated on an annual basis
- Again, the counter-balance between the legislature and the executive may have been commendable but it was to prove inherently unstable in practice.

Role of Bonaparte

- A supreme self-propagandist, he seemed to offer the strength and charisma which the Directory and the legislative councils singularly lacked
- Afraid that his spectacular victories in Italy during 1795 might be jeopardised by the election of a right-wing government less sympathetic to conducting a war against monarchical states, Bonaparte threw his support behind the Directory who effectively annulled the election results by purging right-wing deputies
- The 1788 and 1799 elections were similarly 'adjusted'
- The Consulate – with Bonaparte as First Consul – came into being. A notably more authoritarian constitution was promulgated by referendum, supported by a populace tired of weak and ineffectual government and the instability it had brought between 1795 and 1799.

24. The candidate assesses the validity of the statement that the Bourgeoisie gained most from the French Revolution, by using evidence and arguments such as:

The impact of the Revolution on the bourgeoisie

- The Revolution instigated a fundamental shift in political and economic power from the First and Second Estates to the Bourgeoisie
- The ending of feudalism in August 1789 heralded profound social and economic change (eg facilitating the development of capitalism) whilst the Declaration of the Rights of Man and the Citizen later in the month did the same for political life. In both cases the main beneficiaries were the Bourgeoisie
- Successive constitutions and legislative reforms throughout the 1790s favoured the Bourgeoisie above all other social groups by emphasising the notion of a property-owning democracy with voting rights framed within property qualifications, whilst the ending of trade restrictions and monopolies favoured an expanding business and merchant class
- France had moved from a position of privileged estates to one where increasingly merit was what counted. It was the educated Bourgeoisie who were best placed to benefit from this profound change in French society.

The impact on other sections of Society

The peasantry

- In contrast to the Catholic Church and the nobility the position of the peasantry was in many ways strengthened by the Revolution. The ending of feudalism in August 1789 removed many of the legal and financial burdens which had formed the basis of peasant grievances in the Cahiers des Doleances presented to the Estates-General in 1789
- The revolutionary land settlement, instigated by the nationalisation of church lands in November 1789, had transferred land from the nobility and the clergy to the peasantry to their obvious advantage. It should be noted, however, that not all peasants benefited equally from this. Only the well-off peasants could afford to purchase the Church lands which had been seized by the National Assembly.

The urban workers

- At key points throughout the Revolution overt demonstrations of discontent by the urban masses – particularly in Paris – impacted on key events as successive regimes framed policy with an eye to appeasing the mob.

However, any modest gains by the urban poor were short-lived. A decade of almost continuous wars in the 1790s had created shortages and inflation which hit the urban poor particularly hard

- The passing of the Chapelier Law in May 1791, by a bourgeois-dominated National Assembly protecting the interests of industrialists, effectively banned the formation of trade unions and thereafter the Revolution brought few tangible economic or political gains for urban workers.

The impact of the Revolution on the First Estate

- The Catholic Church was a key pillar of the Ancien Regime. The Upper Clergy (usually drawn from the ranks of the traditional nobility) enjoyed considerable wealth and status based on a raft of privileges and tax exemptions. These privileges and exemptions were swept away by the Revolution and the position of the Catholic Church within France by 1799 was far less assured than it had been under the Ancien Regime

- The Civil Constitution of the Clergy (July 1790) polarised attitudes towards the place of the Catholic Church within French society and promoted conflict between opposing factions through the rest of the period to 1799. In November 1789 Church lands were nationalised, stripping the Church of much of its wealth. The net result of all of this was that the Church never regained its primacy within the French state and can be seen to have lost far more than it gained.

The impact of the Revolution on the Second Estate

- The aristocracy had enjoyed similar privileges and tax exemptions to those of the Catholic Church under the Ancien Regime. Advancement in the key positions of the State, the Army and, indeed the Church, depended more often on birth than merit. The traditional nobility monopolised these key positions and sought at all times to defend its favoured position. Again, the Revolution swept away aristocratic privilege even more completely than that of the clergy

- The ending of feudalism in August 1789 marked the prelude to a decade when the status of the nobility in France effectively collapsed. In 1790 outward displays of 'nobility' such as titles and coats of arms were forbidden by law and in 1797, after election results suggested a pro-royalist resurgence, the Convention imposed alien status on nobles and stripped them of French citizenship

- The Revolution brought in a regime where careers were open to talent regardless of birth or inheritance and the traditional aristocracy simply ceased to exist. Having said that, some nobles simply transformed themselves into untitled landlords in the countryside and continued to exercise significant economic and political power.

Germany 1815 – 1939

25. The candidate assesses how strong nationalism was in Germany, using evidence and arguments such as:

Supporters of nationalism

- Liberal nationalists – a united Germany should have a Liberal constitution that would guarantee the rights of citizens
- Cultural nationalists – unity was more important than individual rights and that what mattered was the preservation of German identity and culture
- Economic nationalists – unity would remove the trade barriers between states and this would allow economic growth and prosperity
- To encourage trade Prussia formed a customs union in 1818 that by the 1830s was called the Zollverein; the Zollverein helped nationalist ideas to spread

- Nationalist ideas were spread by philosophers, historians, poets and dramatists who influenced the literate middle classes and especially the students: Jahn and the burschenschaten movement; Wartburg in 1817; Hamburg in 1832; Young Germany in 1833; the Rhine Movement in 1840
- Fichte described 'Germany' as the Fatherland where all people spoke the same language and sang the same songs
- German poets and authors, such as the Grimm brothers, and composers such as Beethoven, encouraged feelings of national pride in the German states
- In 1830 anti-French feelings promoted 'the watch on the Rhine' and nationalist festivals such as Hambach (1832) also encouraged nationalist feelings.

Opponents of nationalism

- One-fifth of the population of the Austrian empire were German; the Austrian Emperor feared nationalism would encourage them to break away and join Germany; this would leave Austria weaker and cause other national groups in the Empire to demand their independence
- In 1815 Metternich became worried about the growth of liberal and nationalist student societies
- In 1819 Carlsbad Decrees banned student societies and censored newspapers
- The following year the power of the Diet was increased so that soldiers could be ordered to stop the spread of new ideas in any of the German States
- The particularism of the various German states – autonomous and parochial in many ways
- Popular apathy – most Germans had little desire to see a united Germany
- France and Russia feared that a strong, united Germany would be a political, economic and military rival to them.

Attitudes of peasants

- Golo Mann wrote that most Germans 'seldom looked up from the plough'. He doubted the influence of artists and intellectuals whom most Germans knew little or nothing about; nationalism attracted mainly the educated/business/middle classes
- But by the late 1840s peasants were demanding that remaining feudal dues should be cancelled by their German princes.

Political turmoil in the 1840s

- Trade depression, unemployment and high food prices because of bad harvests led to revolutions throughout Europe
- In the German Confederation nationalists and liberals saw their chance; the rulers of the small states fled; elections were held to local assemblies and then to a national convention to create a united Germany; this convention or parliament met at Frankfurt.

The Frankfurt Parliament, divisions

- This was the first serious attempt to challenge Austria's political power in Germany and Austrian opposition to the liberals and nationalists
- Failure of the Frankfurt Parliament – lack of clear aims and no armed force to enforce its decisions
- Nationalists could not agree on the size of a new Germany – should it include Austria and the Hapsburg lands and Prussia's Polish possessions?
- Should it be governed by a King or be a republic or a mixture of both?
- The Protestants of the North distrusted the Southern Catholics.

The collapse of the revolution in Germany, 1848-1849

- Frankfurt Parliament failed to satisfy the needs of the starving workers who had helped create the revolution

- Parliament had to rely on the Prussian army to put down a workers' revolt
- Self-interest of German rulers led to opposition to the actions at Frankfurt
- Frederick William, King of Prussia, tried to take advantage of the defeat of the 1848 revolution to increase Prussian power to exclude Austria from the Confederation – the Erfurt Parliament
- Austria was still too strong in 1850 and was able to force Prussia to back down; at Olmutz it was agreed to return to the Constitution of 1815.

26. The candidate evaluates the extent to which the weaknesses of the Weimar Republic were the major reason for the rise of the Nazi Party between 1919 and 1933, using evidence and arguments such as:

Weaknesses of the Weimar Republic
- 'A Republic without Republicans'/'a Republic nobody wanted' – lack of popular support for the new form of government after 1918
- 'Peasants in a palace' – commentary on Weimar politicians
- Divisions among those groups/individuals who purported to be supporters of the new form of government eg the socialists
- Alliance of the new government and the old imperial army against the Spartacists – lack of cooperation between socialist groups – petty squabbling rife
- The Constitution/Article 48 ('suicide clause') - arguably Germany was too democratic. 'The world's most perfect democracy – on paper'
- Lack of real, outstanding Weimar politicians who could strengthen the Republic, Stresemann excepted
- Inability (or unwillingness) of the Republic to deal effectively with problems in German society
- Lukewarm support from the German Army and the Civil Service.

Other factors

Resentment towards the Treaty of Versailles
- The Treaty of Versailles: acceptance by Republic of hated terms
- Land loss and accepting blame for the War especially hated
- Led to growth of criticism; 'November Criminals', 'Stab in the back' myth.

Social and Economic difficulties
- Over-reliance on foreign investment left the Weimar economy subject to the fluctuations of the international economy
- 1922/23 (hyperinflation) - severe effects on the middle classes, the natural supporters of the Republic; outrage and despair at their ruination
- The Great Depression of 1929 – arguably without this the Republic might have survived. Germany's dependence on American loans showed how fragile the recovery of the late 1920s was. The pauperisation of millions again reduced Germans to despair
- Propaganda posters with legends such as "Hitler – our only hope" struck a chord with many
- The Depression also polarised politics in Germany – the drift to extremes led to a fear of Communism, which grew apace with the growth of support for the Nazis.

Appeal of the Nazis after 1928
- Nazi Party had attractive qualities for the increasingly disillusioned voting population: They were anti-Versailles, anti-Communist [the SA took on the Red Front in the streets], promised to restore German pride, give the people jobs
- The Nazis put their message across well with the skilful use of propaganda under the leadership of Josef Goebbels

- The SA were used to break up opponents meetings and give the appearance of discipline and order
- Gave scapegoats for the population to blame from the Jews to the Communists.

The role of Hitler
- Hitler was perceived as a young, dynamic leader, who campaigned using modern methods and was a charismatic speake
- He offered attractive policies which gave simple targets for blame and tapped into popular prejudice.

Weaknesses and mistakes of others
- Splits in the left after suppression of Spartacist revolt made joint action in the 1930s very unlikely.
- Roles of von Schleicher and von Papen. Underestimation of Hitler
- Weakness/indecision of Hindenburg.

27. The candidate evaluates the validity of the statement that the 'Nazis gave the people what they wanted' as a reason for the Nazis maintaining power between 1933 and 1939, using evidence and arguments such as:

Success of Economic policies
- Nazi economic policy – attempted to deal with economic ills affecting Germany, especially unemployment
- Nazis began a massive programme of public works; work of Hjalmar Schacht
- Nazi policy towards farming eg Reich Food Estate – details of various policies
- Goring's policy of 'guns before butter'. Popular once foreign policy triumphs appeared to justify it.

Other factors

Social policies
- Creation of the *volksgemeinschaft* (national community)
- Nazi youth policy
- Nazi education policy
- Nazi policy towards the Jews-first isolate, then persecute and finally destroy
- Nazi family policy – Kinder, Kirche, Kuche
- Kraft durch Freude programme
- A Concordat with the Catholic Church was reached; a Reichsbishop was appointed as head of the Protestant churches.

Success of foreign policy
- Nazi success in foreign policy attracted support among Germans; Rearmament, Rhineland, Anschluss
- 'Much of Hitler's popularity after he came to power rested on his achievements in foreign policy' (Welch).

Establishment of totalitarian state
- Political parties outlawed; non-Nazi members of the civil service were dismissed
- Nazis never quite able to silence opposition to the regime
- Speed of takeover of power and ruthlessness of the regime made opposition largely ineffective
- Anti-Nazi judges were dismissed and replaced with those favourable to the Nazis
- Acts Hostile to the National Community (1935) – all-embracing law which allowed the Nazis to persecute opponents in a 'legal' way.

Fear and state terrorism
- The use of fear/terror through the Nazi police state; role of the Gestapo
- Concentration camps set up; the use of the SS.

Crushing of opposition
- Opponents liable to severe penalties, as were their families
- Opponents never able to establish a single organisation to channel their resistance – role of the Gestapo, paid informers
- Opposition lacked cohesion and a national leader; also lacked armed supporters
- Lack of cooperation between socialists and communists – role of Stalin considered.

Propaganda
- Use of Nuremburg Rallies
- Use of Radio
- Cult of the Leader: the Hitler myth
- Use of the Cinema: Triumph of the Will, the Eternal Jew, etc
- Role of Goebbels.

Italy 1815 – 1939

28. The candidate assesses the success of supporters of Italian nationalism up to 1850, using evidence and arguments such as:

Supporters of nationalism

Educated middle class
- Risorgimento saw 'patriotic literature' from novelists and poets including Pellico, and Leopardi. These inspired the educated middle class
- Gioberti, Balbo and Mazzini promoted their ideas for a national state, this inspired nationalism amongst the middle classes.

Liberals
- Some liberals and business classes were keen to develop an economic state. Napoleon Bonaparte had built roads and encouraged closer trading. One system of weights, measures and currency appealed.

Popular sentiment
- French revolutionary ideals had inspired popular sentiment for a national Italian state.
- There was a growing desire for the creation of a national state amongst students; many joined Mazzini's 'Young Italy'
- Operas by Verdi and Rossini inspired growing feelings of patriotism
- The use of Tuscan as a 'national' language by Alfieri and Manzoni spread ideas of nationalism
- Membership of secret societies such as the Carbonari grew. Members were willing to revolt and die for their beliefs which included desire for a national state.

Opponents

Austria
- Resentment against Austria and its restoration of influence in the Italian peninsula and their use of spies and censorship, helped increase support for the nationalist cause. However, any progress made by nationalists was firmly crushed by the Austrian army. Strength of the Quadrilateral. Austrians never left Italian soil. Carbonari revolts in Kingdom of Naples 1820-1821, Piedmont 1821, Modena and the Papal States 1831 all crushed by Austrian army. During 1848-1849 revolutions, Austrian army defeated Charles Albert twice – Custoza and Modena, retook Lombardy and destroyed the Republic of St Mark.

Italian princes and rulers
- Individual rulers were opposed to nationalism and used censorship, police and spies as well as the Austrian army, to crush revolts 1820-1821, 1830 and 1848-1849.

Attitude of the peasants
- The mass of the population were illiterate and indifferent to politics and nationalist ideas. They did revolt during bad times as can be seen in 1848 – but their revolts were due to bad harvests and bad economic times and were not inspired by feelings of nationalism.

Position of the Papacy
- Pope Pius IX. Nationalist movement had high hopes of New Pope Pius IX, initially thought of as a liberal and sympathetic to nationalist cause. Hopes dashed when Pope Pius IX denounced the nationalist movement during 1848-49 revolutions.

Failures of 1848 – 1849 revolutions
- These showed that nationalist leaders would not work together, nor did they seek foreign help thus hindering progress. Charles Albert's 'Italia farad a se' declared that Italy would do it alone – she did not. Lombardy and Venetia suspected Charles Albert's motives and were reluctant to work with him. Venetians put more faith in Manin
- All progress was hampered when Pope Pius IX denounced nationalism. Charles Albert hated Mazzini and would not support the Roman Republic. Austrian military might based on the Quadrilateral defeated Charles Albert twice – at Custoza and Modena, retook Lombardy and destroyed the Republic of St Mark
- The French crushed the Roman Republic.

29. The candidate evaluates the accuracy of the claim that the appeal of fascism was the main reason why Mussolini came to power in Italy by 1925, using evidence and arguments such as:

Appeal of the Fascists
- They exploited weaknesses of other groups by excellent use of Mussolini's newspaper 'Il Popolo D'Italia'
- The Fascio Italiano di Combattimento began as a movement not a political party and thus attracted a wide variety of support giving them an advantage over narrower rivals
- By 1921 – fascism was anti-communist, anti-trade union, anti-socialist and pro-nationalism and thus became attractive to the middle and upper classes
- Fascism became pro-conservative, appealed to family values, supported church and monarchy; promised to work within the accepted political system. This made fascism more respectable and appealing to both the monarchy and the papacy
- Squadristi violence was directed against socialism so it gained the support of elites and middle classes
- Violence showed fascism was strong and ruthless. It appealed to many ex-soldiers
- Fascists promised strong government. This was attractive after a period of extreme instability
- Fascists promised to make Italy respected as a nation and thus appealed to nationalists
- Fascist policies were kept deliberately vague to attract support from different groups.

Other factors

Role of Mussolini
- Key role in selling the Fascist message: Powerful orator – piazza politics
- He seized his opportunities. He changed political direction and copied D'Annunzio
- He used propaganda and his newspaper effectively and had an ear for effective slogans
- He dominated the fascist movement kept support of Fascist extremists (Ras)
- He relied on strong nerve to seize power and to survive the Matteotti crisis
- Mussolini manipulated his image, kept out of violence himself but exploited the violence of others.

Weaknesses of Italian governments
- Parliamentary government was weak – informal 'liberal' coalitions. Corruption was commonplace (trasformismo). Liberals were not a structured party. New parties formed: PSI (socialists), PPI (Catholic Popular Party) with wider support base threatening existing political system
- WWI worsened the situation; wartime coalitions were very weak. 1918; universal male suffrage and 1919 Proportional Representation; relied on 'liberals' – unstable coalitions. Giolitti made an electoral pact with Mussolini (1921); Fascists gained 35 seats then refused to support the government. Over the next 16 months, three ineffective coalition governments
- Fascists threatened a 'March on Rome' – King refused to agree to martial law; Facta resigned; Mussolini was invited to form coalition. 1924 Acerbo Law.

Resentment against the Peace Settlement
- Large loss of life in frustrating campaigns in the Alps and the Carso led to expectation that these would be recognised in the peace settlement; Wilson's commitment to nationalist aims led to the creation of Yugoslavia and a frustration of Italian hopes of dominating the Adriatic
- 'Mutilated victory' – Italian nationalists fuelled ideas that Italy had been betrayed by her government.

Role of the King
- The King gave in to Fascist pressure during the March on Rome. He failed to call Mussolini's bluff
- After the Aventine Secession the King was unwilling to dismiss Mussolini.

Economic difficulties
- WWI imposed serious strain on the Italian economy. The government took huge foreign loans and the National Debt was 85 billion lira by 1918. The Lira lost half of its value, devastating middle class savers. Inflation was rising; prices in 1918 were four times higher than 1914. This led to further major consequences:
  - no wage rises
  - food shortages
  - two million unemployed 1919
  - firms collapsed as military orders ceased.

Social and economic divisions
- Membership of trade unions and PSI rose – strikes, demonstrations, violence. 1919/20 'Biennio Rosso' in towns – general strike 1920; army mutiny; occupation of factories
- Industrialists/middle classes were fearful of revolution. Governments failed to back the police so law and order broke down
- In the countryside, there was seizure of common land – peasant ownership increased.

Weaknesses and mistakes of opponents
- D'Annunzio's seizure of Fiume was not stopped by the government
- Government failed to get martial law to stop fascist threat. Some liberals supported the Acerbo Law
- Socialist General Strike July 1922 – failed. Socialists' split weakened them; refused to join together to oppose fascism
- Liberals fragmented into four factions grouped around former PMs. They were too weak to effectively resist. Hoped to tame Fascists
- PPI were divided over attitude to fascism – right wing supported fascism. Aventine Secession backfired; destroyed chance to remove Mussolini.

30. The candidate evaluates how important the use of fear and intimidation was in maintaining Fascist control over Italy between 1922 and 1939, using evidence and arguments such as:

Fear and intimidation
- Mussolini favoured complete State authority with everything under his direct control. All Italians were expected to obey Mussolini and his Fascist Party
- The squadristi were organised into the MVSN – *Milizia Voluntaria per la Sicurezza Nazionale* – the armed local Fascist militia (Blackshirts). They terrorised the cities and provinces causing fear with tactics such as force-feeding with toads and castor oil
- After 1925–6 around 10,000 non-Fascists/opposition leaders were jailed by special tribunals
- The Secret police, OVRA was established in 1927 and was lead by Arturo Bocchini. Tactics included abduction and torture of opponents. 4000 people were arrested by the OVRA and sent to prison
- Penal colonies were established on remote Mediterranean islands such as Ponza and Lipari. Conditions for those sentenced to these prisons were primitive with little chance of escape
- Opponents were exiled internally or driven into exile abroad
- The death penalty was restored under Mussolini for serious offences but by 1940 only ten people had been sentenced to death.

Other relevant factors

Establishment of the Fascist state
- Nov/Dec 1922 Mussolini was given emergency powers. Nationalists merged with PNF 1923. Mussolini created MSVN (fascist militia) – gave him support if the army turned against him – and Fascist Grand Council – a rival Cabinet. These two bodies made Mussolini's position stronger and opposition within PNF weaker. The establishment of a dictatorship began:
- 1926 – opposition parties were banned. A one party state was created
- 1928 – universal suffrage abolished
- 1929 – all Fascist Parliament elected.

Crushing of opposition
- Liberals had divided into four factions so were weakened
- The Left had divided into three – original PSI, reformist PSU and Communists – they failed to work together against Fascists
- Pope forced Sturzo to resign and so PPI (Catholic Popular Party) was weakened and it split
- Acerbo Law passed. 1924 elections – Fascists won 66% of the vote
- Opposition parties failed to take advantage of the Matteotti crisis. By walking out of the Chamber of Deputies (Aventine Secession) they gave up the chance to overthrow Mussolini; they remained divided – the Pope refused to sanction an alliance between PPI and the socialists. The King chose not to dismiss Mussolini
- Communists and socialists did set up organisations in exile but did not work together. Communist cells in northern cities did produce some anti-fascist leaflets but they suffered frequent raids by OVRA
- PPI opposition floundered with the closer relationship between Church and State (Lateran Pacts).

Social controls
- Workers were controlled through 22 corporations, set up in 1934; overseen by National Council of Corporations, chaired by Mussolini
- Corporations provided accident, health and unemployment insurance for workers, but forbade strikes and lock-outs
- There were some illegal strikes in 1930s and anti-Fascist demonstrations in 1933 but these were limited

- The majority of Italians got on with their own lives conforming as long as all was going well. Middle classes/ elites supported fascism as it protected them from communism
- Youth knew no alternative to fascism, were educated as Fascists and this strengthened the regime. Youth movements provided sporting opportunities, competitions, rallies, camps, parades and propaganda lectures – 60% membership in the north.

Propaganda
- Press, radio and cinema were all controlled
- Mussolini was highly promoted as a 'saviour' sent by God to help Italy – heir to Caesar, world statesman, supreme patriot, a great thinker who worked 20 hours a day, a man of action, incorruptible.

Foreign policy
- Mussolini was initially extremely popular, as evidenced by huge crowds who turned out to hear him speak
- Foreign policy successes in the 1920s, such as the Corfu Incident, made him extremely popular. He was also able to mobilise public opinion very successfully for the invasion of Abyssinia
- Mussolini's role in the Munich Conference of 1938 was his last great foreign policy triumph
- As Mussolini got more closely involved with Hitler his popularity lessened. His intervention in Spain proved a huge drain on Italy's resources. The invasion of Albania was a fiasco. The Fascist Grand Council removed him in 1943.

Relations with the Papacy
- Lateran treaties/Concordat with Papacy enabled acceptance of regime by the Catholic majority
- Many Catholics supported Mussolini's promotion of 'family values'.

Economic and social policies
- Fascists tried to develop the Italian economy in a series of propaganda-backed initiatives eg the 'Battle for Grain'. While superficially successful, they did tend to divert resources from other areas
- Development of transport infrastructure, with building of autostrade and redevelopment of major railway terminals eg Milan
- One major success was the crushing of organized crime. Most Mafia leaders were in prison by 1939
- Dopolavoro had 3.8 million members by 1939. Gave education and skills training; sports provision, day-trips, holidays, financial assistance and cheap rail fares. This diverted attention from social/economic problems and was the Fascist state's most popular institution.

Russia 1881 – 1921

31. The candidate evaluates the importance of working class discontent in causing the 1905 revolution in Russia, using evidence and arguments such as:

Discontent of Working Class
- At the start of the 1900s there was industrial recession which caused a lot of hardship for the working class
- The working class complaints were long hours, low pay, poor conditions, the desire for a constitutional government and an end to the war with Japan
- There was a wave of strikes in Jan 1905 with nearly half a million people on strike (10 times the number in the previous decade)
- In October there were two and half million people on strike as well as demonstrations
- Soviets were speaking for the workers and expressing political demands.

Other Factors

Discontent with Repressive Government and its policies
- There was discontent amongst various factions in Russian society
- The middle class and some of the gentry were unhappy with the government at the time
- The middle class was aggrieved at having no participation in government, and angry at the incompetence of the government during the war with Japan
- There was propaganda from middle class groups, Zemstva called for change, the Radical Union of Unions was formed to combine professional groups
- Students rioted, and carried out assassinations
- The gentry tried to convince the Tsar to make minor concessions
- Political groups did not really play a role although they encouraged peasant unrest, and strikes in the urban areas
- The Mensheviks had influence in the soviets and the Bolsheviks were involved in the Moscow Rising
- Russification: The National minorities were aggrieved at the lack of respect for their culture language and religion, and the imposition of the Russian language
- The National minorities harboured a great desire for independence or at least greater autonomy and began to assert themselves, such as Georgia which declared its independence.

Economic problems
- Worsening economic conditions such as famines in 1897, 1898 and 1901 had led to shortage and distress in the countryside. Urban workers conditions and pay also dreadful
- Economic recession between 1899 and 1903 led to growing unemployment throughout the Empire.

Discontent amongst the Peasants
- The peasants had several grievances such as Redemption payments, high taxes, Land Hunger and poverty
- There was a wave of unrest in 1902 and 1903, which had gradually increased by 1905 There were various protests like timber cutting, seizure of lords' land, labour and rent strikes, attacks on landlord's grain stocks, landlords estates seized and divided up
- There were claims that peasants should boycott paying taxes, redemption payments and refuse to be conscripted to the army.

War with Japan
- The war with Japan was a failure and humiliation for the country and moreover this was compounded by the heavy losses suffered by the Russian army
- The war was initially to distract the public from domestic troubles by rallying patriotism
- The incompetence of the government during the war made social unrest worse rather than dampening it
- Troops suffered from low morale after the defeat and there were complaints about poor pay and conditions
- There were some sporadic but uncoordinated revolts although nothing too major
- There were mutinies by troops waiting to return from the war and on the Trans Siberian Railway
- In June there was the Potemkin mutiny although the planned general mutiny did not follow
- Generally though most of the troops remained loyal (unlike 1917).

Bloody Sunday
- 22nd Jan 1905 Father Gapon, an Orthodox priest attempted to lead a peaceful March of workers and their families to the Winter Palace to deliver a petition asking the Tsar to improve the conditions of the workers
- Marchers were fired on and killed by troops

- Many of the people saw this as a brutal massacre by the Tsar and his troops
- Bloody Sunday greatly damaged the traditional image of the Tsar as the "Little Father", the Guardian of the Russian people
- Reaction to Bloody Sunday was strong and was nationwide with disorder strikes in urban areas, terrorism against government officials and landlords, much of which was organised by the SRs
- The situation was made worse by the defeat to Japan in 1905
- The assassination of government minister Plehve.

32. The candidate evaluates the extent to which the Bolsheviks gained power due to the weaknesses of the Provisional Government, using evidence and arguments such as:

Weaknesses of the Provisional Government
- The Provisional Government was an unelected government; it was a self-appointed body and had no right to exercise authority, which led it into conflict with those bodies that emerged with perceived popular legitimacy
- The Provisional Government gave in to the pressure of the army and from the Allies to keep Russia in the War
- Remaining in the war helped cause the October Revolution and helped destroy the Provisional Government as the misery it caused continued for people in Russia
- General Kornilov, a right wing general, proposed to replace the Provisional Government with a military dictatorship and sent troops to Petrograd
- Kerensky appealed to the Petrograd Soviet for help and the Bolsheviks were amongst those who helped
- Some Bolsheviks were armed and released from prison to help put down the attempted coup.

Other Factors

Appeal of the Bolsheviks
- Lenin returned to Russia announcing the April Theses, with slogans such as "Peace, Land and Bread" and "All Power to the Soviets" which were persuasive
- Lenin talked of further revolution to overthrow the Provisional Government and his slogans identified the key weaknesses of the Provisional Government
- The Bolsheviks kept attending the Petrograd Soviet when most of the others stopped doing so and this gave them control of the Soviet, which they could then use against the Provisional Government
- The Bolsheviks did not return their weapons to the Provisional Government after they defeated Kornilov
- Bolsheviks were able to act as protectors of Petrograd.

Dual power – The role of the Petrograd Soviet
- The old Petrograd Soviet re emerged and ran Petrograd
- The Petrograd Soviet undermined the authority of Provisional Government especially when relations between the two worsened
- Order No.1 of the Petrograd Soviet weakened the authority of the Provisional Government as soldiers were not to obey orders of Provisional Government that contradicted those of the Petrograd Soviet.

Economic problems
- The workers were restless as they were starving due to food shortages caused by the war
- The shortage of fuel caused lack of heating for the workers in their living conditions
- The shortage of food and supplies made the workers unhappy and restless
- The Bolsheviks' slogans appealed to them such as the workers control of industry.

The Land Issue
- All over Russia peasants were seizing nobles land and wanted the Provisional Government to legitimise this
- The failure of the Provisional Government to recognise the peasants' claims eroded confidence in the Provisional Government
- Food shortages caused discontent, and they were caught up by revolutionary slogans such as "Peace, Land And Bread".

The July Days
- The Bolsheviks staged an attempt to seize power, rising in support of the Kronstadt sailors who were in revolt
- The revolt was easily crushed by the Provisional Government but showed increasing opposition to the PG, especially from the forces
- The revolt also showed that the PG was still reasonably strong and able to crush opposition such as the Bolsheviks who now appeared to be weakened.

33. The candidate evaluates how important the use of terror by the Reds was in allowing them to win the Civil War, using evidence and arguments such as:

Terror (Cheka)
- The Cheka was set up to eradicate any opposition to the Reds
- There was no need for proof of guilt for punishment to be exacted
- There was persecution of individual people who opposed the Reds as well as whole groups of people, which helped to reduce opposition due to fear, or simply eradicate opposition
- The Cheka group carried out severe repression
- Some of the first victims of the Cheka were leaders of other political parties
- 140,000 were executed by 1922 when Lenin was happy that all opposition had been suppressed.

Other Factors

Organisation of the Red Army
- The Red Army was better organized than the White Army and better equipped and therefore able to crush any opposition from the White forces
- Use of ex-officers from old Imperial Army
- Reintroduction of rank and discipline
- Role of Commissars.

Role of Trotsky
- Trotsky had a completely free hand in military matters
- HQ was heavily armed train, which he used to travel around the country
- He supervised the formation of the Red Army, which became a formidable fighting force of three million men
- He recruited ex-Tsar army officers and used political commissars to watch over them, thus ensuring experienced officers but no political recalcitrance
- He used conscription to gain troops and would shoot any deserters
- Trotsky helped provide an army with great belief in what it was fighting for, which the Whites did not have.

Disunity among Whites
- The Whites were an uncoordinated series of groups whose morale was low
- The Whites were a collection of socialists, liberals, moderates etc who all wanted different things and often fought amongst themselves due to their political differences. All of the Whites shared a hatred of Communism but other than this they lacked a common purpose
- No White leader of any measure emerged to unite and lead the White forces whereas the Reds had Trotsky and Lenin.

Superior Red resources
- Once the Reds had established defence of their lines they were able to repel and exhaust the attacks by the Whites until they scattered or surrendered
- With the major industrial centres in their land (Moscow and Petrograd) the Reds had access to factories to supply weapons etc and swiftly move due to their control of the railways.
- Control of the Railways meant they could transport troops and supplies quickly and efficiently and in large numbers to the critical areas of defence or attack
- The decisive battles between the Reds and Whites were near railheads
- The Reds were in control of a concentrated area of western Russia, which they could successfully defend due to the maintenance of their communication and supply lines
- Having the two major cities of Moscow and Petrograd in their possession meant that the Reds had the hold of the industrial centres of Russia as well as the administrative centres
- Having the two major cities gave the Reds munitions and supplies that the Whites were unable to therefore obtain.

Foreign Intervention
- The Bolsheviks were able to claim that the foreign "invaders" were imperialists who were trying to overthrow the revolution and invade Russia
- The Reds were able to stand as Champions of the Russian nation from foreign invasion
- The help received by the Whites from foreign powers was not as great as was hoped for
- The Foreign Powers did not provide many men due to the First World War just finishing and their help was mostly restricted to money and arms.

Propaganda
- Whites were unable to take advantage of the brutality of the Reds to win support as they often carried out similar atrocities
- The Whites were unable to present themselves as a better alternative to the Reds due to their brutality
- The Reds kept pointing out that all of the land that the peasants had seized in the 1917 Revolution would be lost if the Whites won. This fear prevented the peasants from supporting the Whites.

Leadership of Lenin
- Introduction of War Communism
- By forcing the peasants to sell their grain to the Reds for a fixed price the Reds were able to ensure that their troops were well supplied with and well fed
- The Whites' troops were not as well supplied and fed as the Reds' troops
- Skilled delegation and ruthlessness.

USA 1918 – 1968

34. The candidate evaluates how far it can be argued that the activities of the Ku Klux Klan as the most important obstacle to the achievement of Civil Rights for black people up to 1941, using evidence and arguments such as:

Activities of the Ku Klux Klan
- Founded in 1860s to prevent former slaves achieving equal rights
- Suppressed by 1872, but in the 1920s there was a resurgence
- Black population in South terrified to campaign for civil rights by actions of KKK
- By 1925 it had three million members, including the police, judges and politicians
- Secret organisation with powerful members

- 1923 Hiram Wesley Evans became the Klan's leader
- Methods horrific: included beatings, torture and lynching
- Roosevelt refused to support a federal bill to outlaw lynching in his New Deal in 1930s – feared loss of Democrat support in South
- Activities took place at night – men in white robes, guns, torches, burning crosses
- The 'second' Klan grew most rapidly in urbanizing cities which had high growth rates between 1910 and 1930, such as Detroit, Memphis, Dayton, Atlanta, Dallas and Houston
- Klan membership in Alabama dropped to less than 6,000 by 1930. Small independent units continued to be active in places like Birmingham.

Other Factors

Legal impediments
- 'Jim Crow Laws' – separate education, transport, toilets etc – passed in Southern states after the Civil War
- 'Separate but Equal' Supreme Court Decision 1896, when Homer Plessey tested their legality
- Attitudes of Presidents eg Wilson 'Segregation is not humiliating and is a benefit for you black gentlemen'.

Lack of political influence
- 1890s: loopholes in the interpretation of the 15th Amendment were exploited so that states could impose voting qualifications
- 1898 case of Mississippi v Williams – voters must understand the American Constitution
- Grandfather Clause: impediment to black people voting
- Most black people in the South were sharecroppers they did not own land and some states identified ownership of property as a voting qualification
- Therefore black people could not vote, particularly in the South, and could not elect anyone who would oppose the Jim Crow Laws.

Divisions in the black community
- Booker T Washington, accomodationist philosophy, regarded as an 'Uncle Tom' by many
- In contrast W E B De Bois founded the NAACP – a national organisation whose main aim was to oppose discrimination through legal action. 1919 he launched a campaign against lynching, but it failed to attract most black people and was dominated by white people and well off black people
- Marcus Garvey and Black Pride – he founded the UNIA (Universal Negro Improvement Association) which aimed to get blacks to 'take Africa, organise it, develop it, arm it, and make it the defender of Negroes the world over'.

Popular prejudice
- After the institution of slavery the status of Africans was stigmatised, and this stigma was the basis for the anti-African racism that persisted
- The relocation of millions of African Americans from their roots in the Southern states to the industrial centres of the North after World War I, particularly in cities such as Boston, Chicago, and New York (Harlem). In northern cities, racial tensions exploded, most violently in Chicago, and lynchings – mob-directed hangings, usually racially motivated – increased dramatically in the 1920s.

35. The candidate evaluates the importance of the emergence of effective black leaders in the growing demand for Civil Rights between 1945 and 1968, using evidence and arguments such as:

The emergence of effective black leaders
- Martin Luther King – inspirational. Linked with SCLC. Peaceful non violence and effective use of the media
- Malcolm X – inspirational, but more confrontational. Articulate voice of Nation of Islam

- Stokely Carmichael – Black power and rejection of much of MLK's non violent approach. A direct ideas descendant of Marcus Garvey
- All leaders attracted media coverage, large followings and divided opinion across USA
- Black Panthers attracted attention but lost support by their confrontational tactics
- Other leaders and organisations eclipsed by media focus on main personalities.

Other factors

Effective black organisations formed
- 1957 Martin Luther King and other black clergy formed the Southern Christian Leadership Conference (SCLC) to coordinate the work of Civil Rights groups
- King urged African Americans to use peaceful methods
- 1960 a group of black and white college students organised Non-violent Coordinating Committee (SNCC) to help the Civil Rights movement
- They joined with young people from the SCLC, CORE and NAACP in staging sit-ins, boycotts marches and freedom rides
- Combined efforts of the Civil Rghts groups ended discrimination in many public places including restaurants, hotels, and theatres.

Continuing racial discrimination pushed many black Americans to demand civil rights
- The experience of war emphasised freedom, democracy and human rights yet in USA Jim Crow laws still existed and lynching went unpunished
- The Emmet Till murder trial and its publicity
- Education: 1954 Brown v Board of Education of Topeka; 1957 Little Rock Central High School
- Transport: 1955 Rosa Parks and the Montgomery Bus Boycott.

Influence of Second World War
- Black soldiers talked about 'the Double-V-Campaign': Victory in the war and victory for Civil Rights at home
- Philip Randolph is credited with highlighting the problems faced by black Americans during World War Two
- Planned March on Washington in 1941 to protest against racial discrimination
- Roosevelt's response – Executive order 8802
- Roosevelt also established the Fair Employment Practices Committee to investigate incidents of discrimination
- Creation of the Congress of Racial Equality (CORE) 1942
- Beginning of a mass movement for Civil Rights.

36. The candidate assesses the extent to which the Civil Rights campaigns of the 1950s and 1960s resulted in significant improvements in the lives of black Americans, using evidence and arguments such as:

Aims of Civil Rights movement
- Were mainly pacifist and intended to bring Civil Rights and equality in law to all non-white Americans
- More radical segregationist aims of Black Radical Movements.

Role of NAACP
- Work of NAACP in the Brown v Topeka Board of Education, 1954
- Work of NAACP in the Montgomery Bus Boycott, 1955.

Role of Congress of Racial Equality [CORE]
- Organised sit-ins during 1961 and freedom rides
- Helped organise march on Washington
- Instrumental in setting up Freedom Schools in Mississippi.

Role of SCLC and Martin Luther King
- Emergence of Martin Luther King and the SCLC
- Little Rock, Arkansas - desegregation following national publicity
- Non-violent protest as exemplified by Sit-ins and Freedom Rides
- Birmingham, Alabama 1963: use of water cannon: Reaction of Kennedy
- March on Washington, August 1963 - massive publicity
- Martin Luther King believed that the Civil Rights Act of 1964 'gave Negroes some part of their rightful dignity, but without the vote it was dignity without strength'
- March 1965, King led a march from Selma to Birmingham, Alabama, to publicise the way in which the authorities made it difficult for black Americans to vote easily.

Changes in Federal Policy
- Use of executive orders: Truman used them to appoint black appointments, order equality of treatment in the armed services: Kennedy signed 1962 executive order outlawing racial discrimination in public housing, etc
- Eisenhower sent in army troops and National Guardsmen to protect nine African-American students enrolled at Little Rock Central High School: Kennedy sent troops to Oxford, Mississippi to protect black student: James Meredith
- Johnson and the 1964 Civil Rights Act banning racial discrimination in any public place, Voting Rights Act of 1965: by end of 1965 over 250,000 Blacks newly registered to vote, Affirmative Action, etc.

Social, Economic and Political changes
- Civil Rights Acts of 1964 and 1965 irrelevant to the cities of the North
- Economic issues more important in the North
- Watts riots and the split in the Civil Rights movement
- King and the failure in Chicago
- Urban poverty and de facto segregation still common in urban centres – failure of King's campaign to attack poverty.

Rise of black radical movements
- Stokely Carmichael and Black Power
- Malcolm X publicised the increasing urban problems within the ghettos of America
- The Black Panthers were involved in self-help schemes throughout poor cities
- Kerner commission 1968 recognised US society still divided.

Appeasement and the Road to War, to 1939

37. The candidate assesses the extent to which fascist powers used diplomacy to achieve their aims using evidence and arguments such as:

Fascist diplomacy as a means of achieving aims:
- Aims can be generally accepted as destruction of Versailles, the weakening of democracies, the expansion of fascist powers and countering communism
- Diplomacy and the protestation of 'peaceful' intentions and 'reasonable' demands
- Appeals to sense of international equality and fairness and the righting of past wrongs eg Versailles
- Withdrawal from League and Disarmament Conference
- Anglo German Naval Treaty 1935 - Germany allowed to expand navy. Versailles ignored in favour of bi lateral agreements. A gain for Germany
- Prior to Remilitarisation of Rhineland Hitler made offer of 25 year peace promise
- Diplomacy used to distract and delay reaction to Nazi action.

Economic reasons
- Use of economic influence and pressure, eg on south-eastern European states

- Aid supplied to Franco (Spain) was tactically important to Hitler. Not only for testing weapons but also access to Spanish minerals.

Pacts and alliances
- The German-Polish Non-Aggression Pact between Nazi Germany and Poland signed on January 26, 1934 – normalised relations between Poland and Germany, and promised peace for 10 years. Germany gained respectability and calmed international fears
- Rome-Berlin axis – treaty of friendship signed between Italy and Germany on 25 October 1936
- Pact of Steel an agreement between Italy and Germany signed on May 22, 1939 for immediate aid and military support in the event of war
- Anti-Comintern Pact between Nazi-Germany and Japan on November 25th, 1936. The pact directed against the Communist International (Comintern) but was specifically directed against the Soviet Union. In 1937 Italy joined the Pact Munich Agreement – negotiations led to Hitler gaining Sudetenland and weakening Czechoslovakia
- Nazi Soviet Non-Aggression Pact August 1939 – both Hitler and Stalin bought time for themselves. For Hitler it seemed war in Europe over Poland unlikely. Poland was doomed. Britain had lost the possibility of alliance with Russia.

Rearmament
- Open German rearmament from 1935
- The speed and scale of rearmament, including conscription
- The emphasis on air power and the growing threat from the air
- By 1939, Hitler had an army of nearly 1 million men, over 8,000 aircraft and 95 warships
- Mussolini embarked on a rearmament programme to protect Italy from worldwide depression. His building of a modern navy seriously threatened British domination of the Mediterranean as a result.

Military threat and force
- Italy's naval ambitions in the Mediterranean – 'Mare Nostrum'
- Italian invasion of Abyssinia – provocation, methods, and relatively poor performance against very poorly equipped enemy
- German remilitarisation of Rhineland – Hitler's gamble and timing, his generals' opposition, lack of Allied resistance
- Spanish Civil War – aid to Nationalists, testing weapons and tactics, aerial bombing of Guernica
- Anschluss – attempted coup 1934; relations with Schuschnigg; invasion itself relatively botched militarily; popularity of Anschluss in Austria
- Czechoslovakia – threats of 1938; invasion of March 1939
- Italian invasion of Albania – relatively easy annexation of a client state
- Poland – escalating demands; provocation, invasion
- The extent to which it was the threat of military force which was used rather than military force itself – eg Czechoslovakia in 1938; and the extent to which military force itself was effective and/or relied on an element of bluff – eg Rhineland.

38. The candidate assesses the validity of the statement that the Munich agreement of 1938 was a "reasonable settlement under the circumstances", using evidence and arguments such as:

Munich reasonable under circumstances
- Czechoslovakian defences were effectively outflanked anyway following the Anschluss
- Britain and France were not in a position to prevent German attack on Czechoslovakia in terms of difficulties of getting assistance to Czechoslovakia
- British public opinion was reluctant to risk war over mainly German-speaking Sudetenland

- Military unpreparedness for wider war – especially Britain's air defences
- Lack of alternative, unified international response to Hitler's threats
- Failure of League of Nations in earlier crises
- French doubts over commitments to Czechoslovakia
- US isolationism
- British suspicion of Soviet Russia
- Strong reservations of rest of British Empire and Dominions concerning support for Britain in event of war
- Attitudes of Poland and Hungary who were willing to benefit from the dismemberment of Czechoslovakia
- Munich bought another year for rearmament which Britain put to good use
- Views of individuals, politicians and media at this time.

Munich not reasonable
- A humiliating surrender to Hitler's threats
- Another breach in the post-WW1 settlement
- A betrayal of Czechoslovakia and democracy
- Czechoslovakia wide open to further German aggression as happened in March 1939
- Further augmentation of German manpower and resources
- Furtherance of Hitler's influence and ambitions in Eastern Europe
- Further alienation of Soviet Union
- Poland left further exposed
- A British, French, Soviet agreement could have been a more effective alternative
- Views of individuals, politicians and media at this time.

39. The candidate evaluates the extent to which the occupation of Czechoslovakia in March 1939 led to the outbreak of World War Two six months later, using evidence and arguments such as:

The occupation of Bohemia and the collapse of Czechoslovakia
- British and French realisation, after Hitler's breaking of Munich Agreement and invasion of Czechoslovakia in March 1939, that Hitler's word was worthless and that his aims went beyond the incorporation of ex-German territories and ethnic Germans within the Reich
- Promises of support to Poland and Rumania
- British public acceptance that all attempts to maintain peace had been exhausted
- Prime Minister Chamberlain felt betrayed by the Nazi seizure of Czechoslovakia, realised his policy of appeasement towards Hitler had failed, and began to take a much harder line against the Nazis.

Other factors

British abandonment of the policy of Appeasement
- Events in Bohemia and Moravia consolidated growing concerns in Britain
- Czechoslovakia did not concern most people until the middle of September 1938, when they began to object to a small democratic state being bullied. However, most press and population went along with it, although level of popular opposition often underestimated
- German annexation of Memel (largely German population, but in Lithuania) further showed Hitler's bad faith
- Actions convinced British government of growing German threat in south-eastern Europe
- Guarantees to Poland and promised action in the event of threats to Polish independence.

Importance of Nazi-Soviet Pact
- Pact – diplomatic, economic, military co-operation; division of Poland
- Unexpected – Hitler and Stalin's motives

- Put an end to British-French talks with Russia on guarantees to Poland
- Hitler was freed from the threat of Soviet intervention and war on two fronts
- Hitler's belief that Britain and France would not go to war over Poland without Russian assistance
- Hitler now felt free to attack Poland
- But, given Hitler's consistent, long-term foreign policy aims on the destruction of the Versailles settlement and lebensraum in the east, the Nazi-Soviet Pact could be seen more as a factor influencing the timing of the outbreak of war rather than as one of its underlying causes
- Hitler's long-term aims for destruction of the Soviet state and conquest of Russian resources - lebensraum
- Hitler's need for new territory and resources to sustain Germany's militarised economy
- Hitler's belief that British and French were 'worms' who would not turn from previous policy of appeasement and avoidance of war at all costs
- Hitler's belief that the longer war was delayed the more the balance of military and economic advantage would shift against Germany.

British diplomacy and relations with the Soviet Union
- Stalin knew that Hitler's ultimate aim was to attack Russia
- Lord Halifax, the British Foreign Secretary was invited by Stalin to go to Russia to discuss an alliance against Germany
- Britain refused as they feared Russian Communism, and they believed that the Russian army was too weak to be of any use against Hitler
- In August 1939, with war in Poland looming, the British and French eventually sent a military mission to discuss an alliance with Russia. Owing to travel difficulties it took five days to reach Leningrad
- The Russians asked if they could send troops into Poland if Hitler invaded. The British refused, knowing that the Poles would not want this. The talks broke down
- This merely confirmed Stalin's suspicions regarding the British. He felt they could not be trusted, especially after the Munich agreement, and they would leave Russia to fight Germany alone. This led directly to opening talks with the Nazis who seemed to be taking the Russians seriously by sending Foreign Minister von Ribbentrop and offering peace and land.

The position of France
- France had signed an agreement with Czechoslovakia offering support if the country was attacked. However, Hitler could all but guarantee that in 1938, French would do nothing as their foreign policy was closely tied to the British
- French military, and particularly their airforce, allowed to decline in years after 1919
- After Munich, French more aggressive towards dictators and in events of 1939 were keen on a military alliance with the Soviet Union, however despite different emphasis on tactics were tied to the British and their actions.

Developing crisis over Poland
- Hitler's long-term aims for the destruction of Versailles, including regaining of Danzig and Polish Corridor
- British and French decision to stick to their guarantees to Poland.

Invasion of Poland
- On 1 September 1939, Hitler and the Nazis faked a Polish attack on a minor German radio station in order to justify a German invasion of Poland. An hour later Hitler declared war on Poland stating one of his reasons for the invasion was because of "the attack by regular Polish troops on the Gleiwitz transmitter"
- France and Britain had a defensive pact with Poland. This forced France and Britain to declare war on Germany, which they did on September 3.

The Cold War 1945 – 1989

40. The candidate assesses how effectively the Soviet Union controlled Eastern Europe up to 1961, using evidence and arguments such as:

The international context
- 1955 - emergence of Nikita Khrushchev as leader on death of Stalin. He encouraged criticism of Stalin and seemed to offer hope for greater political and economic freedom across the Eastern European satellite states
- Speech to 20th Party Congress, Feb 1956: Khrushchev attacked Stalin for promoting a cult of personality and for his use of purges and persecution to reinforce his dictatorship. Policy of de-Stalinisation
- Development of policy of peaceful co-existence to appeal to the West
- Development of policy of different roads to Socialism to appeal to satellite states in Eastern Europe who were becoming restless.

Demands for change and reaction: Poland (1956)
- Riots sparked off by economic grievances developed into demands for political change in Poland
- On the death of Stalinist leader Boleslaw Bierut in 1956 he was replaced by Wladyslaw Gromulka, a former victim of Stalinism which initially worried the Soviets
- Poles announced their own road to Socialism and introduced extensive reforms
- Release of political prisoners (and Cardinal Wyszynski, Archbishop of Warsaw); collective farms broken up into private holdings; private shops allowed to open, greater freedom to factory managers
- Relatively free elections held in 1957 which returned a Communist majority of 18
- No Soviet intervention despite concerns
- Gromulka pushed change only so far. Poland remained in the Warsaw Pact as a part of the important 'buffer zone'. Political freedoms were very limited indeed. Poland was a loyal supporter of the Soviet Union until the 1980s and the emergence of the Solidarity movement.

Demands for change and reaction: Hungary (1956)
- Hungarians had similar complaints: lack of political freedom, economic problems and poor standard of living
- Encouraged by Polish success, criticism of the Stalinist regime of Mátyás Rákosi grew and he was removed by Khrushchev
- Popular upsurge of support for change in Budapest led to a new Hungarian government led by Imre Nagy, who promised genuine reform and change
- Nagy government planned multi-party elections, political freedoms, the withdrawal of Hungary from the Warsaw Pact and demands for the withdrawal of Soviet forces
- Nagy went too far. The Soviet Union could not see this challenge to the political supremacy of the Communist Party and the break-up of their carefully constructed buffer zone. They intervened and crushed the rising brutally
- Successful intervention, but lingering resentment from mass of Hungarian people, through some economic flexibility allowed the new regime of Janos Kadar to improve economic performance and living standards.

Demands for change and reaction: Berlin (1961)
- Problem of Berlin – a divided city in a divided nation
- Lack of formal boundaries in Berlin allowed East Berliners and East Germans to freely enter the West which they did owing to the lack of political freedom, economic development and poor living standards in the East

- Many of those fleeing (2.8 million between 1949 and 1961) were skilled and young, just the people the communist East needed to retain. This was embarrassing for the East as it showed that Communism was not the superior system it was claimed to be
- Concerns of Ulbricht and Khrushchev: attempts to encourage the Western forces to leave Berlin by bluster and threat from 1958 failed
- Kennedy of America spoke about not letting the Communists drive them out of Berlin. Resultant increase in tension could not be allowed to continue
- Building of barriers: barbed wire then stone in August 1961 to stem the flood from East to West
- Success in that it reduced the threat of war and the exodus to the West from the East to a trickle
- Frustration of many in East Germany. Propaganda gift for the US and allies.

Military and ideological factors
- Buffer zone could not be broken up as provided military defence for Soviet Union
- Use of force and Red Army to enforce control in late 40s and early 50s
- Need to ensure success of Communism hence policy.

Domestic pressures
- Intention to stop any further suffering of Soviet Union in aftermath of WW2 made leadership very touchy to change
- Some economic freedoms were allowed, but at the expense of political freedoms
- Need to stop spread of demands for change.

41. The candidate evaluates the extent to which the superpowers' attempts to manage the Cold War between 1962 and 1985 were prompted by the economic cost of the arms race, using arguments and evidence such as:

Economic cost of arms race
- Developments in technology raised the costs of the arms race
- The development of Anti-Ballistic Missile technology and costs of war led to SALT 1 and the ABM treaty
- Limiting MIRV and intermediate missile technology led to SALT 2
- The cost of 'Star Wars' technology also encouraged the Soviet Union to seek better relations
- Khrushchev's desire for better relations between the Superpowers in the 50s and 60s was, in part, about freeing up resources for economic development in the USSR. He hoped this would show the superiority of the Soviet system
- Gorbachev wanted to improve the lives of ordinary Russians and part of this was by reducing the huge defence budget eg Intermediate Nuclear Forces Treaty, December 1987.

Other factors

Mutually Assured Destruction
- The development of vast arsenals of nuclear weapons from 1945 by both Superpowers as a deterrent to the other side; a military attack would result in horrific retaliation
- So many nuclear weapons were built to ensure that not all were destroyed even after a first-strike, and this led to a stalemate known as MAD. Arms race built on fear.

Dangers of military conflict as seen through Cuban Missile Crisis
- The threat of nuclear war seemed very close on the discovery of Soviet nuclear missiles on Cuba in 1962. Before Khrushchev backed down nuclear war was threatened. It also illustrated the lack of formal contact between the Superpowers to defuse potential conflicts

- Introduction of a 'hot-line' between the Kremlin and White House in order to improve communication between the Superpowers. Khrushchev and Kennedy also signed the Limited Nuclear Test Ban Treaty, the first international agreement on nuclear weapons.

Technology: The importance of verification
- American development of surveillance technology (U2 and satellites) meant that nuclear weapons could be identified and agreements verified
- Example of U2 flight over Cuba where Anderson photographed nuclear sites
- Also U2 and satellite verification to make sure the Soviets were doing as promised at the negotiating table
- Some historians think Arms Control would never have taken root, but for the ability of the sides to verify what the other was doing.

Co-existence and Détente
- Policies of co-existence and détente developed to defuse tensions and even encourage trade
- Role of others like Brandt in West Germany in defusing tension through their policies of Ostpolitik, etc.

42. The candidate evaluates the role of Gorbachev in ending the Cold War using evidence and arguments such as:

Role of President Mikhail Gorbachev
- Gorbachev saw that the USSR could not afford a new arms race. The Soviet economy was at breaking point. Commitments to the arms race and propping up allied regimes meant consumer goods and other things such as housing that mattered to Russian people were neglected
- Gorbachev implemented policies of Perestroika and Glasnost which aimed to reform the Soviet economy and liberalise its political system
- Gorbachev worked to improve relations with the USA. He took ideology out of his foreign policy, as exemplified by arms agreements to allow the USSR to concentrate on internal matters: Intermediate Nuclear Forces Treaty, Dec 1987, Nuclear Weapons Reduction Treaty, 1989
- Gorbachev told leaders of the satellite East European states in March 1989 that the Soviet army would no longer help them to stay in power.

Other factors

Role of President Ronald Reagan
- Unlike many in the US administration Reagan actively sought to challenge Soviet weakness and strengthen the west in order to defeat Communism. In 1983 he denounced the Soviet Union as an 'Evil Empire'
- Programme of improving US armed forces, including nuclear weapons and he proposed a Star Wars missile shield to challenge the belief in MAD (SDI). He was very charming when he met Gorbachev and visited the Soviet Union.

Western economic strength
- Allowed America to embark on the Star Wars weapons programme
- Perception of the affluent West through television and consumer goods undermined Communist claims of the superiority of their economic system.

Withdrawal of the Soviet Union from Afghanistan
- Symptom of the problems of Soviet Union
- Intervention in Dec 1979: conflict with the Mujaheddin. Russian army morale crumbled when over 20,000 Soviet soldiers died, as did support at home
- The conflict showed the weaknesses of the Soviet economy. War led to a slump in living standards for ordinary Russians
- Russians began to question the actions of their own government. Gorbachev withdrew troops in 1988.

Failure of Communism in Eastern Europe
- Strong Polish identity and history of hostility with Russia. By 1970s, Poland in economic slump. Emergence of opposition around Gdansk in 1980: industrial workers strike led by Lech Walesa, who argued for the creation of an independent trade union. Solidarity grew to nine million members in a matter of months. Movement suppressed in 1981 by General Jaruzelski's government
- Multiparty elections in Poland, after Soviet troops left, victory for Solidarity.
- Czechoslovakia, political prisoners released in November 1989 and by the end of the month, the communist government had gone. No Soviet intervention
- Opening of the Berlin Wall: division of Germany finally came to an end
- Soviet domination ended
- Perestroika and Glasnost and end of Communist rule in USSR.

HIGHER HISTORY PAPER 2 2012

SPECIAL TOPIC 1: THE WARS OF INDEPENDENCE, 1286 – 1328

1. The candidate makes a judgement on the extent to which **Sources A** and **B** agree about the Scots' attempts to protect their independence in terms of:

Overall both sources generally agree that the Scottish Guardians were concerned about maintaining the independence of Scotland. **Source B** offers a more detailed summary of how the kingdom would function under a dual monarchy and seems to suggest more optimism than the frank statements of the actual treaty.

Source A	*Source B*
• No one of the kingdom of Scotland shall be held to answer outwith that kingdom for any agreement entered into, or for any crime committed, or in any other cause contrary to the laws and customs of that kingdom	• Persons in Scotland who had been accused of a crime or sued at law should not have to answer in a court outside their country
• The rights and liberties and customs of Scotland shall be wholly preserved	• The guardians above all anxious to do nothing that might impair the "rights" or the integrity of Scotland
• We promise that the kingdom of Scotland shall remain separate and divided from the kingdom of England	• The treaty envisaged two feudal kingdoms – England and Scotland – ruled separately
• We grant that no tenant-in-chief of the king of Scotland shall be forced to go outside the kingdom to do homage or fealty.	• Tenants in chief of the Scots Crown need do homage for their lands in Scotland only.

2. The candidate makes a judgement as to how useful **Source C** is as evidence of the subjugation of the Scots by Edward I in 1296 in terms of:

Points from the source which show the candidate has interpreted the significant views:

- **Origin** – Primary source written in the early 14th century by the canon of Guisborough Priory in the Bruce lands of Yorkshire. The chronicle details events throughout the period of the Scottish wars (though there is a gap between 1316 and 1326); it is generally considered a reliable document. Events detailed during the reign of Edward I are a contemporary record of events.
- **Possible purpose** – Walter's work is a record of English history, dating from the conquest in 1066, as with many chronicles it is an attempt to set the world in context. The Guisborough Priory suffered during the Scottish wars, and housed many refugees from other religious houses during the wars. There could be a trace of bias due to this.
- **Content** –
  - When the city was taken more than 8,000 were killed
  - Taking of hostages like Lord William Douglas
  - Taking the oaths of loyalty from two hundred men.

Points from recall which support and develop those from the source:
- Despite the Scots' early confidence, and the fortification of Berwick, the city fell quickly to Edward's more professional and experienced army
- The garrison of the castle surrendered under the laws of chivalry and Edward allowed them to go, but the townsmen and Burghers were slaughtered
- Edward forced the women and children to abandon their homes and re-populated Berwick with people from Northumbria.

Points from recall which offer a wider contextualisation such as:
- The Earl of Surrey defeated the Scottish army at Dunbar, many Scottish knights and nobles were captured
- Edward I captured important castles such as Roxburgh, Edinburgh and most importantly Stirling, there was no attempt at resistance at Stirling
- Edward's march northward to Elgin, and the acceptance of oaths of loyalty from nobles along the way (Ragman's Roll)
- King John's humiliating surrender at Kincardine Castle (Toom Tabard)
- Edward's removal of the Stone of Destiny and Scottish legal documents to prevent an inauguration of a future king
- The appointment of the Earl of Surrey as Lieutenant of Scotland
- Any other relevant points.

3. The candidate makes a judgement as to how far **Source D** shows the changing military balance between Scotland and England, 1298-1301 in terms of:

Points from the source which show the candidate has interpreted the significant views:
- The Scots army is forced to retreat north, deploying scorched earth tactics. It can be surmised that this would have had a negative impact on the people living in the area as well as the local economy
- Edward seized and repaired Stirling Castle, a vital stronghold in the defence of Scotland
- Edward holds a parliament at Carlisle and divides Scottish land out amongst his supporters
- Wallace is forced to resign as Guardian because he cannot work with the jealous nobles.

Points from recall which support and develop those in the source:
- It was not Wallace's decision to attack that was the mistake, but his tactics at the Battle of Falkirk that cost him his victory and his position as Guardian of Scotland
- Wallace understood the power of the English cavalry. His tactics of fortifying the positions of the schiltrons behind stakes and ropes meant that they were essentially impregnable as far as the English cavalry were concerned, but easy targets for the Welsh archers
- Despite the crushing defeat at Falkirk, there was no capitulation before Edward, as there had been after Dunbar.

Points from recall which offer a wider contextualisation such as:
- New Guardians were chosen, including Bruce and Comyn, and later Bishop Lamberton
- They planned to attack Roxburgh castle, still in English hands, but a pre-emptive strike by Edward forced them to retreat to their own lands and organise their defences. Unlike Wallace who had no lands to defend, these lords were concerned about more than just the independence of Scotland
- The Scots did have some success, Bruce, Comyn and Lamberton were able to capture Stirling Castle in late 1299 and succeeded in harassing Edward's armies with small forces operating out of Scotland's rugged terrain. In the Southwest the Galloway hills and in the central borders, Selkirk Forrest offered ideal bases for hit and run activities

- However, they also had their share of misfortunes. The highly important castle of Caerlaverock was captured in 1300 by Edward; its fall meant that the Scots army had to flee across the moors to avoid destruction
- Distrust and arguments between Bruce and Comyn
- Bruce eventually resigned his Guardianship and instead settled for defending his lands in the south west
- By the end of 1300 the Scottish resistance was in balance. Edward had succeeded in defeating the Scots at Falkirk and thus had forced Wallace's resignation, but the Scots continued to fight tenaciously. However the arguments in the Scottish camp weakened their ability to present a united front against Edward
- Any other relevant points.

4. The candidate makes a judgement on how fully **Source E** explains the reasons for the ultimate success of Bruce in maintaining Scotland's independence in terms of:

Points from the source which show the candidate has interpreted the significant views:
- Robert rewarded his followers from lands of his enemies and thus ensured their loyalties
- Robert raided northern England to try and force the English king to negotiate
- Robert negotiated an uneasy truce with England in 1323
- Robert negotiated a mutual defence treaty with France in 1326 as part of his policy to ensure a stable inheritance for his son.

Points from recall which support and develop those in the source:
- Bannockburn represented a major victory for Robert, it was the start of his fearful reputation as a great warlord who couldn't be beaten
- Bannockburn had more of an impact on domestic politics in Scotland than any real long term military benefits. Robert passed legislation forbidding nobles holding land in both England and Scotland
- Robert took land from the disinherited at Cambuskenneth and shared it among his supporters to gain loyalty
- The war in the north of England was a significant and often overlooked aspect of the Scottish wars.

Points from recall which offer a wider contextualisation such as:
- As well as the 1315 invasion, Robert attacked England no fewer than 5 times (1316, 1318, 1322, 1323 and 1328)
- The campaign of 1322 was particularly impressive and culminated in the battle of Old Byland, which almost saw a repeat of Bannockburn and the capture of Edward II
- In 1320 the Declaration of Arbroath, a rebuttal to the papal decrees against Robert, was dispatched to Rome along with other letters. It is often seen as a key defence against English insistence that the papacy intervene on their behalf. By 1323 papal attitude to Scotland had significantly improved
- The campaign of 1328, following the murder of Edward II by Isabella and Mortimer is a final decisive move by Robert
- He re-opened his Irish campaign with a new army invading Ulster, at the same time his most trusted lieutenants raided northern England, skilfully running rings around Mortimer and the young newly crowned Edward III
- Robert's announcement that he intended to annex Northumbria eventually forced Isabella and Mortimer to sign the Treaty of Edinburgh 1328
- Edward Bruce invaded Ireland to take war to English and create a pan-Celtic alliance. Overran Ulster quickly, but became bogged down
- Any relevant recall 1306 – 14
- Any other relevant points.

SPECIAL TOPIC 2: THE AGE OF REFORMATION, 1542-1603

1. The candidate makes a judgement on how far **Sources A** and **B** agree about the changes brought about by the Treaty of Edinburgh in terms of:

Overall both sources look at and agree about the changes brought about by the Treaty of Edinburgh of 1560 signed between England and France.

However, **Source A** says that while Scottish nobles and people had to fulfil and observe the terms set out in the treaty while **Source B** says that king and queen were obliged to fulfil their treaty obligations due to the Scots' obedience and loyalty.

Source A	*Source B*
• All warlike operations shall cease	• Truce arranged between England and France
• All military forces of each party shall withdraw from the realm of Scotland	• All foreign soldiers were to withdraw from Scotland
• King Francis and Queen Mary shall abstain from using or carrying the said title or arms of the kingdom of England or Ireland	• Francis II and Mary, Queen of Scots, would abstain from displaying the English arms with those of Scotland
• Francis and Mary will fulfil all those things which were granted to the nobility and people of Scotland provided that the nobility and people of Scotland fulfil and observe what was contained in those conventions and articles.	• Francis and Mary would fulfil all their treaty obligations since the Scots had spontaneously and freely professed and acknowledged their obedience and loyalty towards their king and queen.

2. The candidate makes a judgement on how useful **Source C** is in explaining Mary's difficulties in ruling Scotland, in terms of:

Points from the source which show the candidate has interpreted the significant views:

- **Origin** – The source was written by James Melville, a trusted member of Mary's household who witnessed the murder of David Riccio.
- **Possible Purpose** – To explain the reasons behind the murder of David Riccio and the difficulties Mary faced from the nobles within her court.
- **Content**
  - David Riccio as Mary's secretary was envied and hated by the nobility
  - Mary's husband, Darnley, agreed to the murder of Riccio which Scottish Lords had planned so that they could control the court and parliament
  - Mary was unable to save Riccio and kept as captive.

Points from recall which support and develop those in the source:
- As the Queen's husband, Darnley wanted the 'crown matrimonial'. Mary refused as she believed he was unfit to rule
- As Darnley became more resentful, ambitious Scottish nobles encouraged his anger and Darnley joined a plot to murder Riccio
- George Douglas took Darnley's knife to strike the first blow. He left the knife in Riccio's body to show that Darnley was involved in the murder
- During the struggle, Mary was seized and threatened. Her life was in danger and so was the life of her unborn child.

Points from recall which offer a wider contextualisation:
- Many nobles including Mary's half-brother, the Earl of Moray hated Darnley and they viewed the marriage unfavourably. This led to the Chaseabout Raid in 1565 and although Mary demonstrated her authority over the nobles, she lost the support of many powerful men
- Mary had called a Parliament to punish said nobles by confiscating their titles and property. They offered to help Darnley if he intervened to prevent this. The murder took place two days after the Parliament opened
- While some nobles hoped to benefit from her death; others planned to imprison her and make her child their ruler because they would gain from another minority
- Rivalry between noble families would be one of the main sources of trouble in Mary's reign
- Religion was the most serious problem of Mary's reign. A Catholic Queen ruling a Protestant country was viewed with suspicion by the Kirk
- Mary favoured French influences and often preferred to hide away with servants
- Queen Elizabeth viewed Mary, her cousin and heir, with suspicion. Mary feared that her cousin might assist Scottish Protestants to rise against her
- Mary a woman
- Any other relevant points.

3. The candidate makes a judgement on how far **Source D** illustrates the efforts of James VI to control the Kirk in terms of:

Points from the source which show the candidate has interpreted the significant views:
- When local feuding between the Catholic Earl of Huntly and the Protestant Earl of Moray led to the latter's murder, the incident was used by the Kirk to gain concessions in the Golden Act
- Despite the Golden Act, James never conceded the principle of royal supremacy over the Kirk
- James made a number of successful efforts to tighten royal control over the general assembly and re-establish diocesan episcopacy
- James appears frustrated by the lack of respect he receives from his subjects and is determined to bring Scotland's remote localities under more direct royal control.

Points from recall which support and develop those in the source:
- Relations with the Kirk deteriorated after 1592, leading to conflict in 1596
- James' belief in the divine right of monarchs clashed with Melvillians' view that the Monarch should be accountable to the authority of the Kirk
- In his writings, James asserted that no human institution could limit the powers of a monarch
- Extreme Presbyterians/Melvillians were marginalised on account of James' views
- Further detail of Trew Law and Basilikon Doron.

Points from recall which offer a wider contextualisation such as:
- The Second Book of Discipline (1578) had proposed a Presbyterian Kirk which could make the church independent of the King and his nobility
- By 1581 plans to establish 13 Presbyteries appeared to challenge royal authority
- In 1584, all ministers were required to accept the 'Black Acts' abolishing Presbyteries and asserting royal authority over the Kirk
- In 1592 the 'Golden Act' accepted the recovery of Presbyterian influence within the Kirk, but did not reduce the power of the King

- James sought to extend the power of the monarch and bishops over the Kirk by: having bishops recognised as moderators of Presbyteries; allowing them to hear cases of excommunication and deposition of ministers
- Elders were excluded from Presbyteries and the monarch had the power to determine time and place of the General Assembly
- James would have the General Assembly meeting in Perth or Aberdeen where he could expect more ministers would support the King
- As a result of rebellion in December 1596, James fled from Edinburgh, but this made him more determined to control the Kirk
- 1597 riot in Edinburgh after a sermon preached against the King. James VI had the ministers of Edinburgh briefly imprisoned. The King ordered that no minister was to be appointed without his consent
- In 1597, Andrew Melville was deposed as rector of St Andrews
- James attended every General Assembly from 1597 to 1603, by which time assemblies were becoming more agreeable to the King's aims
- James preferred form of Church government was by bishops and in 1600 he appointed three bishops to Parliament
- Any other relevant points.

4. The candidate makes a judgement on how fully **Source E** explains the impact of the Reformation on the lives of the people of Scotland in terms of:

Points from the source which show the candidate has interpreted the significant views:
- There was a new religious fervour demonstrated by support for Presbyterian beliefs
- Congregations had the right to choose their own minister
- The place of music in the lives of people generally and in the church services was to suffer
- There remained a compassionate attitude towards representatives of the Catholic faith.

Points from recall which support and develop those in the source:
- Emphasis was placed upon attendance at daily and Sunday services. There were to be no distractions which might detain a congregation from their duties
- The *Second Book of Discipline* led indirectly to a regular meeting of ministers from 10 to 20 parishes for discussion of doctrine, which became the presbytery
- The Kirk removed all organs from places of worship
- It proved impractical to dispossess the Catholic clergy of their benefices so they were allowed to retain two-thirds of their revenues for life
- Concessions made to Catholic clergy, on the grounds of old age or ill-health.

Points from recall which offer a wider contextualisation such as:
- At the beginning of 1560, Scotland was a Catholic country with a Protestant minority. By 1603, it was a Protestant country with a small Catholic minority
- The Reformation did not lead to a significant transfer of wealth from the Church and much of the lands of the Catholic Church remained in the hands of the nobility
- The new church still had the problem of not having enough revenue for the parishes
- James VI was reluctant to enforce anti-Catholic laws
- Kirk sessions were instruments of moral and religious control
- The elaborate interiors of Catholic churches were replaced with plain, whitewashed parish kirks
- Observance of Catholic festivals and saints' days and festivals were discouraged

- Literary works and Kirk sermons were conducted in English rather than Latin. (The only Protestant Bibles available to lowland Scots were in English)
- Assistance given to the poor from the friaries ended. New plans to help the poor by the Presbyterian church faced difficulty
- The aim of a school in every parish not achieved but some advances were made in central Scotland
- Literacy rates improved during this period
- Many of the issues prevalent within the Catholic Church prior to the Reformation remained, such as: attendance; poverty of some parishes; and poor quality of preaching
- Scots merchants continued to trade with England and trading ports across the North Sea
- Scots focused on trade with the Protestant Dutch
- Trade with France continued despite the change in religion – although pro-French foreign policy was replaced with pro-English under James
- Any other relevant points.

SPECIAL TOPIC 3: THE TREATY OF UNION, 1689-1740

1. The candidate makes a judgement on how far **Sources A** and **B** agree about worsening relations between Scotland and England in terms of:

Overall **Source A** and **Source B** agree that Scotland's economy was affected by England; **Source A** attributes this to a combination of factors and **Source B** suggests that English actions were responsible.

Source A	*Source B*
• Scotland tipped over the edge of an economic abyss	• Scots aware of sinking economic condition of their nation
• English wars leading to damaging loss of French trade	• Visible damage both to trade and wealth of Scotland
• Protective tariffs blocked the export of certain Scottish goods	• Problems owing to the disadvantage of tariffs
• Outcome was incorporating union with England.	• One way for Scots to restore themselves was incorporating union and alliance with England.

2. The candidate makes a judgement on how useful **Source C** is as evidence of attitudes towards the union, in terms of:

Points from the source which show the candidate has interpreted the significant views:
- **Origin** – Petition sent by Stirling Town Council during debates.
- **Possible purpose** – To give reasons for opposing union with England.
- **Content** –
  - Treaty will bring insupportable taxation which will ruin manufacturing
  - Burghs will lose right to be represented in legislative power
  - Scotland will be suppressed as its parliament is extinguished with fatal consequences.

Points from recall which support and develop those in the source:
- Royal burghs would be deprived of rights
- Fear of loss of European trade
- British parliament would favour English trade over Scottish.

Points from recall which offer a wider contextualisation such as:
Attitudes against union:
- English currency, weights and measures to be introduced

- Public opinion against union
- Reduction in status of Scottish nobility in British parliament
- Scots Episcopalians opposed union and Hanoverian succession – only Stuart dynasty might restore episcopacy to Scottish church
- Protestants feared a British parliament dominated by Anglican Episcopalian church with bishops' seats in the House of Lords
- Fear of 'Scotlandshire'
- Scots' liberties at risk.

Attitudes for union:

- Advantages in commerce and trade
- Economy would improve – national product would increase
- Scotland's trade would catch up with other European nations'
- Free trade with English colonies
- Protection of being in Great Britain
- Common interests already with England
- Advantages of Scottish politicians being part of the court of the king in London
- Hanoverian succession offered security to Protestantism
- Threat from "Popery" reduced
- Property preserved
- Any other relevant points.

3. The candidate makes a judgement on how far **Source D** explains the passage of the Treaty of Union through the Scottish Parliament in terms of:

Points from the source which show the candidate has interpreted the significant views:

- Opposition was divided and poorly led by unpredictable Hamilton
- Hamilton may have been bribed by the Court party
- Hamilton refused to participate in planned walkout of parliament
- Failure of armed rising proved that opponents of union were not willing to engage in violence.

Points from recall which support and develop those in the source:

- Hamilton divided opponents of union and obstructed arguments against union
- Bribery of Scottish ministers/politicians
- Disagreement amongst opponents of union unable to act together
- Political management was vital to make the outcome certain
- Court party fundamental to final victory.

Points from recall which offer a wider contextualisation such as:

- The Equivalent: £398,085.10s to cover the taking on of English debt
- Expectation of the Equivalent influenced support for treaty in parliament
- Those who lost out to Darien failure were beneficiaries
- Payment made to wool industry as well as payment of Scottish public debt
- Unspecified payments made to Scottish Commissioners for Union
- £20,000 paid to various Scottish politicians through Earl of Glasgow
- Court members voted consistently through all Articles of the Treaty
- Promise of favours, pensions, military patronage, high-ranking positions and cash ensured government majorities
- Threats of loss of civil list pension
- Squadrone Volante's hold on balance of power key to Court party's success
- Some Squadrone members believed they would share the Equivalent

- Assurances that new parliament would support Scots economy over taxation
- Scottish parliament given incentive of free trade with England and its colonies
- Last minute concessions from English on issues such as salt, wool and liquor
- Seats in House of Lords for 16 Scottish peers
- Other Scots peers to retain privileges – Treaty appealed to self-interest
- Act of Security for the Kirk would allow Church of Scotland to continue
- Rights of burghs and Royal Burghs to remain
- Inherited offices for Lords to continue
- Scots laws and Scottish courts to remain
- Security of liberty and stability under one parliament
- English forces moving north and fear of invasion if no treaty was agreed
- Peace secured by being part of Great Britain
- Role of Daniel Defoe in informing the English government during Treaty's passage through the Scottish Parliament
- Any other relevant points.

4. The candidate makes a judgement on how fully **Source E** explains the effects of Union up to 1740 in terms of:

Points from the source which show the candidate has interpreted the significant views:

- Scotland not extinguished, it retained identity, attitudes, ideas; traditions were not eradicated
- Treaty did exert strong Anglicising influence
- Guarantees to Scottish legal system and Church had influence on Scotland
- Continuation of Scottish systems of education and local government were significant achievement of Union.

Points from recall which support and develop those in the source:

- Scottish tradition still evident in culture, music, art, literature, law, religion, education; Scottish Enlightenment, Scott, Smith, Hume, Burns
- Influence of English agricultural techniques and innovations.

Points from recall which offer a wider contextualisation such as:

- Political effects: 1711 – parliament banned Scottish peers with English titles
- Highland clans divided between Hanoverian and Jacobite loyalties
- 1713 – motion to repeal Act of Union defeated by 4 votes
- Whig election victory in 1715 led to government delaying Malt Tax
- 1725 – Secretary of State for Scotland replaced by Home Secretary
- Economic effects: Scottish industry could not compete with English competition; only small number of Scots engaged successfully with colonies
- Taxes led to increases in smuggling and loss of revenue for government
- Paper industry failed; Scottish linen industry suffered
- Merchant shipping benefited, particularly trade with Baltic and Caribbean
- Tobacco industry developed in Glasgow
- Agriculture improved; increased investment; 1727 – Royal Bank of Scotland
- 1730s – favourable economic climate; industries such as linen recovered
- Jacobite reaction: Jacobites led national sentiment in literature and songs
- 1708 – abortive French-sponsored invasion by the Old Pretender

- Jacobite rising of 1715; Earl of Mar played leading role; Battle of Sheriffmuir in November 1715 claimed as victory by both government and Jacobites
- 1716 Disarming Act banned holding of weapons by Highlanders
- 1719 – failed attempt at rising in north-west Scotland by Earl Marischal
- Other effects: claims of the unpopularity of union made vocally by opponents
- 1712 – House of Lords became court of appeal for Scottish cases
- 1724 – outbreak of fence-smashing by levellers; 1725 – Shawfield riots in response to Malt Tax; 1736 – Porteous riots in Edinburgh
- Military road-building; establishment of forts in Highlands
- 1710 – Tories in parliament failed to remove Church of Scotland's privileges; 1711 – Greenshields case; 1712 – Toleration Act and Patronage Act
- 1722 Marrow affair in Church of Scotland; 1733 secession from state church
- Initial dissatisfaction with the Equivalent being unpaid
- Scots joined East India Company in large numbers
- Increased Baltic trade
- Any other relevant points.

SPECIAL TOPIC 4: MIGRATION AND EMPIRE, 1830–1939

1. Overall: The sources agree about the push factor of poverty and the pull factor of prosperity. Although almost a hundred years apart both sources remark on the poverty of life in rural Scotland with high unemployment and the difficulty of providing for families. In contrast both sources comment on the opportunities to be had in Canada, particularly the availability of employment and land for farming.

Source A	Source B
• Occupying a farm that does not pay him in Scotland	• The pay is good as experienced men can at the very start earn £5 to £6 a month in Canada
• Quite unable to support his family in Scotland	• The inability of the crofts to satisfy the hunger of the families in Scotland
• So much land lies in Canada to occupy	• The men also have the prospect of becoming tenant farmers and later on owners of their own farms in Canada
• A farmer continuing to remain in Scotland even when unemployed.	• Lack of employment generally in Scotland.

2. The candidate makes a judgment on how useful **Source C** is as evidence of the assimilation of immigrants into Scottish society in terms of:

Points from source which show the candidate has interpreted the significant views:
- **Origin** – memories of an immigrant child and his assimilation into Scottish society in the 1920s and 30s.
- **Possible purpose** – to record the experiences of his family arriving in Glasgow in the 1920s and how they became established in their new home.
- **Content** –
  - I found myself surrounded by classmates chanting at me because I was a foreigner
  - Our family moved house a few times in an effort to improve our lot
  - In no time at all I was a complete Glaswegian.

Points from recall which support and develop those in the source:
- Assimilation of Italians helped by popularity of ice cream parlours and fish and chip shops
- Young Italians soon adopted local speech patterns due to frequency of contact in catering trade
- Some tension between Catholic Italians and Presbyterian Scots. Italian cafés criticised by Scottish Presbyterian church leaders for opening on the Sabbath
- Italian café owners also met with criticism from local people who claimed the cafés were sometimes the scenes of unruly behaviour. Glasgow Herald article claimed ice cream parlours were morally corrupt and reported the 'ice cream hell'
- There was a greater degree of acceptance of Italian cafés from the Temperance Movement as the cafés chose not to sell alcohol.

Points from recall which offer a wider contextualisation such as:
Catholic Irish:
- Often resented as competition for jobs
- Blamed for spread of diseases and poverty
- Catholic Irish workers were also accused of being strike-breakers and being willing to work for less money than Scottish workers
- Often blamed for being 'benefit scroungers' claiming poor relief after 3 years residence
- The Education (Scotland) Act 1918 allowed Catholic schools into the state system funded through education rates. It also gave the schools the right to give Catholic religious instruction and select their own teachers
- The Catholic Irish had a shared experience with the Scottish worker in that they were affected by industrialisation, urbanisation, as well as fighting together during the First World War
- Even into the 1930s Catholic Irish faced persecution, sometimes organised by Church of Scotland.

Protestant Irish:
- Irish Protestants had a lot in common with the average Scot – long term and deeply embedded cultural interaction between Ulster and lowland Scotland
- Much easier assimilation because of religion
- The first Scottish Orange Lodge opened in 1800 in the weaving centre of Maybole in Ayrshire. The growth of the lodge system in Scotland shows the spread of Irish Protestantism.

Jews:
- Prejudice and discrimination affected the Jews in Scotland – The Daily Record – Aug 1905 'Alien Danger: Immigrants infected with loathsome disease'
- Anti-Semitism never that widespread, possibly owing to low numbers of Jewish immigrants in relation to other groups
- Very few Jews received any help from local poor relief. It was members of the Jewish community that helped each other eg The Glasgow Jewish Board of Guardians and the Hebrew Ladies Benevolent Society in 1901 were dealing with 500 cases of needy Jews.

Lithuanians:
- Between 1860s and 1914 about 7000 Lithuanians decided to settle in Scotland
- Scots complained about the Lithuanians being dirty and immoral but soon most were accepted
- Settlements in mining areas of central Scotland such as Coatbridge
- At first Lithuanians used as strike breakers but soon Lithuanians joined with the local workers and joined the strikes
- Many Lithuanians integrated by changing surnames to Scottish names

- During Great War Lithuanians between eighteen and forty-one faced the choice of conscription into the British Army or deportation for military service in Russia. Of the 1,800 Lithuanians who were called up, 700 joined the British Army and 1,100 chose to be deported to Russia
- Any other relevant points.

3. The candidate makes a judgement on how far **Source D** shows the contribution of Scots to the growth and development of the Empire in terms of:

Points from the source which show the candidate has interpreted the significant views:
- The most obvious field of Scottish achievement in Australia was farming/sheep grazing and the wool trade
- Scots also invested heavily in mining/the Gold Rush of the 1850s brought to Australia a considerable number of Scottish miners
- Shipping and trade were other areas of enterprise in which Scots excelled; example of McIllwrath McEachan and Burns Phillips
- Scots played large part in creating the sugar boom of the 1880s in Northern Queensland.

Points from recall which support and develop those in the source:
Examples of Scots contributing to economic growth and development in Australia:
- Many Scots sheep and cattle farmers squatted on land until allowed to buy squatters licenses
- After gold discovered in Victoria and New South Wales, many gold camps were recognisably "Scottish"
- Role of Church of Scotland in developing education in Australia, eg Australia College, Scots College in Melbourne, and influence of development of Melbourne and Sydney universities.

Points from recall which offer a wider contextualisation such as:
Examples of Scots contributing to Canada:
- Scots gave a thorough and honest character to Canadian business and financial life
- George Stephen organising finance and creation of Canadian Pacific Railroad
- Scots' control of the fur trade
- Contribution to laws and learning/education (eg McGill University).

Examples of Scots contributing to New Zealand:
- Scots founded banks and financial institutions as well as having a political impact
- Scottish influence on NZ education.

Examples of Scots contributing to India:
- Scots' impact on education, the development of the banking system.
- Many Indian institutions such as elite schools, universities and press owed much to Scottish emigrants
- Scots' contribution to development of tea plantations and the jute industry
- Any other relevant factors.

4. The candidate makes a judgement on how fully **Source E** explains the effects of migration and Empire on Scottish society, in terms of:

Points from the source which show the candidate has interpreted the significant views:
- The movement of the Irish changed the population balance of several lowland towns
- A huge reservoir of Irish labour which … was ready and willing to move anywhere and do anything to find work

- Huge construction schemes of nineteenth century relied on this vast labour
- The Irish presence vital to an understanding of Scottish culture as Catholic Irish have played such an influential role in the evolution and shaping of Scottish society ranging from literature to music and on to football.

Points from recall which support and develop those in the source:
- Details of economic contribution of Irish immigrants to Scottish industrial development
- Development of Celtic, Edinburgh Hibernian, Dundee United, etc
- The Education (Scotland) Act 1918 allowed Catholic schools into the state system funded through education rates. It also gave the schools the right to give Catholic religious instruction and select their own teachers. Resentment in Scotland for 'Rome on the Rates'
- Sectarian divisions, Orange v Green.

Points from recall which offer a wider contextualisation such as:
- One in four immigrants from Ireland were Protestant and brought their own distinct culture which had an impact in Scotland, especially through the Orange Lodge
- Large numbers of poorer Jews arrived between 1880 and 1914 – by 1919 over 9000 lived in Glasgow alone. Most lived in the Gorbals and maintained separate identity – eg spoke Yiddish, the Jewish language
- Jewish immigrants tended to work in particular jobs such as peddling and hawking (selling door to door)
- Sweated labour was associated with immigrants and Jews in particular: tailoring and cigarette making
- Impact of Lithuanians to the economy through the coal-mining industry around Coatbridge
- In 1861 there were about 120 Italians in Scotland, by 1901 the Italian population was 4051
- Italians were usually found in catering trades, especially ice cream and fish and chips
- Italian businesses met with success – number of Italian cafés/takeaways in Glasgow increased: 1903 – 89, 1905 – 337, broadening the average Scots social experience
- In addition to catering, Italians became established as hairdressers – they established the College of Italian Hairdressers in Glasgow in 1928 adding another distinct contribution to Scotland
- Role of Empire in making Scots rich
- Role of Empire as a market for Scottish goods and emigrants
- Empire helped the export orientated Scottish economy to develop, at least up until 1914, especially in production of shipping, locomotives, etc
- Empire as a source of competition to Scottish economy: farm produce from Australia, Jute mill development in India, etc
- Any other relevant points.

SPECIAL TOPIC 5: THE IMPACT OF THE GREAT WAR, 1914 – 1928

1. The candidate makes a judgement as to how far **Sources A** and **B** agree about the experience of Scots on the Western Front in terms of:

Overall: **Source A** and **Source B** offer some similar and some contrasting opinions on the experience of Scots on the Western Front with regard to the taking of Hill 70. **Source A** reflects the tenacity and dogged determination required by the Scots during a long and difficult attack whilst **Source B** skirts over difficulties and gives the impression of an easier, successful attack. Both agree that the pipes played during the attack and that no reinforcements arrived.

Source A	Source B
• We made for the top of Hill 70 through murderous rifle and machine gun fire	• For a time there was a kind of Bank Holiday crowd on Hill 70 as the German machine gunners … initially dared not fire
• We made for the top to the sound of the pipes and led by our brave old colonel	• Shriller than the scream of shells was the skirl of pipes going with them
• We were desperate for reinforcements but no help could we see	• We must hold on until the reinforcements arrive. None came
• Shows determination of Scots; "A Cameron never can yield". This time we meant to do or die.	• Shows determination, 'to go all out and press onto Hill 70.'

2. The candidate makes a judgement on how useful **Source C** is as evidence of the impact of the war on Scottish women in terms of:

Points from source which show the candidate has interpreted the significant views:
- **Origin** – Glasgow Herald, daily Scottish newspaper. Contemporary source.
- **Possible purpose** – To report on the opposition in Glasgow to increased rents and the eviction of tenants.
- **Content** –
  - Reports on the first attempt to enforce eviction of a woman in Merryland Street, Glasgow who had not been paying her rent
  - Role of Mrs Barbour of the GWHA addressing demonstration of strikers
  - Details methods used by demonstrators, mainly women.

Points from recall that support and develop those in the source:
- Rent Strikes took place following large increases in rents and increased cost of living. Women at home with men away particularly vulnerable
- Rent Strikes began in May 1915; 25,000 tenants joined the movement by the end of the year
- Rent Strikes saw a prominent role played by women – formation of tenants' strike committees, Glasgow Women's Housing Association and many local "Women's Housing Associations"
- Roles of Mary Barbour, Helen Crawfurd, Agnes Dollan and Jessie Stephens
- Agitation, Rent Strikes and role of women in other areas such as Aberdeen and Dundee.

Points from recall which offer a wider contextualisation such as:
- Migration of thousands of workers into munitions districts had led to acute housing shortages
- War led to women being more involved in local politics and changing male attitudes
- The war led to dilution of labour and the employment of more women for example at Gretna in the huge munitions works
- Anti-war groups formed like the No Conscription League: leading role of women in these groups
- Role of women as workers on the land, etc
- Any other relevant points.

3. The candidate makes a judgement on how far **Source D** illustrates the economic difficulties faced by Scotland after 1918 in terms of:

Points from the source which show the candidate has interpreted the significance views:
- Many of the changes brought by the war were temporary
- The war shifted the balance of international trade against Scottish shipbuilders
- War shifted the balance against textile manufacturers
- The war demonstrated the fragility of the Scottish heavy industry base.

Points from recall which support those in the source:
- War affected Britain's ability to trade. Loss of markets had a long term effect on industry
- Concentration on a narrow group of heavy industries meant Scotland was affected badly when the post-war boom turned into a slump. Exemplification, such as decline in shipbuilding
- Dundee jute companies saw price collapse with removal of trade restrictions on India
- The textile industry in Scotland had a varied experience – wool price rose but falling exports of cotton and woollen goods.

Points from Recall which offer a wider contextualisation such as:
- War delayed long-standing structural problems for the Scottish economy and its reliance on a narrow range of heavy industries that were reliant on exports
- Initial post-war boom in some industries like ship-building – warship yards built passenger liners and merchant ships to replace those lost
- Mines were nationalised and the miners made good wages. After the war the mines returned to their original owners. Lack of investment and fierce foreign competition resulted in decline
- The Admiralty cancelled the cost-plus system and went back to competitive tendering for orders: The demand for ships, and therefore steel, declined
- Yards suffered because of labour disputes and a shortage of material
- Wages were cut in autumn of 1921, men were laid off and Yarrow's closed. Industrial unrest and late delivery of ships damaged the Clyde's reputation
- Other countries increased their steel-making as well as their ship-building capacity. Falling demand for ships affected steel
- Jute prices collapsed after the war. Trade restrictions removed. Competition from abroad. Resulting in unemployment, social misery and discontent
- In Dundee, several firms went into liquidation others amalgamated, to form Jute Industries Ltd
- The collapse of foreign markets for herring from Germany, Poland, Czechoslovakia, Bulgaria, Russia and the Baltic greatly affected the industry. European countries started to compete
- Cheap foreign imports of food like refrigerated meat from Argentina and frozen lamb and tinned fruit from Australia and New Zealand competed with indigenous agriculture when trade was resumed after the war
- Any other relevant points.

4. The candidate makes a judgement on how fully **Source E** describes the impact of the war on political developments in Scotland in terms of:

Points from the source which show the candidate has interpreted the significance views:
- The war years showed that support for Scottish home rule continued
- Arthur Henderson and the Labour leadership in London were forced to concede a separate Scottish Council of Labour
- The war undermined the organisation of Scottish Liberalism, but also much of its moral authority
- The ILP was able to emerge as the natural successor to liberal radicalism.

Points from recall which support those in the source:
- Home rule still prominent. September 1918 the Scottish Home Rule Association formed
- The Labour Party manifesto of 1918 included a commitment to home rule for Scotland
- The ILP MPs from Clydeside elected November 1922 were committed to home rule
- Initial instances of radicalism after war: 1919 – George Square
- In the 1922 election Labour made the breakthrough as the second political party
- ILP members' activities – involved in resisting the Munitions Act of 1915; in opposing the introduction of the dilution of labour; anti-conscription…
- ILP in Scotland had many women prominent in the party such as Mary Barbour, Agnes Dollan and Helen Crawfurd.

Points from recall which offer a wider contextualisation such as:
- It was difficult for Home Rule to make progress in Westminster parliament
- Private members' Home Rule bills failed
- Support for Home Rule waned within the Labour Party
- Glasgow University Scottish National Association formed 1926
- 1927 Jon McCormack and Roland Muirhead, formed the National Party of Scotland. It distanced itself from the Labour Party. Drew support from intellectuals like Hugh McDiarmid
- Some Liberals and Conservatives formed the Scottish Party at the end of the 1920s and proposed some form of devolution in an effort to attract Liberal and Unionist supporters
- The Labour Party emerged as an important political force with seven seats in Scotland, winning as many votes as the Conservatives. Continued success in the 1922 election
- The role of Manny Shinwell, Willie Gallacher, John MacLean
- In Scotland the ILP was to the fore, campaigning on major issues. Membership increased
- Clydeside ILP MPs confronted Conservatives and Liberals, even leadership of PLP. MPs on issues of poverty and unemployment
- The Conservative Party was strengthened as they worked hard to gain middle class support, helped by Presbyterian churches. Scottish legal system also had strong links with the Conservatives
- Events in Ireland – growing fears in Scotland of extremism
- Any other relevant points.

Hey! I've done it

Acknowledgements

Permission has been sought from all relevant copyright holders and Bright Red Publishing is grateful for the use of the following:

SQP

An extract from 'William Wallace: Braveheart' by James Mackay, published by Mainstream Publishing 1996 (p 2); An extract from 'Robert Bruce, King of Scots' by Ronald McNair Scott, published by Hutchinson 1982 (p 2); An extract from 'James VI of Scotland' by Caroline Bingham, published by Weidenfeld and Nicolson 1979 © Caroline Bingham. Reproduced with permission (p 5); An extract from 'Andrew Fletcher and the Treaty of Union' by P.H. Scott, published by The Saltire Society 1992 (p 7); An extract from 'Scotland's Relations with England' by William Ferguson, published by The Saltire Society 1977 (p 8); An extract from 'The Scottish Nation 1700–2000' by T.M. Devine (Allen Lane and the Penguin Press 1999, Penguin Books 2000). Copyright © T.M. Devine, 1999. Reproduced by permission of Penguin Books Ltd (p 9); An extract from 'The Catholic Irish in Scotland: In Search of Identity' by Tom Gallagher, quoted in 'Irish Immigrants and Scottish Society in the Nineteenth and Twentieth Centuries', edited by T M Devine, published by John Donald 1991. Reproduced by permission of Birlinn Ltd. www.birlinn.co.uk (p 9); An extract from 'The Emperor's New Kilt' by Jan-Andrew Henderson, published by Mainstream 2000 (p 10); An extract from 'The Complete Odyssey, Voices from Scotland's Recent Past', edited by Billy Kay, published by Polygon 1996. Reproduced by permission of Birlinn Ltd. www.birlinn.co.uk (p 10); An extract from 'McCrae's Battalion: The Story of the 16th Royal Scots' by Jack Alexander, published by Mainstream 2003 (p 12); Two extracts from 'Voices from War: Personal recollections of war in our century by Scottish men and women' by Ian MacDougall, published by The Mercat Press 1995. Reproduced by permission of Birlinn Ltd. www.birlinn.co.uk (p 12); An extract from 'Scotland: A New History' by Michael Lynch, published by Pimlico 1992. Reprinted by permission of The Random House Group Ltd (p 13); An extract from 'Revolt on the Clyde' by Willie Gallacher published by Lawrence & Wishart Ltd, 1936. Reproduced with permission (p 13).

2011 Paper

An extract from 'Kings and Queens of Scotland' by Richard Oram, published by The History Press Ltd 2006 (p 2); An extract from 'Medieval Scotland Kingship and Nation' by Alan Macquarrie, published by The History Press Ltd 2004 (p 2); An extract from 'Wars of Scotland, 1214–1371' by Michael Brown, published by Edinburgh University Press 2004 (p 3); An extract from 'Mary Queen of Scots: A Study in Failure' by Jenny Wormald, published by Hamlyn 1988 © I. B. Tauris & Co Ltd (p 4); An extract from 'Scotland James V to James VII, History of Scotland' by Gordon Donaldson, published by Oliver & Boyd 1965 © The Estate of Gordon Donaldson (p 4); An extract from 'Scotland's Society and Economy in Transition 1500–1760' by Ian Whyte, published by Palgrave Macmillan, 1997. Reproduced with permission of Palgrave Macmillan (p 5); An extract from 'The Scottish Nation 1700–2000' by T.M. Devine (Allen Lane and the Penguin Press 1999, Penguin Books 2000). Copyright © T.M. Devine, 1999. Reproduced by permission of Penguin Books Ltd (p 6); An extract from 'The Scots and the Union' by Christopher A. Whately, published by Edinburgh University Press 2007 (p 6); An extract from 'Scotland: A New History' by Michael Lynch, published by Pimlico 1992. Reprinted by permission of The Random House Group Ltd (p 7); An extract from 'Irish Catholics in the West of Scotland', in the book 'New Perspectives on the Irish in Scotland' by Martin J. Mitchell, published by John Donald 2008. Reproduced by permission of Birlinn Ltd. www.birlinn.co.uk (p 8); An extract from 'Settlers–New Zealand Immigrants from England, Ireland and Scotland, 1800–1945' by Jock Phillips and Terry Hearn, published by Auckland University Press 2008 (p 8); An extract from 'A History of Scotland' by J. D. Mackie and revised by Geoffrey Parker and Bruce Lenman (Penguin Books, 1978) Copyright © J.D. Mackie, Geoffrey Parker and Bruce Lenman 1978 (p 9); An extract from the diary of Private Thomas McCall, taken from 'Everyman at War', edited by C.B. Purdom, published by J.M. Dent, London 1930. Public Domain (p 10); An extract from 'In War's Wake' by Nicholas Morgan, taken from 'The Sunday Mail Story of Scotland' Vol 4 part 44. Reproduced by permission of Scottish Daily Record and Sunday Mail Ltd (p 10); An extract from 'The Flowers of the Forest: Scotland and the First World War' by Trevor Royle, published by Birlinn 2006. Reproduced by permission of Birlinn Ltd. www.birlinn.co.uk (p 10); An extract from 'Scottish Journey' by Edwin Muir, published by Mainstream 1996 (p 10); An extract from 'The Scottish Nation 1700–2000' by T.M. Devine (Allen Lane and the Penguin Press 1999, Penguin Books 2000). Copyright © T.M. Devine, 1999. Reproduced by permission of Penguin Books Ltd (p 11).